The Speediest Land Traveller

A HISTORY OF ALBERTA AUTO RACING

by

RICHARD McDONELL

To Rob,

Best wishes,

Dick McDonell

June/05

To Diane: Without your support, neither racing
nor writing would have happened.
—R. M.

Editor: Neall Calvert
Indexer: Sheilagh Simpson
Designer: Andrew Johnstone
Printed in Hong Kong

Granville Island
Publishing
Suite 212 – 1656 Duranleau
Vancouver, B.C. V6H 3S4
Tel: (604) 688-0320
info@granvilleislandpublishing.com
www.granvilleislandpublishing.com

Library and Archives Canada Cataloguing in Publication

McDonell, Richard, 1946-
The speediest land traveller : a history of Alberta auto racing / by

Richard McDonell.

Includes index.
ISBN 1-894694-35-X

1. Automobile racing--Alberta--History. I. Title.

GV1034.15.A1M32 2005   796.72.092   C2005-900845-8

ACKNOWLEDGMENTS

When work began on this project, I knew virtually nothing of the history of auto racing, aside from those events I had personally witnessed or been involved with. I still have a long way to go, but what I have learned and put into this book is a credit to the following people, racers for the most part, but also others who, though removed from the sport, chipped in with their knowledge of history, computers, photography, archives, medicine, publishing, and law.

A collective thank you is also due two internet forums to which I subscribe, and whose members are a fount of knowledge on all manner of auto racing minutiae: Canadian Motor Sport History Group and Racing History Group.

Writing a book may seem to be a solitary pursuit, but if that book is a history, it really takes a small army to get the job done. Here, in alphabetical order, is the roll call for my army, with apologies to any I may have missed.

Dale Armstrong, CMHF*
John Barnaschone
Jane Barrett, *Road & Track* magazine
Allen Berg
Ben Berg
Shawn Bishop
Jo Blackmore
Gordie Bonin, CMHF
Reg Bowett
Buddie, Trevor and Wheeler Boys

Gavin Breckenridge
Dr. Lance Bredo
Bob Brockington
Sharon Butala, O.C.
Neall Calvert
Bob Cantin,
Terry Capp, CMHF, and Rachelle Capp
Dr. Vinay Chafekar
Richard Chevalier
Marcel Chichak
John Clark

---

*CMHF indicates Honourable Member, Canadian Motorsport Hall of Fame

Owen Clark
Boots Cooper
Reed Daniels
Michael Dawe
Ted Dawson
Mike Dean
Daniel Ding
Ben Docktor
Ron Doherty
George "TheCar"
    Daszkowski
Robin Edwardes
Gerry Emonds
Tim Erlam
Beth Ernst, Red Deer
    Court House
Bernie Fedderly, CMHF
Ron Ferworn
Ken Finnigan
Ross Fletcher
Duke Foster
Dave Fowler
Barry Fox
Paul Frère
Tim and Ruth Gee
Geoff Goodwin
Terry Goyman
Terry Graham
Terry Gray
Eric Grochowski, Calgary
    Sports Car Club
Chuck Grote
Bruce and May
    Anne Hampton
Ron Harris
Stella Heberling

Rod Henderson
Ron Hodgson, CMHF
Richard Houghton
Bill Hull
Peter Jack
Frank Janett
Gordon Jenner, CMHF
Tom Johnston, CMHF
Andrew Johnstone
Don Jorgensen
Walt Kammer
Reg Kostash
Dr. Bob Lampard
Daniel Langdon
Claude Lapalme
Graham Light, CMHF
Donald MacKay
Jim Martin
Ian McArthur
John and Paulette McEachran
Gene McMahon
Wayne Meadows
Jim Milligan
Ed Moody
Blaine Newton
Liz Oglu
Kirsten Olson, Alberta
    Legal Archives
Jack Ondrack
Ray Peets, CMHF, and
    Marlene Peets
Barry Powers
Bill Powers
Brian Pratt
Don Radbruch
Arnold Rasmussen

Eldon Rasmussen, CMHF,
    and Dianne Rasmussen
Gordon Rasmussen
Lena Running Rabbit
Vern Schultz
Don Sharp
Laura Siebenga
Sheilagh Simpson
George Sitko
Ken Staples
Suzanne Stewart
Bob Stokowski

Terry Sturgeon
Art Suderman
Gail Terner
Rod Traptow
Iain Tugwell
Leonard Vaselenak
Frank and Marilyn Weiss
Eric Wilberg
Prof. Patricia Yongue

MAP OF ALBERTA, CANADA

TABLE OF CONTENTS

Acknowledgments iii
Map of Alberta vi
About the Author ix
Preface x

1. The Beginning 1
2. Of Stampedes and Depressions 12
3. Model T Ford Racing 26
4. After T, What Next? 35
5. Frank Janett 42
6. Men In Drag 54
7. Arrival of the Sports Cars 67
8. Eldon Rasmussen 83
9. Edmonton International Speedway, Part 1 94
10. Ray Peets 108
11. The Boys 118
12. A Racer and a Gentleman: Buck Heberling 127
13. Calgary Tracks 134
14. Shell 4000 and the Evolution of Rallying 148
15. Oval Track Feature Racers: CAMRA and Beyond 160
16. Life After Racing: Frank Weiss 170
17. 300-mph Man Dale Armstrong 181
18. Edmonton International Speedway,
    Part II: Too Close to Town 193
19. Allen Berg 202
20. Tim Gee 212
21. Docktor Prescribes a Race Track 221
22. "240 Gordie" 230
23. Pro Sports Cars 241
24. Capp and Fedderly 261
25. Vintage on the Prairie: The Sports Cars Mature 270
26. Capital City Raceway 280
Epilogue 287
Glossary of Racing Terms 289
Bibliography 297
Index 298

The author, c. 1956. *(From the collection of Helen and the late Duncan McDonell)*

ABOUT THE AUTHOR

The older I get, the faster I was.
—Ontario motor racing columnist Dave Boon
(as quoted in *Old Autos* newspaper)

Richard D. (Dick) McDonell first became interested in car racing when an older cousin took him to a race at Edmonton's Speedway Park in 1956. He began racing in 1965 on ice and competed in sports car races for the next seven years, racing as often as his limited mechanical skills and funds would allow. He took several class wins in various races, and in 1968 claimed second place in C Sedan Class in the Prairie Region Championship, driving a Ford Cortina graciously loaned to him by his new bride, Diane.

In 1972, Dick left the sport to pursue various extracurricular activities such as a career, marriage, buying a house, and raising children. In 1990, he returned to racing, this time on oval tracks. He raced I.M.C.A. modifieds for six seasons, and re-retired in September 1995 as Race City Speedway Champion.

Dick McDonell has written for a number of motor racing and trade publications over many years, but this is his first book.

Dick and his wife, Diane, live in Red Deer and have two grown children, Colleen and Andrew. Dick is involved in property investment, condominium planning, Rotary, attending auto races, and restoring his 1971 Datsun 240Z and 1978 Mercedes-Benz 450 SEL.

PREFACE

There are only three real sports: mountain climbing, bull-fighting, and automobile racing. All the rest are merely games.
—Ernest Hemingway (possibly apocryphal)

The idea of writing a book such as this came to me towards the end of the 1995 racing season. It was my sixth consecutive year of racing International Motor Contest Association (I.M.C.A.) oval-track modifieds, and thirteenth year overall in racing. I was 49 years old, and had just acquired my first pair of eyeglasses. Racing was still going well, but the numbers on my birth certificate were telling me that the ten to fifteen thousand dollars a year the sport was costing should really be going into retirement savings. Further pangs of guilt were coming from repeatedly causing my wonderful, never-complaining wife, Diane, to attend weddings and other important occasions alone, and somehow explain to friends and family that I found racing cars many miles from home more important. Clearly it was time; I had been selfish for too long. In late July I told Diane and my mechanic, Dave Whitford, that this would be the last season.

Ceasing active participation in a sport one loves is not all that hard. Look at the sports pages, and almost every day someone hangs up his cleats, skates, gloves, helmet, or whatever. But really breaking away from the sport, and more importantly its people, is the challenge. I suggest to the reader that the challenge is particularly great in auto racing, if only because of the remarkable people found there.

A little over two decades ago, the late Peter Gzowski wrote a book on horse racing. To research his book, he spent months literally living with horse-racing people, and the result was the eminently readable *Unbroken Line*. Around the same time, he also wrote *The Game of Our Lives*, a book about major-league hockey. Again he became part of the community he was writing about. He travelled with the Edmonton Oilers for most of the 1980–81 season, even skating with them at informal practices. Some time after these two books were published, he was asked in an interview which of the two groups of people, horse racers or hockey players, he found most interesting. His answer was the horse racers. He went on to explain—and as the interview I refer to was on radio rather than in writing, I am paraphrasing and interpreting here—that he found the racers to be a far more individualistic collection of personalities. Whereas the hockey players, who were paid a salary normally negotiated on their behalf by an agent, were first and foremost a team, with their actions, travels, schedules, and playing assignments directed by that team, the horse racers, by contrast, for the most part woke up every morning effectively unemployed. If a horseman wanted work as a trainer, jockey, warm-up rider, or stablehand, he had to go out and find that work. He was paid for what he did today, not for what someone imagined and hoped he would accomplish over the course of a season. The horsemen were survivors, and to use a hackneyed phrase, they had "street smarts." In this respect, car racers, who put a large investment at risk every time they drive onto a track, think nothing of working until midnight for days on end to get their cars ready for a race, and must spend many hours doing their own sales calls if they want sponsors to lessen their financial burden, are much like Peter Gzowski's self-motivated horse racers.

It is my contact with these remarkable people that I did not want to lose. It is their many stories that I wanted to tell. Having done a little writing in the past, I decided that this book would be the way to accomplish that goal.

My original idea was to record in detail the year-by-year, day-by-day history of the sport in this province, but it took me very little time to realize that this was firstly impractical, and secondly would create some pretty dull reading. For over six decades, there has been racing many evenings and every weekend on tracks throughout the province. There have been drag races, dirt track races, asphalt oval races, ice races, and sports car races, all involving thousands of cars and drivers. All the data from all those events could probably be indexed and published, but who would want to read it? And what would it have to say about the development of the sport, and about the people that made it happen? "Very little," was my single answer to my two questions. Far better, I decided, to concentrate first on the events that shaped the sport, and second on the exceptional people who through their natural gifts and their determination to succeed have left their marks on the history of racing.

During the writing of this book, I was contacted by Calgary radio station QR-77, inviting me to an interview on their sports talk show. The first question put to me was, "Racing car history in Alberta—is there really enough material for a book?" I'm not sure exactly how I answered, but on reflection the proper response would have been to say that a book such as this can only scratch the surface of the sport. Any number of anecdotes used herein could be expanded to chapters, and chapters to books. We have almost 100 years of history to work with, and we have people deserving of their own biographies, and events worthy of volumes.

I am grateful to the many people I interviewed in researching this book. Of the dozens of people I contacted, only two declined to speak to me, and for the most part I was welcomed and given access to whatever archival material I wanted. If I liked racers before I began this project, I now love them. I particularly want to mention Donald MacKay of Edmonton, the publicist and promotions manager for Speedway Park, Edmonton International Speedway, and later Capital Raceway. He was one of the first people I interviewed. After not hearing from me for several years, during which time I had become sidetracked by any number of other projects, he called, much to my surprise, and in so many words kick-started me into completing the 90 percent of this book I had yet to touch. Thanks, Don. I hope you enjoy the book.

Red Deer, Alberta
November 2004

CHAPTER I

THE BEGINNING

When a man has an automobile,
the first thing he runs into is debt.
— Bob Edwards, writing in the *Calgary Eye Opener*

The first automobile in Canada was built in 1867—two months after Confederation—by watchmaker Henry Seth Taylor (1833–1887) in Stanstead, Quebec. This was a steam-powered buggy, and by most definitions, did not qualify as an automobile.[1] Real automobiles have internal-combustion engines, and the first of that kind in the world was a motorcycle created in Germany in 1885 by Gottlieb Daimler. Within a year, he and Karl Benz, working independently and unknown to one another, had built the world's first two cars.

At that time, the population of Calgary was 506. The site of the future city of Red Deer, populated then by one family, was about to be enlarged by a detachment of militia pitching its tents near the shore of the river, in fear that the Louis Riel–led North West Rebellion would move first west to Edmonton, then south to Calgary. Edmonton was officially a hamlet, but some still referred to it as Fort Edmonton. Lethbridge was little more than a decade removed from the last great Indian battle. The first self-propelled vehicles, steam-

---

1. Taylor's vehicle was a lighter and apparently quicker version of the steam-powered three-wheel gun carriage built in France in 1770 by Nicolas Joseph Cugnot. By all accounts, Taylor's car ran well, but it had no brakes. On its first downhill trip, the car went out of control and crashed. Dejected, Taylor stripped off the boiler and installed it in his yacht.

powered locomotives to be precise, were now able to cross Canada. In these circumstances it is understandable that the works of Daimler and Benz did not cause much of a stir among the residents of that part of the North West Territories we now know as Alberta.

In 1895, the first-ever automobile race was held on public roads, from Paris to Bordeaux to Paris. There appears to have been no coverage of the event in Edmonton or Calgary newspapers, perhaps reflective of the fact that the arrival of the first car was still seven years away.

In the August 8, 1902 issue of the *Calgary Eye Opener* appeared the news that Billy Cochrane of High River had taken delivery of an automobile—albeit not a modern internal-combustion model: a Stanley[2] Steamer. This is the first record of a car, either steam or internal-combustion, in Alberta, and it would be another two years before there were enough of them to fill a double garage. In May of 1904, Joseph Morris of Edmonton drove his Ford from Strathcona, across the Low Level Bridge and up the hill to Jasper Avenue. At around the same time, John Prince of Calgary became the proud owner of Calgary's second car, a Rambler.

Nature being what it is, any time there are two or more of people, animals or vehicles, there will soon be either a fight or a race. In the case of Alberta, the latter took just two years.

On July 4, 1906, expatriate Americans held their annual "Ex-American Day" celebration, and in addition to the usual parade, speeches, athletic contests, and pony races, they staged a two-mile race for touring cars and a one-mile event for runabouts. These races, described in the Calgary *Daily Herald* as "a great novelty," took place on the fairgrounds oval. The touring car race, which appears to have been the first to run, was won by J. J. Young, ahead of R. White. The runabout race was won by W. Hillier, with Stewart MacKid second. The races, again in the words of the *Herald*, "attracted much attention."

Edmonton was only two days behind in holding its first race. On July 6 at the first Provincial Fair, following an 18-car parade

2. Some records indicate the car was a White Steamer or a Locomobile, rather than a Stanley.

July, 1906: Edmonton's first race at the exhibition fairgrounds. While the archival caption on the photo identifies this as being a race, closer examination of the picture and of the newspaper coverage of the day would indicate it was more likely the 18-car parade that preceded the race. *(Alberta Provincial Archives, B-8778)*

Barney Oldfield and entourage in Winnipeg, September 1912. Oldfield is third from left; J. R. Hamill of Calgary is far left. *(Glenbow Archives, Calgary)*

Lethbridge Fair, 1912: Barney Oldfield tries out the track. Building complex in background burned down in 1920s. *(Glenbow Archives, Calgary)*

Charisma, Barney Oldfield–style. Arriving in Calgary, 1912. *(Glenbow Archives, Calgary)*

past the grandstand, races were held, each scheduled for five laps of the half-mile fairgrounds oval. Whether by rule or otherwise, each competing car carried four occupants. The first race was won by C. Watt, in a time of 4 minutes 40 seconds, followed by L. York. The second heat was won by J. H. Morris (department store owner Joe Morris of 1904 fame) in a Buick, in a time of 5 minutes flat. It is interesting to note how closely the speed of these cars compares to that of horses running on the same track. The cars were turning laps in a range of 56 to 60 seconds. A decent one-mile (two-lap) time for a winning saddle horse was 2 minutes, 20 seconds, or 70 seconds per lap.

The two heat winners, Watt and Morris, were to decide the match in a final five-lap race. Morris dropped out with mechanical problems after one mile, and Watt took the win. Other competitors identified in the Edmonton papers that day were E. J. Taylor (Ford), K. A. McLeod (Buick), and W. Oliphant (Darrocq).

The Edmonton *Journal* declared, "In future, no fair will be complete without this exciting feature." Indeed, Edmonton auto enthusiasts wasted little time in organizing their second race meet. On Labour Day, September 3, they held another parade, but this time only two cars agreed to race. The "gaily-decorated" entry of Moser and Ryder came out ahead of the July winner, Mr. Watt. The newspapers of the day did not bother mentioning the make of vehicle driven by either competitor, but the *Journal* did dwell extensively on the decoration of the Moser and Ryder car. While the entrants gave no reason for their choice of blue and purple ribbons, the *Journal* opined that the colours, being those of the Elks Lodge, represented the elk, a primitive beast. The automobile, on the other hand, "is the latest and most perfect invention," therefore the idea was "to represent the old and the new."

Sure, why not?

In spite of the *Journal's* prediction about "this exciting feature," there were no races at the next Provincial Fair, even with enthusiast J. H. Morris being named exhibition president. After a promising start, the sport appears to have fallen into a period of dormancy over the next few years.

In Calgary in 1909, Mr. J. Jackson, manager of the local McLaughlin-Buick dealership, attempted to create a car race track but was unsuccessful. Undeterred, in 1910 he publicly challenged anyone interested to an open road race, "you name the distance." Messrs. Hatfield and Bell accepted the challenge and put up a $1,000 wager for a race on open roads from Calgary to Lethbridge, a distance of roughly 150 miles (243 km). The race was to take place Christmas Day, but Superintendent Deane of the North West Mounted Police stepped in, reminding all that he was obliged to enforce the rural speed limit of 20 miles per hour (30 kmh), and would soon put a stop to any open-road race.[3]

Still eager to prove the performance of his products, Jackson publicly claimed that the McLaughlin-Buick was the only car that could climb Brickman Hill in Calgary, and he went so far as to try to change the name of the escarpment to "Buickman Hill." He was quickly challenged by the Hayes dealer, Mr. Grasswick, who not only drove one of his cars up the hill, but also took a full load of passengers with him.

Professional racing made its debut in 1912 when the inimitable—although some might prefer the word insufferable—Barney Oldfield brought his travelling automotive circus to Alberta. Barney Oldfield advertised himself as a daredevil racer, but his racing talent, while not insignificant, came a distant second to his skill as a promoter, and particularly a self-promoter. Twice he competed in the Indianapolis 500, in 1914 and 1916, finishing a respectable fifth both times. This seems to have been the pinnacle of his success in genuine competition. He was the first man to lap the Indianapolis Motor Speedway at 100 miles per hour (161 kmh), but to do so he used his aging Christie, a car he knew could not possibly last the 500-mile (805-km) race distance. For qualifying and racing he used another car and was officially clocked at 94.3 miles per hour (152 kmh).

In 1912, while under suspension from the American Automobile Association for his "outlaw" racing activities, he and his racing entourage toured Western Canada, beginning in

---

3. *Sport in Early Calgary,* William M. McLennan, Fort Brisebois Publishing.

Vancouver, then travelling to Calgary July 27, Edmonton July 31, and later on to Regina, Winnipeg, and back to Lethbridge. In Calgary an estimated 10,000 people paid 50 cents each to watch the Oldfield racers stage their standard-format race card on the Victoria Park oval. In the end, Barney managed to bravely come from behind and eke out a victory over his competitors, who not coincidentally were also his employees and clearly understood the terms of their engagement.

While in Calgary, Oldfield was contacted by real-estate developer Daniel Webster Trotter, who through his South-East Calgary Corporation had purchased a tract of land in what is now the Ogden area. Across the centre of his land, Trotter had built a straight, flat road, two miles long, and named it Gridiron Speedway. In 1911, the Calgary Motor Racing Association, under the leadership of Daniel Trotter, had held one-mile time trials on Gridiron Speedway; but now with Oldfield in town Trotter sensed an opportunity to attract wider attention to his development. He asked the racer if he would use the road to set a speed record—a world record, if that were possible. This suited Barney perfectly, as world records were his specialty. Over almost two decades, he claimed to have set hundreds of world records. Some were for a half-mile straight, others for one mile, some on banked ovals, some on a flat ovals, some on dirt, some on various types of pavement. In fairness, many of the records he claimed were indeed verified by the American Automobile Association, but by 1912 that organization had suspended Oldfield. The AAA had little interest in his various records, and it didn't really matter to Barney whether or not they recognized his claims.

The earliest date Oldfield could accommodate Trotter was August 10, as he had his previous commitment to stage a race in Edmonton. The Edmonton show was set for the South Side Athletic Park on July 31. The advance promotion referred to Oldfield as "a daredevil shaking dice with death" and promised "spectacular, nerve-tingling, death-daring" entertainment. And yes, a world record was offered.

Surprisingly, in that era of booster-journalism, the Edmonton *Journal* questioned Oldfield on the exact nature of the record he proposed to set. The *Journal* pointed out that the American Automobile Association did not recognize half-mile tracks, and went on to say there were different kinds of half-mile tracks. Edmonton's was a flat track of hard dirt—how did it compare to tracks of cinder? Or soft earth? Or to banked tracks? Oldfield, not seeking any A.A.A. recognition, wouldn't be drawn into details. What he did know was that the Toronto papers were carrying a story of a closed-track "world record" being set on that city's fairgrounds oval the previous weekend by Louis Disbrow.[4] That was all Barney needed for a target. "I will go after a new record, and I will get it," declared the daredevil.

Some 4,000 Edmontonians put down a dollar each (grandstand and parking included)[5] to watch the show, and by all accounts they were only mildly disappointed when the self-proclaimed Speed King fell some 3½ seconds short of Disbrow's record.

Back in Calgary, Oldfield had Trotter prepare the gravel track as smoothly as was possible with the road machinery of the day. The morning of August 10 saw some 4,000 spectators gathered along the sides of Gridiron Speedway to witness the spectacle of a world speed record being set.

The first record to fall was for one mile, a distance covered by Oldfield, after a running start, in 41 ⅘ seconds for an average speed of just over 86 miles per hour (139.5 kmh). Next came the half mile, which took just 18 ⅕ seconds, or a remarkably quick 98.9 miles per hour (160.2 kmh). Both records were set in his front-wheel-drive Christie. The car had been built in 1908 and sold by the factory with a claim of 200 horsepower—a figure widely questioned in the racing community. By the time Barney got the car to Alberta, it had magically increased to 300 horsepower.

The reasons for Oldfield choosing these particular distances are unclear. With a running start, did the distance really mean anything?

---

4. Disbrow's everlasting claim to fame will be that in the inaugural Indianapolis 500 in 1911, he moved from fifth on the starting grid to first by the first corner, and led the first-ever turn of that race.

5. Interestingly, this is the same admission charged at Breckenridge Speedway in Edmonton four decades later.

Presuming the measured distances were towards the end of his runs, he would have had more time to build speed before entering the timed section on the half-mile than on the one-mile. This would explain the higher speed on the shorter run, and it might answer why the Calgary *Herald* claimed that all four wheels left the ground at one point on the half-mile. Having said that, there are no photographs showing the car in the air, and it seems unlikely it would have happened on a road that had received the special treatment Trotter is said to have afforded this one. It may well have been journalistic license on the part of the *Herald* reporters, but if that were the case, their efforts paled in comparison to the work of reporter Maj. J. B. Jeffery of the Chicago *Press* who wrote, "South-East Calgary now owns the two great world's records, and the fastest track in the world." He then became truly hyperbolic and proclaimed, "It was a beautiful day with the afternoon bathed in golden sunshine, and every moment jewelled with a joy for this interesting and spectacular drama of sport, which doubtless will never again be witnessed in the history of the world."

Well. Perhaps we should end our book right here.

But there is more to tell.

While, understandably, Barney Oldfield made the front page of the August 11 Calgary *Daily Herald*, large numbers of local motorists also found themselves featured there, and the next day as well. Developing a technique that is still being used and refined by police forces around the world today, Calgary officers, using a stopwatch, nabbed 55 motorists for speeding, going to or coming from Gridiron Speedway. Of the lot, only five were found to be travelling under 20 miles per hour (32 kmh), against a speed limit of 15 mph (24 kmh).

Fines handed out by a Police Court magistrate with the curious name of Colonel Sanders ranged from $15 to $25. Once the last of the miscreants had been dealt with, Sanders is reported in the *Herald* to have asked the equally unlikely-named prosecutor, Inspector Nutt, "Didn't you get Mr. Oldfield?"

Came the inspector's reply, "Mr. Oldfield was the slowest driver that crossed our trap."

* * *

The enthusiasm generated by the Oldfield visit made it inevitable that there would be local racing. The Calgary Auto Club organized its first race meet in 1913 on the Victoria Park oval. Auto dealer Carl Grasswick won two five-mile races and a ten-mile race and was declared "Alberta Champion." Mrs. Carl Grasswick drove in the "slow race," thus becoming the first female race driver in Alberta.

In 1914, Motor Supply Company of Calgary offered an award for a speed trial: Calgary–Lethbridge–Medicine Hat–Calgary. The Cadillac of Messrs. McLeod and Williamson took up the challenge and completed the route in 18 hours, 24 minutes. In short order, several attempts to break the new record were made, but all ended in breakdowns until Mr. F. Keeton of the Keeton Motor Car Company came to Calgary with one of the cars from his factory in Brantford, Ontario. His first attempt failed, but on the second try he covered the route in 16 hours, 56 minutes, an average speed of almost 31 miles per hour (49 kmh). While all this was going on, there was no mention in the press of Superintendent Deane and his edict of 1909.

This photo has been published in various media, purporting to show Oldfield setting either of his world records at Gridiron Speedway in southeast Calgary. Both records, however, were set in a front-wheel-drive Christie, and that is not the car in this picture. More likely, the shot is of one of Oldfield's sidekicks, either Lew Heinemann in a Prince Henry Benz, or Bill Fritsch in a Cino. The stated location and the date, August 10, 1912, appear to be accurate. Note the lack of concern for either driver or spectator safety. *(Glenbow Archives, Calgary)*

Curiously, in light of Mrs. Grasswick's accomplishment the previous year, a touring show called The Western Canada All-Star
Racing Team came to Alberta in 1914, advertising, "Miss Lillian
Bennett, the only female racing driver in the world." Calgary garage
owner George Webber competed with the visitors and, much to
their chagrin, won the three races he entered.

By then, World War I had begun and organized racing remained
dormant for three years.

OF STAMPEDES AND DEPRESSIONS

These races are scarcely anything else than hippodrome affairs, as we get them here.
—Wetaskiwin farmer J. H. Hodson, in a letter to Edmonton Exhibition Association, 1925

It might be hard to imagine the Calgary Exhibition without the Calgary Stampede, but prior to 1923, the two lived quite separate lives. The Exhibition had been operating since 1886, while the first Stampede didn't take place until 1912. The Exhibition was the property of the farmers, ranchers, and landed gentry of Southern Alberta. The Stampede had been started on the initiative of an ex-cowboy turned promoter named Guy Weadick.

In 1917, in spite of almost 30 years of successful fairs, the Exhibition's directors found themselves worrying about the lack of any recent growth in attendance. In fact, finances had become so tight that for two years in a row the board had asked the general manager to accept a pay cut of $500.[1]

All of which is not to say that the Exhibition had nothing to recommend it. Its livestock judging events were highly regarded, and the midway with its various sideshows certainly appealed to many

---

1. Minutes of the board of directors of the Calgary Exhibition Association.

people—but there was still a large part of the population of Southern Alberta that found nothing of interest at the annual fair.

At the April 15, 1917 meeting of the board, the Attractions Committee brought forward the possibility of staging car races. There was general agreement, and the 1917 racing-prize budget was amended so that $5,000 would go to the harness races, $4,500 to the running races (saddle horses), and $784 to automobile races. A Chicago promoter named Geo. Huff Durward was to be contracted to bring in the racing show. Five days later, however, car racing was again on the board's agenda, Mr. Durward apparently having told the directors what they could do with their $784. The board just couldn't drop the idea, though, as new information clearly showed that auto racing was the way of the future. Contact with other fairs in North America found that when they scheduled auto races on their slow days, "this new feature was practically always successful, and in many instances resulted in building up these particular days to be the largest days of the fair."[2] The decision was made to schedule races on July 4 and 5, and this time to contract the International Motor Contest Association "which is an association of Fairs and Expositions of which we are a member" to organize them.[3] The board's minutes go on to say, "Arrangements for this contest will be under the supervision of Mr. Alex J. Sloan who has charge of practically all of the automobile races at state fairs, and arrangements have been completed to have 6 or 8 professional drivers of international reputation and some of the best racing cars on the continent present for these races. We look confidently to this feature to assist materially in building up the entertainment side of the exhibition." As if an omen of what was to happen in July, the minutes conclude, "It is of course necessary that the drivers should be professional drivers, as it would be absolutely unwise to permit amateur racers on half-mile tracks."

So as not to put the entire burden of improving attendance on the auto racers, the board decided to offer as additional attractions

---

2. Minutes of the board of directors, April 1917.

3. The minutes do not explain how the Exhibition could be a member of I.M.C.A., and not have known about it.

Gruber's Animals, Dixon's Mule Derby, and the Waterson Bros. Upside-Down Feature Jugglers.

International Motor Contest Association was not in reality "an association of Fairs and Expositions," but rather a travelling auto race show, operated by Alex Sloan. Sloan had done well touring the United States since 1915 but now, with Calgary onside, he would be able to add a Western Canada loop to his schedule, with Edmonton, Red Deer, Regina, and Winnipeg included.

In its July 2 issue, the *Morning Albertan* enthusiastically reported, "Speed demons, entered in the auto races which will be held Wednesday and Thursday, and their mechanicians[4], began to arrive in the city Saturday night." Entries included Fred Horey, "the dirt track champion" in a F.I.A.T., Dave Koetzla and George Clark in Cases, Ben Giroux with a Sunbeam, Jules Ellingboe in a Briscoe, Floyd Willard in a Prince Henry, Chad Jewett driving a Ford, and Bob Kline with a S.C.A.T.[5]

The Calgary Exhibition had effectively leased a packaged show from I.M.C.A. and its president Sloan, and it is probably accurate to say that the drivers were totally unknown to the population of Calgary. Who were they?

The best scale by which to judge drivers of this era is the Indianapolis 500. It had in six years become the foremost professional auto race in North America and attracted the best drivers from America, Canada, and Europe. George Clark qualified 27th for the 1913 500, and finished 10th. Ellingboe first made it to the 500 in 1921, qualifying 5th, but dropping out after only 49 laps. He raced there through most of the 1920s, finishing a career-high 11th in

---

4. This is an archaic term that was briefly popular in the era of World War I and was gradually replaced with "mechanic" over the decade of the 1920s.

5. At the time of these races, there were roughly 2,500 automobile manufacturers in North America, and identifying these race cars is at best, an inexact science. Having said that, Horey's F.I.A.T. was an Italian car; the Cases were purpose-built race cars, purchased by Sloan after mediocre finishes in the 1913 Indianapolis 500, from the company that later achieved fame in the manufacture of farm tractors; the Sunbeam was an English car, made by the same company that produced sports cars in the 1950s and '60s; the Briscoe was likely a limited-production, or even a one-off hot rod made by Benjamin Briscoe after his acrimonious 1913 split with Maxwell Cars; the Prince Henry was probably a modified Ford; and the S.C.A.T. an Italian car properly called a Societa Ceirano Automobili Torino.

Starting line-up for the first I.M.C.A. race in Calgary, 1917. Near driver, in car #17, is Fred Horey. Regrettably, the author has been unable to identify the other drivers. *(Glenbow Archives, Calgary)*

Rolling start, 1918, Calgary, Dave Koetzla on pole. Starting-flag colour is yellow, as per I.M.C.A rules of the time. Other flags were red for stop, green for last lap, white for "stop at your pit for consultation," black with a white centre for "you are being passed," and chequered for end of the race. *(Glenbow Archives, Calgary)*

Mlle. Mazie performing her crash-through-the-burning-fence act in 1934. The same stunt would claim her life before the year was out.

Elfreida Mais, a.k.a. Mlle. Mazie, c.1925. Man beside her is believed to be fellow racer George Clark. *(Both photos from collection of the late Christine Horey Logan, courtesy Grace Jones and Don Radbruch)*

1924. There is no record of the remaining 1917 Calgary racers ever competing in the Indianapolis 500, but Horey (or H'Orey, as he spelled it), a Winnipeg native who raced in the U.S. as "The Canadian Champion," went on to a long and illustrious career specializing in dirt tracks, and in 2003 he was inducted into the Sprint Car Hall of Fame in Knoxville, Iowa. These drivers were for the most part adventurous young men who had found an exciting way to make a living in an era when most people worked long hours and days for poor pay in boring, repetitive, and often dangerous jobs. They were indeed "professional racing drivers," but they appear for the most part to have had no particular qualifications in their trade aside from the experience they picked up running with Sloan's travelling show.

The evening *Daily Herald* was no less enthusiastic than the *Morning Albertan* about the races, stating that the events "Will be the Greatest Auto Races Ever Staged in Canada." Given that there is precious little evidence of the *Herald* covering other motor racing in the country in those days, it is difficult to determine just how they arrived at this conclusion.

The *Herald* added a second automotive article to its front page that day: "Lady Motorist Makes a Record Run from Banff." Dr. Rosamond Leacock of Calgary, in a Ford, accompanied by Miss M. Muir of the *Herald*, left Banff at 2:45 p.m. and arrived in Calgary at 6:55 p.m. on roads described as "excellent." The ladies made a ten-minute stop in Cochrane, leaving them with an actual driving time of four hours flat.

The papers also reported that for the second day of racing, Thursday, July 5, the touring professionals were to be joined by two "local autoists," George Webber in a Mercer and Fred Seigel with a McLaughlin Special. Webber was the owner of a Calgary garage and the man who had so embarrassed another travelling race show in 1913, while Seigel was advertised as being the former "head tester" of the McLaughlin factory in Oshawa.

At the Victoria Park oval on July 4, I.M.C.A.'s J. Alex Sloan (not "Alex J." as shown in the Exhibition Board minutes) took on the dual role of starter and starting judge, while Calgary's Mayor M. C.

Costello honoured the meet by acting as referee. His Worship apparently didn't take his official responsibilities too seriously, though, and was seen making a wager with a police officer prior to one of the races.

No attendance figures are available, but the *Albertan* headline of the next day referred to an "immense throng."

Prize money for the two-day show was advertised as being $3,000, but portions of that appear to have been payable only if certain records were set. The "Official World's Time Trials" took place as the fifth heat on the first afternoon of racing and offered $500 for a world's record, $200 for a Canadian record, and $100 for fastest time of the day. For some reason, the distance was advertised as "1 to 5 miles," but was run as a five-mile heat. Dave Koetzla was the winner, setting a "Canadian National" record, but there is no mention in the press of a world record, which would seem to indicate that the actual amount of prize money paid out was closer to $2,500 than $3,000. Nevertheless, good money for the era; far more than the $784 the board had budgeted in April and in fact more than some oval tracks pay today.

The remaining heats were a mix of Australian Pursuit (cars begin at set positions around the track; if you get passed, you're out of the race), wheel change (13 ⅕ seconds for Ben Giroux vs. the world record of 11 ⅘), and straight heat races of between three laps and five miles each.

The second day of racing was the final day of the 1917 Exhibition. It was also the day the two locals, George Webber and Fred Siegel,[6] were supposed to compete. Contrary to their own motion of April 20 regarding amateur drivers, the board had either explicitly or by its silence permitted the entry of the two. Sloan wanted no part of them, and he apparently pressured the board in that direction. In response, the board hastily called a noon meeting on July 4 at which, in a triumph of muddleheaded thinking, it agreed that at the following evening's show there would be a match race between Webber and Siegel for a $100 prize, and a second race for the two amateurs against two of the professionals, with the top

---

6. In various news reports, the name is spelled both Siegel and Seigel.

World War I air ace Captain Fred McCall tried racing in the 1920s. This photo is believed to have been taken in Regina. *(Glenbow Archives, Calgary)*

three men being awarded $75, $50, and $25 respectively. Their motion concluded "Amateur competitors to drive separately." How that was to be achieved in the second race was not explained.

For reasons ostensibly related to safety—many racing accidents are caused by leaders lapping back-markers—but possibly out of fear that one or both of the Calgarians just might have been able to keep up with his professionals, Sloan adamantly refused to go along with the board's feeble attempt at compromise. If the locals took to the track, his men would park. The board finally acquiesced, and while Webber reluctantly accepted the decision, Siegel would have none of it. Waiting until race and track officials were otherwise engaged, Siegel drove his car onto the track and began lapping. His demonstration of race-driving prowess ended abruptly when he hooked a wheel on an inside fence post, flipped over, and was killed. Sloan's hard-line position was vindicated, and he was quoted the next day as saying, "After seeing him enter the turn, I made the statement in front of five spectators, 'He will be lucky if he ever gets around that turn.'"

An example of local racing in the Depression years. This small group from the Magrath area apparently stripped down some old cars and raced on a track marked out in a wheat field. *(Photos courtesy Alexander Galt Museum Archives)*

Another potential disaster was averted when the plan to have American barnstorming pilot Miss Katherine Stinson fly her airplane around the track, in a match race against George Clark, was cancelled because of high winds.

Once the serious racing started, George Clark set fastest time of the day with a 1-minute, 7-second mile (53.6 mph or 86.8 kmh), some ⅖ second quicker than Horey, but a full second slower than his own first-day clocking of 1:08.

Aside from the incident with the unfortunate Mr. Siegel, the two days of racing appear to have gone off without a mishap, and the Exhibition had achieved everything that it wanted. In its year-end review, the board was able to show an increase in gate and grandstand revenue of $6,868.70 and commented that this was "largely attributable to the very successful automobile races." Spending on prizes was up $4,021 over 1916 and, again, this appears to be mainly the result of the races. J. Alex Sloan and I.M.C.A. were invited back for 1918.

The I.M.C.A. crew quickly loaded their cars on the train north and, on July 7, put on a one-day show at the Exhibition in Red Deer, where the *Advocate* reported, "The horse racing was poor owing to only one day's purses being provided, but the auto races on Saturday more than made up for any lack. They were a novel and thrilling feature and will repay repetition next year: the auto racer is far and away the speediest land traveller."

The next stop was Edmonton, where the population and press received the racers no less enthusiastically. Coverage in the Edmonton *Journal* began when the cars were unloaded at the rail yards. The *Journal* promised that the first day of racing, Friday the 13th of July, would be a "Gladsome Day," and that every car "is certain to be in perfect mechanical condition." This optimism somehow seemed appropriate in light of the *Journal*'s further pronouncement that the Exhibition oval "is said to be the best short distance track in Canada or the western part of the United States." Who really said that, or upon what factors their judgement was based—given that the no serious race car had ever turned a wheel on the track—is not stated.

As for the races, they appear to have been a great success for the Exhibition. Reporter F. H. McPherson of the *Journal* declared in the July 14 edition, "The races drew like a porous plaster, attracting perhaps the biggest crowd that had tested the capacity of the grandstand and infield since the plant was opened in 1910." However, the *Journal*'s earlier judgement of the suitability of the track for cars had changed dramatically in five days, and it was now regarded as "not an autoist's dream, lacking the necessary banking at the turns." Floyd Willard was the hero of the first day's racing, taking his Prince Henry to two wins.

Wins on the second day of racing were shared among Clark, Giroux, Horey, Koetzla, and Willard. If the races were legitimate, Sloan certainly had gathered a competitive group of drivers.

The following year, from July 1 to 3, the two Calgary papers breathlessly carried running accounts of which famous drivers had arrived in town for another two days of racing, although on July 2, the motorists were temporarily bumped off the front sports page by the news that the night before, one J. P. Taylor had set a new sackrace record of 32 seconds for 196 yards, eclipsing the old record which had stood since 1884.

The previous year's races had been so popular that reserved seating was now advertised. Ticket orders were received from as far away as Lethbridge and Camrose.

With ten of his drivers in town, J. Alex Sloan inspected the track on July 3, and while happy for the light rain overnight, felt that more water and some calcium chloride would be needed to maintain texture and keep down the dust for the following day's racing. The Exhibition board complied with his requests, and all was set for the Thursday and Friday events.

Ellingboe and Cline (or "Kline" as it was spelled in some reports) were back for a second year in Calgary, accompanied by Vern Soules, Bill Endicott, Larry Doyle, Clifford Toft, Leon Duray, Arthur Chevrolet, Ben Gotoff, and Sig Haugdahl. No mention was made this year of any participation by local drivers.

Of the 1918 recruits, Duray is perhaps the most interesting. Born near Chicago as George Stewart, his name was changed to

Leon Duray by Sloan, who wanted to add some foreign flair to his races. Sloan even made up a fake biography, giving "Duray" credit for service as a French Air Force pilot in World War I. After beating around the dirt tracks of North America for years, Stewart/Duray finally made it to the Indianapolis 500 in 1922. In a pattern he was to repeat over the next decade, he qualified 4th in his Frontenac-Chevrolet but ended up 22nd, having completed just 94 of 200 laps. His stated philosophy of "win, blow, or put a hole in the fence" was already beginning to show itself, but give the man his due, he was fast. In 1928, driving one of Harry Miller's engineering master-pieces, he set a one-lap Indianapolis record of 124.02 miles per hour (201 kmh) that was to stand until 1938—the longest of any record at that track—and then followed up the same year with a World Closed Course Record of 148.17 mph (240 kmh) on the 2 ½-mile (4 km) high-banked Packard test track.

Of the remaining Class of '18, Endicott and Chevrolet were undistinguished veterans of the first 500 in 1911. Endicott later finished 5th in 1912, while Chevrolet's real success came in 1921 as owner of Tommy Milton's 500-winning Frontenac.

After the first night of racing, the *Morning Albertan* reported, "Alberta people like automobile races." The grandstands were packed, and spectators lined the fence almost the entire length of the track. J. Alex Sloan estimated the crowd at 18,000. The big winner of the day was Haugdahl, who took the Australian Pursuit race and the ten-mile feature in his F.I.A.T.

Again in 1918, the I.M.C.A. cars were hauled first to Red Deer and then to Edmonton for the following week's festivities, but this year they had company. Katherine Stinson, the American aviatrix who had tried to race her plane against the cars at Calgary in 1917, was to perform on the Saturday evening race card. The 1918 format also featured the Alberta Sweepstakes, which offered points towards the "World Championship," and more prize money than the previous year.

Stinson not only performed her aerobatic tricks in front of the grandstand, she also borrowed Leon Duray's car and set what was announced as a women's world record for one mile (2 laps) at one minute, 15 ⅕ seconds.

While wins in the various races were fairly evenly spread among the various drivers, Ben Gotoff won the Alberta Sweepstakes feature.

Racing continued to be a featured attraction at the Calgary and Edmonton Exhibitions in much the same fashion for the following five years, but its pre-eminent position took a plunge in 1923 when the board of directors of Calgary Exhibition merged their fair with the Stampede of Guy Weadick. Prime grandstand time was now reserved for rodeo events, with the cars moved to the end of the fair, once the horses had left. Sloan and his I.M.C.A. show continued to come to Alberta, and by all accounts brought better cars with more experienced drivers and staged faster races every year—Haugdahl set a sequence of three credible Canadian one-mile records in 1922–24, culminating in a one-minute-flat in Edmonton in a Miller Special in 1924—but there was no mistaking the fact that racing was becoming a sideshow.

In 1925, Sloan, apparently recognizing he had a problem, added two attractive women, Miss Elfreida Mais, and "European Champion" Miss Marion Martin, to his stable of drivers. Also appearing that year were Johnny DePalma, the cousin of Indianapolis 500 winner Ralph DePalma, and ex–Regina Pat hockey player Emory "Spunk" Collins, who would return to Alberta almost a quarter-century later. Nevertheless, when the *Journal* ran a feature article in 1925 asking what could be done to improve the fair, one prominent suggestion was to eliminate auto races and revert to more agrarian events, or even a Chautauqua (educational meeting). The novelty was wearing thin.

To be sure, there were attempts to organize indigenous racing, with tracks created in wheat fields and pastures, but these efforts lacked organization and failed to establish the sport as a regular participant and spectator activity.

Travelling racing shows continued to come to Alberta, but more as a spectacle than a sport. Promoters coupled races with such seedy acts as "Rose Marie, who holds the world's record for eating more peanuts per mile than any other monkey race driver" (1928), and Mlle. Mazie,[7] whose specialty was to drive a car through a wood-plank fence that had been soaked in gasoline and set on fire (1934).

When there was actual racing, the continued lack of local participation meant no favourites to cheer for, and the once-a-year schedule left plenty of time for interest to wane.

The 1930s were terrible years for the economy of Western Canada, and it took a war to fix that. Just as it did to fix auto racing.

---

7. American racing historian Don Radbruch believes that "Mlle. Mazie" was the same person as Elfreida Mais. He points out that by 1934, Elfreida Mais was performing the same crash-through-the-burning-board-fence stunt as Mlle. Mazie, and in fact was killed doing just that at Birmingham, Alabama later in 1934.

CHAPTER 3

MODEL T FORD RACING

Did we follow the rules? Hell no,
but who was going to catch you?
— Auto racer Frank Janett

By 1940 there was still no indigenous racing in Alberta. In the manner of the nomadic carnivals, circuses, and Chautauquas that visited as many towns as possible in the Prairies' short summer, auto racers in the province were but transient showmen, little different from Barney Oldfield of three decades earlier.

Curiously, the onset of World War II provided the spark to get the sport started. In 1941, the Lions Club of Calgary had committed itself to supporting a charity for children in Britain orphaned by the war. As a fundraiser, they struck upon the idea of staging a car race. But what kind of race? With all machinery production in the country dedicated to the war effort, any competing vehicles would have to be pre-existing units, preferably with a large supply of parts already available. The obvious fit was the Model T Ford.

Again, because of the demands of the war effort, there was no way a new track could be built, and the Stampede Fairgrounds at Victoria Park had served the sport well before, so arrangements were made to stage the event there.

By today's standards, the rules were incredibly lax. The cars were required to use stock Model T mechanical parts. Roofs and windshields had to be removed. The cars could be stripped and their springs

Start of the 1942 Labour Day race, Calgary. Note vast differences in levels of car preparation. *(Glenbow Archives, Calgary)*

No roll bar, no seat belt, no helmet…no body! Len Erlam at Calgary, c. 1945. *(Tim Erlam collection)*

Consistently-fast Tom Fraser of Standard showing fine dirt-track form, Calgary, c. 1945. *(Glenbow Archives, Calgary)*

Same car, six months later. Tom Fraser had the mail-delivery contract for the Standard area, and converted his racer to a tracked snowmobile to get the job done. *(Glenbow Archives, Calgary)*

re-curved, but there was no requirement for any sort of safety equipment. The usual driver attire consisted of a cloth or leather helmet, goggles and coveralls, although one debonair fellow, W. A. Wocknitz of Magrath, Alberta, drove the first race in a suit, tie, and bowler hat.

Some 12,000 spectators showed up for the first Model T races on September 1, 1941. Thirty-three cars started the 200-lap, 100-mile event. When it was over, half the cars had been wrecked, but $5,000 had been raised for the bombing victims of Britain. Leading Aircraftman (LAC) Norman Price of Windsor, Ontario took home first prize of $250, beating out the aforementioned Mr. Wocknitz, who after safely driving 100 miles at racing speeds, happily waved his bowler hat to the cheering crowd on the cool-down lap, lost control, and crashed his car. There is no record of whether his second-place prize money was sufficient to cover his medical bills, and his name does not appear in any subsequent race records.

LAC Price, on the other hand, turned out to be something of a trendsetter in that he was the first of a number of servicemen who would do well in Model T races over the next four years. During the war, the Prairie Provinces were the home of the British Commonwealth Air Training Plan (BCATP), and small airbases were built near numerous prairie communities, expressly to train pilots and aircrew for the air forces of the Commonwealth. During the five years the plan lasted, almost 11,000 airplanes were used to train over 137,000 men at such places as Airdrie, Claresholm, Dewinton, Fort MacLeod, and Penhold. What this meant for racing was a huge supply of fit young men, many of whom were becoming skilled mechanics and who, given the opportunity, might just want to get involved in the sport. Many, like LAC Price, did so.

The positive effects of the BCATP on racing continued for many years after the war, when the then-abandoned airfields provided the venues for early drag and sports car races.

The success of the 1941 race made it inevitable there would be a sequel, and on September 7, 1942 a reported 17,000 fans showed up for a three-heat, one-main show on the Calgary oval. In the feature race, Don Robertson led fellow Calgarian Bud Lynch across the line to claim the $100 first prize.

While the size of the crowds at these races may be enough to make a present-day promoter envious, it is important to remember that pari-mutuel betting was available. The Amusements Act of Alberta licensed venues, rather than events, for gambling. As long as the track was able to provide a betting facility for horses, it could offer the same for cars. Perhaps spectator tastes haven't changed all that much over the years. Having said that, it remains that the 1942 Calgary Model T race drew the largest auto-racing crowd in Alberta until the first Edmonton Can-Am sports car race over 26 years later.

If something happens in Calgary, can Edmonton be far behind? In October 1942 Edmonton staged its first Model T race on the exhibition grounds oval. Eighteen racers entertained 8,000 fans in a race won by Sgt. Maj. J. H. Rees of the Royal Canadian Ordnance Corps.

After only two seasons it was obvious that the Lions Clubs of Calgary and Edmonton had a winner with Model T races, and the sport began to spread throughout the province.

Because of wartime gasoline rationing, races were shortened from the original 100-mile distance to typically 20 or 30 miles. With the increasing number of towns hosting events, this probably benefited everyone involved, as it is doubtful that many cars would have lasted long running 100-mile features.

The 1943 season saw tremendous growth in Model T racing, but it also highlighted the reality of the dangers inherent in the sport. In a heat race in Calgary, Corporal Segar had a tire blow out in a corner and he was catapulted from his car. The impact of his landing resulted in the only death to take place in a decade of Model T racing. As a result of the mishap, a rule was instituted requiring cars to arrive at the track early enough to be inspected by officials prior to the race. Remarkably though, the rules continued to make no mention of any safety equipment.

By 1944 the races had created sufficient interest to begin attracting the attention of the business community. Some companies felt that there was greater publicity to be had than merely having a brand name on the side of a dusty car—they could sponsor the race awards. Hudson's Bay Company put up a trophy in its name to be awarded to the Northern Alberta Champion. Maclin Motors, a

With their mechanical skills and daring, students in the British Commonwealth Air Training Program were naturals for Model T races. This group and their newly built racer were posted at Calgary. *(Glenbow Archives, Calgary)*

Arnold (left) and Gordon Rasmussen, c. 1946. In 2003 this car still sat in Gordon's garage near Standard. It was last driven in 2001. *(Glenbow Archives, Calgary)*

Mid 1940s Model T race at High Prairie. *(Provincial Archives of Alberta, A-5278)*

Calgary Ford dealership, donated the Maclin Cup for the winner of the by-now annual Labour Day Race. Maclin received its money's worth, as another 17,000 spectators watched the 1944 running of their race.

Toward the end of World War II, the sport was becoming, if not exactly professional, at least far more serious for the competitors than anything the Lions Club had ever envisaged in 1941. Whereas in the early races, anyone with a modicum of driving skill and a bit of luck had a chance to win (the first seven races were taken by seven different drivers), by late 1944 a hard core of dedicated racers was beginning to dominate. Local servicemen or farmers looking for a novel weekend didn't stand much of a chance of keeping up with the likes of Tom and Bob Villetard, Stan and Ted Reynolds, Vic Bennett, Con Heighington, Gordon Rasmussen, or Tom Fraser. These men knew how to modify and tune their cars to get far more performance than Henry Ford had ever imagined when he designed his masterpiece of practical family transportation.

Some of what the drivers called "tuning" was more like outright modification and appears to have taken advantage of a lack of policing skills among the race organizers. In 1948 George Lemay and Frank Janett, after spending a winter replacing the cast-iron Model T pistons with aluminum Chevrolet pieces, hand-building custom camshafts, offsetting the connecting rod bearings to increase compression, and, in the case of Lemay, gun-drilling the crankshaft to allow for pressure oiling, took their Model T bugs out on the highway and paced them with a speedometer-equipped passenger car. Speeds of 90 miles per hour were reached—something like double the top speed of a stock Model T. At that, George and Frank were still not the fastest of the Model T racers.

Fuel also came in for special treatment, with ether being a popular additive. Gordon Rasmussen remembers so much of it being used that "the pits smelled like a hospital operating room."

Years later, Frank Janett was asked if this kind of mechanical inventiveness was within the rules. "Hell no," he replied. "But who was going to catch you?"

The serious racers also developed driving skills far beyond those of the casual competitor. While we don't have any benchmarks by which to compare Model T drivers to modern dirt trackers, we do know that oval-track racing rewards experience, and by 1945 the winning drivers all had hundreds, perhaps thousands of competition miles behind them.

While most venues followed a proven formula of dirt track events during the summer months, there were occasional novelties. In 1947, a track was ploughed in the snow of the buffalo paddock at Banff and races were held as part of the annual Winter Carnival. Many drivers fashioned crude studded tires by putting bolts into holes drilled in their tires and running liners or "boots" inside to protect the inner tubes.

Toward the end of the decade, Model T racing, novelty events or not, was beginning to grow stale. Pari-mutuel betting was only available at the fairground tracks, and the horse-racing fraternity was becoming vocal in its opposition to sharing the tracks (and betting proceeds) with cars. The better drivers were moving on to newer machinery, and with a growing sense of optimism and prosperity in the province, there was little appeal in using 20- to 40-year-old cars as the basis for a racing class. The crowds were dwindling, and the last-ever Alberta Model T race was held on September 8, 1951 at the track where it all began, the fairgrounds oval in Calgary. The winner was Tom Fraser of Standard.

CHAPTER 4

AFTER T, WHAT NEXT?

You can do anything you want, but
you can't do everything you want.
—George Torok

1951 marked eleven consecutive years of Model T Ford racing in Alberta. The sport that began life as a one-time fund-raiser and had gone on to entertain hundreds of thousands, was growing stale. The cars were now anywhere from 20 to 40 years old, and younger fans, the future of the racing market, did not relate to them. With every passing year, there were fewer parts-donor cars to draw on, and the fields were thinning.

The first post-war race of anything other that Model Ts came in 1949 when Emory Collins led a troupe of I.M.C.A. racers to Alberta. These cars would today be referred to as sprint cars, but that term had not yet come into common use, and perhaps we should digress for a moment to look at the vernacular of the sport.

Prior to the 1930s, there were race cars, period. Out of the Depression of that decade came a need to economize in all aspects of life, including racing, and the midget racer was born. With its lighter weight and smaller engine, the midget burned less fuel, wore out fewer and smaller tires, and was cheaper to haul. The concept was an immediate success. Logically, people then began referring to traditional-size race cars as "big cars," and these were the cars that I.M.C.A. brought to Alberta in 1949. But even within the ranks of big cars, there were divisions. While prior to World War II, professional oval racers often used their same cars for long, paved speedways and shorter dirt tracks, a new generation of constructors in the late 1940s began building specialized chassis for different types of track. Shorter, more upright cars proved more effective on the smaller tracks, particularly dirt, while lower, longer, more aerodynamic cars worked better on bigger, paved tracks. The shorter cars were originally called "dirt cars," but that term was not an effective promotional and advertising tool. In the late '40s the name "sprint cars" was coined, acknowledging the fact that most dirt-track races covered relatively short distances. The divide between the two kinds of "big cars" was neither sudden nor absolute. Short-wheelbase cars continued to appear at the Indianapolis 500 and at other high-speed tracks well into the mid '50s. In fact, it was in just such a car that Troy Ruttman won the event in 1952. The lower, longer, "roadsters" raced only occasionally on dirt.

The I.M.C.A cars that Collins brought to Alberta normally raced on dirt, and they would soon be commonly referred to as sprint cars.

Spectators at the 1949 shows included a number of the men who had driven Model Ts throughout the decade. Impressed by the performance of the I.M.C.A. cars and realizing that their old cars represented a dying breed, many set to work building their own big cars. Len Erlam, Frank Janett, Jack Landage, George Lemay, Jim Orchard, Goldie Patterson, Jim Puller, Bob Rogers, Frank Taylor, Jim Ward, and Lou Weidner were all among the early group of drivers who built cars. Their cars had solid axles front and rear, and the majority were powered by Ford and Mercury flathead V-8s.

The drivers formed the Alberta Auto Racing Association (A.A.R.A.) under president George Lemay and, beginning in 1950, ran their races on fairgrounds ovals in Three Hills, Calgary, Edmonton, Red Deer, Nanton, Lacombe, Brooks, and Lethbridge. In their advertising, A.A.R.A. optimistically referred to their cars as "Indianapolis Speedway–type cars." The strategy appears to have been effective, as the Edmonton and Calgary presses reported crowds as large as 6,000. When I.M.C.A. returned in 1950, A.A.R.A. drivers joined them in Edmonton and Calgary. George Lemay won the A.A.R.A. championship in 1950 and 1951. Joined sometimes by Frank Taylor, he began following the I.M.C.A. tour in '51, and Alberta had its first truly professional race driver, Lemay being able to support himself for half the year from his racing earnings.

George Lemay's car, like the other Alberta cars, was a home-built chassis—a narrowed 1927 Chev frame in this case—with a Ford flat-head V-8 engine. On the I.M.C.A. tour, he was marginally competitive—he always managed to lap fast enough to qualify; however, he wasn't winning. At a race in Oklahoma in 1952, he found himself lapped by the race leaders despite never once lifting his foot off the throttle pedal. More power was obviously needed, and a friend suggested a Ranger aircraft engine. The Ranger was a 440-cubic-inch (7.2-litre), air-cooled, six-cylinder engine. As aircraft engines should be, it was built to last, with low compression, and two complete, separate ignition systems. At 195 pounds (89 kg), it was far lighter than the Ford engine, and it didn't require the extra weight of a radiator. Perhaps best of all, it was cheap. While no record exists of what George Lemay paid for his engine, there were widely circulated stories of these military surplus units selling for as low as $75—with the rest of the airplane thrown in. With his new power source, George was able to run close to the front of I.M.C.A. in 1953, although he did come back to Alberta before the season ended. On home ground, his car was virtually unbeatable.

As exciting as they were, the big/sprint/Indianapolis cars would not last long in Alberta. The horse-racing fraternity, which had watched in sullen silence as Model Ts ate into their pari-mutuel market in the '40s, now found their tracks being literally torn apart by the V-8–driven knobby tires of these new cars. Gavin Breckenridge recalls standing near the rail at the Edmonton track during a practice session in 1951. Next to Gavin was Bill Connelly, an Exhibition Association director. As the cars slid through the corners, hurling chunks of dirt into and over the fence, Connelly said, "This is the last time there will be cars racing on this track." And it was.

That same year, Gavin Breckenridge and Oscar Green opened their new speedway in North Edmonton. The sprint cars appeared at the first race, but their drivers wanted tow money as well as prize

Sprint-car pace lap at Red Deer fairgrounds, c. 1950. Jim Ward centre, Frank Janett outside pole. George Lemay is in the dark car on second row pole. Pole car driver's identity is unknown. *(Frank Janett collection)*

Early '50s race-car transport. This is the trailer and race car of Lou Weidner. There were no ramps; a group of volunteers simply lifted the car onto the deck. *(Lou Weidner collection)*

money, and the partners weren't prepared to do that. The sprint cars did not return.

Meanwhile, midget race cars began to carve a niche in the racing market. Not full-sized midgets—if that is not a contradiction in terms—but rather ¾ midgets, and micro midgets that were the idea of promoter Al Davey. Davey, an aircraft machinist from Moose Jaw, Saskatchewan, felt that the cinder tracks around the perimeters of the Mewata and Clarke football stadiums at Calgary and Edmonton respectively were the right size for these tiniest of race cars.

The ¾ midgets, or "t.q." cars as they were commonly known, weighed 450 pounds (200 kg) and were generally powered by 500-cc motorcycle engines, although at least one had a Crosley car engine. The micros were not much larger than modern-day karts, weighing 250 pounds (114 kg), with Villiers 7.5-horsepower engines. Davey, who had earlier in his career built hand-control systems to enable paraplegics to drive cars, now built ten micros and three t.q. cars, while Tom Fox built a fourth t.q.

While building his racers, Davey contacted the Calgary Stampeders and Edmonton Eskimos and gained their backing to run on the tracks. On June 14, 1951, Davey's midgets held their first race, before a crowd of 2,000 at Clarke Stadium, featuring nine cars with 11 drivers—Davey and his track manager, Pat Higgs, borrowed cars for a match race won by Davey. The feature was an Australian Tag (same as Pursuit) race, won by Jim Dent over Doug Werner, who earlier set fastest time of the evening.

Davey promoted his sport through the summer and fall of 1951 with a continuous flow of media advertising. He also invited reporters to participate in a press and radio championship, with as many as six reporters and photographers competing. The papers reciprocated with a level of coverage not seen since the early days of Model T racing. Initially it paid off, and on July 19, 3,000 Calgarians watched the micros take to the track at Mewata. Again Jim Dent took the feature, with Model T veteran Vic Bennett claiming the Australian Tag race.

Davey's long-range goal was to have midget car racing across the country, and in August he held the organizational meeting of the

Canadian Midget Auto Racing Association in Calgary. Art Cantin, an Edmonton machinist who had done much of the engine work on the cars, was elected president.

August 9 saw 3,500 fans show up at Mewata to watch Keith Perry take the feature, while Tommy Rutter won the Australian Tag. A t.q. car had been promised at this race, but failed to show. Sadly, it would be June of the following year before any of the larger cars were seen on the tracks. The season, which was shortened by a series of rain-outs, ended with Jim Dent winning the championship.

For 1952, Davey increased the size of his ads and added relay races to his program. The micro-car field took on fresh new faces, among them Art Cantin and motorcycle veteran Walt Healey, but overall the car count increased only to 11. The bigger, more expensive ads did not have any apparent effect on crowd size. At season's end, Edmonton driver Pete Sikora won the Davey Trophy as series champion.

By 1953, Davey was struggling. The gate revenue was simply not keeping up with his many expenses. Prize money, advertising, and maintaining and repairing cars for the media races were all financial drains. The tiny micro-midgets were effectively all he had to offer the public as he was never able to field more than three of the faster t.q. cars at one time. The midget race car series ended operations in early 1953, with Al Davey having lost his life savings.

As discussed elsewhere in this book, the first stock car race in Alberta was held in Red Deer in 1950, and by 1951, the new Breckenridge Speedway in Edmonton was running stock cars exclusively. The cars at Breckenridge were not, however, completely stock. Removal of all or part of the fenders, replacement of stock bumpers with more durable steel-pipe bumpers, and removal of window and lighting glass were all either permitted or required on the 10- to 20-year-old racers. The design of Alberta stock cars was already beginning to move more in the direction of modifieds than pure stock. Late-model, full-bodied stock car racing was primarily an American form of the sport, and a touring show came to Alberta in June of 1951. Promoter Frank R. Winkley brought a field of 1946–1951 model cars to Edmonton, Calgary, and Lethbridge to stage 100-lap, 50-mile races on the fairground ovals. The largest crowd was a reported 6,000 in Calgary, but this was apparently not enough to encourage Winkley to return. Unlike the early years of the century in which touring American shows provided the only racing, Model Ts, sprints, midgets, and finally stock cars had shown Albertans they could run their own races, and they would now support their own drivers.

CHAPTER 5

FRANK JANETT

Frank Janett is the grandfather of racing in Western Canada.
—Ron Harris, 2002

Originally, Frank Janett was supposed to be a source of background information for this book, and nothing more, but four hours into a planned 30-minute interview, it had become obvious that the man was a chapter, if not a whole book, himself. Equally adept as racer and raconteur, Frank Janett holds your attention.

Since the early 1940s, Frank Janett's life has been intertwined with the growth of oval track racing in Western Canada. That's unusual, for someone who almost made it to the Olympics as an athlete.

Frank's racing career began in Calgary in the 1930s, on two wheels. In the Depression years, bicycle racing was a major sport with any number of ways for an athletic youth to compete. From 1934 to 1938 Frank raced in an annual Cochrane-to-Calgary event. He also raced from Edmonton to Calgary and participated in unique events such as one that ran from Southwest Calgary to the Elbow River, at which point the competitors had to carry their bikes across the river, then ride up the North Hill. "Sort of like that Ironman thing you see on TV," recalls Frank, "except we didn't have to swim; just wade."

In 1939 Frank won the gold medal for cycling at the Highland Games in Edmonton. This was a major event, and winners were often invited to join the Olympic team. Unfortunately, by autumn, the world was preoccupied with war, and the 1940 Olympics were never held.

In 1941 Frank was a spectator at an event that was to turn him from bicycles to cars forever. The first Model T race was held on the fairgrounds oval at Victoria Park in Calgary that Labour Day, and Frank became hooked. "I figured those fellows had something there," he recalls. Within weeks he had started building his own "bug," as they were called: a stripped-down Model T Ford. Unfortunately, world politics in general and the Royal Canadian Navy in particular had other plans for young Mr. Janett through 1945. Posted to St. John's, Newfoundland, Frank had spent only a little time on the sea when he was approached by an officer who asked if it was true he had been an auto bodyman in Calgary. When Frank confirmed that that was indeed his trade, the officer took him to a fenced compound full of damaged military vehicles and put him to work getting them back on the road. "And that's how I spent the war."

Once he was released from the navy in 1945, Frank wasted little time finishing his Model T racer. By early summer 1946 he was racing his bug on fairground ovals around Alberta, but rarely winning. Within a year he realized he could, and indeed should, be able to get more speed out of the car. Fellow racer George Lemay felt the same way and the two spent the winter of 1947–48 reworking the stock parts of their cars. Camshafts in particular came under scrutiny. There was little in the way of aftermarket performance parts at that time, but shouldn't it be possible, they wondered, to take a stock camshaft, increase the profile of the lobes with brazing, and then file or grind them down for a better-performing lift? And how about the pistons? The Ford's were cast iron, while Chevrolet used aluminum, and they were close to the same size—could they be switched? The two men worked independently on their engines to see who could come up with the best results.

As mentioned earlier, in the spring of 1948 they took their cars out on a highway, accompanied by a friend with a late-model car. Paced by the speedometer-equipped road car, they measured the speed of their racers. George's clocked just over 90 miles per hour

(146 kmh), with Frank coming in about two mph (3 kmh) short of that. They now knew how to make Model Ts go fast, but found they were behind the times, as the public was losing interest in the 30-year-old Fords, and far bigger game was appearing on the horizon.

In 1948 a touring International Motor Contest Association show was staged at the Victoria Park oval. No Model Ts these, but purpose-built race cars with what appeared to Frank like massive reserves of horsepower. He decided he had to have one and spent the winter building. By the following spring, there were between 12 and 14 of the new cars. The Alberta Auto Racing Association was formed, Alberta had sprint car racing, and Frank Janett was part of it.

In 1950, Alberta saw its first-ever stock car race, and Frank found time from his sprint car efforts to show up with his 1939 Ford as the Red Deer Fairgrounds hosted a one-day show with a field of ten very stock cars. Frank remembers that the pre-race preparation of his car consisted of removing the passenger seats, raising the tire pressure, and taking the belt off his trousers to tie the driver's door shut. There was no technical inspection.

Now here is where recollection and history differ. Frank recalls that he won the first-ever stock car race in Alberta, but according to the Red Deer *Advocate* of the day, under the front-page headline "Stock Racing Cars Prove Fine Sport," the first heat race was won by Bob Rogers of Strathmore. In the second race "Frank Janet" (sic) is noted as having smashed through a railing. Frank came back for the fifth race, which he indeed won, setting the fastest time of the day at 57.1 miles per hour. In the feature, Frank finished second to George Lemay, in the words of the *Advocate*, "threatening but never able to overcome the bursts of Lemay's tiny orange racer[1] on the straight stretches."

---

1. The *Advocate's* reference to Lemay's car as "tiny" is troubling. Frank Janett, with no prompting, identified the Red Deer Fairgrounds and July 1950 as the time and place of the first stock car race. The Advocate's headline of "Stock Racing Cars" would appear to confirm that these were, indeed, stock cars. However the description of Lemay's car leaves open the possibility that these were actually the A.A.R.A. sprint cars that would better fit that description. Additionally, the lap speed of 57 mph on a half-mile dirt track seems fast for an early stock car. If Frank Janett's memory and the *Advocate's* headline are incorrect, then the first stock car race in Alberta would have been the travelling show of Frank R. Winkley discussed in Chapter 4.

Frank, right, gives son Paul a lesson in tuning Model T racers, c. 1949. Man in centre is friend Tom Bell. *(Frank Janett collection)*

Frank celebrating a win in Lethbridge, 1951, in "Deacon" Jim Ward's sprint car. Note chequered flag, which appears to be someone's missing tablecloth. *(Frank Janett collection)*

Early Calgary stock car racers, c. 1954. Back row, from left: Frank Janett, Jim Ward, Kelly Save, unknown; front row, from left: George Lemay, Roy Sharratt. *(Frank Janett collection)*

Frank clowning with his poorly-performing CAMRA supermodified, Speedway Park, Edmonton, 1966. White car in background posed for photo with crew belongs to Eldon Rasmussen. *(Frank Janett collection)*

So to be precise, Frank Janett did not win the first-ever stock car race in Alberta. He can, however, lay claim to a heat-race victory, a feature-race second, a fastest lap of the day, and a crash, all on the first day of stock car racing in the province.

Sprint cars continued to be the premier racing class and the prime focus of Frank's considerable energies. George Lemay and Frank Taylor joined I.M.C.A. and toured in the United States. Frank Janett, however, had a young family and a business and elected to stay closer to home and race locally, taking only a few brief trips south.

In 1951, Frank had an accident that caused him to rethink his racing future. In a sprint car race on the Victoria Park oval, while trying to pass another car on the inside line, his left front wheel became caught in the dirt berm running along the base of the fence. The soft earth drew his car into the fence, where it took out a row of posts, some of which pierced the car's thin body shell. One post lacerated his torso, while another ripped flesh from his thigh. The injuries hospitalized Frank, and while he was recuperating, his wife, Bertha, a Newfoundland girl he had met while on service in the war and subsequently married in 1946, let it be known she thought it was time to put an end to this foolish racing business. Sprint car racing was simply too dangerous for a man with responsibilities. Frank wasn't, by his own admission, in much of a position to argue, particularly in light of how close the timber had come to tearing his genitals. The advent of sprint cars had brought with it previously unheard of safety measures such as seat belts and crash helmets, but his own painful injuries were proof that the sport still presented great risks.

Bertha—or Bea as he called her—had always been supportive of Frank's racing, but the boundaries of her patience had been reached. Remembering his stock car experience of a year earlier, he offered that version of the sport with its steel doors and roofs, partially-fendered wheels, and in some cases, roll bars, as a safer option; more appropriate to a man "with responsibilities." Bea reluctantly agreed and the Janett family had found a compromise. "You could never find another woman like her," he recalls with just a tiny catch in his throat. "She just took everything in stride." Bertha Janett died in the mid 1980s.

As luck would have it, regular stock car racing in Calgary was about to begin. The stimulus for stock car racing was the construction of Alberta's first paved race track, Springbank Speedway, on the south outskirts of town.

When Springbank Speedway opened, Frank Janett was offered a ride by wealthy Calgary oilman Carl Nickle. He gladly accepted, but on the condition he could dictate how the car would be prepared and set up for racing. The reason Frank wanted this authority was that his old friend George Lemay had come back from his tours with I.M.C.A. with many ideas he had picked up about chassis set-up and had shared them with Frank. Competing in what was, in Calgary at least, a fledgling sport, but with a reservoir of information gained from others vastly more experienced, Frank found himself with a huge competitive advantage that he was eager to put to work.

After driving his homemade, crudely prepared sprinter on dirt, driving a new stock car on asphalt was, in the man's own words, "like taking candy from a baby." In his first season with the new car, Frank won 13 straight features, including what he considers the greatest victory of his career, the Carl Nickle Trophy, the first-ever 500-lap race in Alberta. This is what he calls the start of "glory days." He ran stock cars through the early and mid 1950s, even winning once in 1954 driving a flathead-6 Dodge at a time when that make of car was rarely ever considered for competition.

But as always, the sport was changing, and true stock cars were evolving into modifieds: cars based on stock components but with fenders removed and extensive modifications to chassis and engines. Later, when modifieds became too hard to regulate, the super-modified was born: basically a sprint car with a full roll cage supporting a token roof. In order to retain some modicum of "stock," the cars were powered by production-based V-8s rather than the Offenhauser fours normally found in sprint cars. Frank evolved with his sport and by the late '50s was driving a super-modified.

Frank became known to track announcers as "Leadfoot Frank"—hardly original, but an accurate description of the man's driving style. He also developed a reputation as a racer who was happy to run in any car made available to him, never back away from a competitor, and have a good time both on and off the track. In the late '50s, a group of racers were partying at a Calgary motel when Frank, thoroughly drunk—a common condition for him in those years—took up a dare to dive into the swimming pool, clothed only in his undershorts. Regrettably, he had forgotten that it was late October, by which time most Calgary swimming pools, this one included, had been drained. The results were dental work, stitches, and a few cracked bones. "Nothing serious," recalls Frank.

Every veteran oval track racer, it would seem, has a favourite Frank Janett story. Eldon Rasmussen's brother Arnold recounts the time in the mid 1960s when Eldon had travelled alone to Vancouver Island for back-to-back races in Nanaimo and Victoria. On Friday night, he had hit the wall, and the car, while repairable, would take more work than one man could do in time to have it ready for the Sunday race. He called Arnold in Calgary to see if he could drive out to the Island in Eldon's dealer-demonstrator Chev to help. Arnold agreed and suggested he could bring Frank Janett with him. Frank was happy to come along and even offered to drive. "You know, that was 700 miles, in a six-cylinder car," recalls Arnold, "and without a word of a lie, Frank drove from Bowness to the Tsawwassen Ferry Terminal in nine hours, five minutes!"

Another anecdote often told about Frank and detailed in the Calgary *Albertan,* concerns a close race between Jim Ward and Frank in the early '50s. The two were friends; so much so that they had on occasion loaned each other their cars. But this time, as they approached the finish line, bumping for position, their wheels tangled, causing the cars to wreck. Both racers jumped from their cars and began throwing punches. Years later, the two men, once again friends, would laugh about the incident. "He was no sportsman," recalled Frank, pointing at Jim Ward. "Just when I had him lined up for a clean punch, he ducked and I broke my knuckle on the guardrail."

"Yeah, but who won the race?" counters Jim Ward. "I did."

On another occasion, Jim Ward had survived a major wreck, but his 1935 Ford was beyond repair. He complained to Frank that he needed another car of the same model to be fitted with his remaining racing parts so he could resume his career. Frank mentioned that he had noticed a '35 parked for many weeks on a nearby street. "Do you think you could find out if the guy will sell it?" asked Jim. Frank was happy to oblige.

The next day he appeared at Jim's garage with the old Ford in tow. "How did you find the owner?" asked Jim.

"How the hell would I know who the owner is?" replied Frank. "It looked abandoned to me." A half-century later, when recounting this story, he wonders aloud if he should still be watching out for the police.

When the Canadian American Modified Association (CAMRA) was formed in 1963, Frank joined their circuit throughout Western Canada and the northwestern U.S. The racing was fast and close, with at least six of its drivers graduating to the Indianapolis 500. In this company, Frank was competitive, but rarely a front-runner.

In 1969 he made the decision to retire from driving and leave the racing to men younger than his half century. His driving career had spanned three decades, beginning with a stripped Model T Ford and ending with a tube-frame racer, its 500-plus horsepower transferred to the pavement by wide slick tires pressed down by the force of a massive rooftop wing.

Simply quitting driving did not end Frank Janett's involvement with the sport he loved; he soon found himself promoting races and working on the executive of CAMRA. Promoting was not always an easy job. As auto racing grew, resistance to its success began to appear in some media sports departments, where stick and ball games were seen as the only real sports. Paying a visit to the sports editor of the Calgary *Herald,* Hal Walker, to drum up publicity for an upcoming CAMRA race, Frank was bluntly told that auto racing was not a sport, and if he wanted publicity, he should go down the hall to the advertising department because there was no room for his event on this man's sports pages. And would he please leave. Now. "Threw me right out of his office," Frank says, with his distinctive chuckle.

Undeterred by such setbacks, he continued in this capacity until 1974, when the fun of promoting races abruptly disappeared. Frank had helped organize a CAMRA race in Cranbrook, BC, and among

CAMRA race, Victoria, 1969, Frank on outside pole. *(Frank Janett collection)*

the competitors were Babe and Jerry Sneva of Spokane, Washington, brothers of future Indianapolis 500 champion Tom Sneva, and sons of Edsel Sneva, Frank's best friend on the CAMRA executive. During time trials, something broke on the right front suspension of Babe's car and the racer cartwheeled off the end of the track, coming to rest nose down in a pond. When safety crew and volunteers got to the car, they found Babe unconscious. The Cranbrook hospital diagnosed head and internal injuries. Once Babe's condition stabilized, he was transferred to a facility near his home, where he died a short time later. Frank is obviously not comfortable talking about this episode, and his career as a promoter ended there.

For the next few years Frank stayed in touch with his sport by helping out any racer who could make use of his varied skills as a mechanic, bodyman, welder, and chassis set-up artist. In 1978 Calgary racer Buddie Boys bought an Indianapolis car and entered it in the 500. Frank was asked to go along as mechanic and quickly agreed. Unfortunately neither Boys nor journeyman driver Bob Harkey was able to qualify the car for the race. Frank went back to Indianapolis later with a fourth Sneva brother, Jan, but once more they failed to qualify. In 1980, Boys and Janett went to Indianapolis again, this time with an all-Calgary team. Driver Frank Weiss passed his rookie driver's test but crashed heavily in practice, destroying the car, and breaking both legs.

In 1983 Frank was invited to become part of a stock car team organized by Calgary businessman and former sports car racer Maurice McCaig. The driver was Buddie Boys' son Trevor. Trevor had enjoyed some success with sprint cars and midgets in the U.S., and Formula Vee in Canadian Automobile Sport Clubs (CASC) Prairie Region races. Everyone involved felt he was now ready to take the next step on the racing ladder, and the team entered the National Association of Stock Car Auto Racing (NASCAR) Winston Cup Series, the biggest league in stock car racing. Once the intrepid Calgarians arrived in the bailiwick of NASCAR in the southeastern United States, they soon found that there was a lot to learn, and no one was giving free lessons. NASCAR was, in Frank's words, "a closed shop." After a few quick doses of humility at the hands of Southern boys, they decided the only way they were going to become competitive was to hire an experienced team. The veteran James Hylton crew was in need of a car and driver, so a deal was struck, with Frank staying on.

"I got an education you wouldn't believe," he recalls. The team competed at all NASCAR venues and began to win places, points, and money; but not races. After two seasons in the south, Frank returned home to Calgary to take care of business and family, but remains proud of his forays into the major leagues of racing. "I got to know all those guys down there," he says. "Hell, I got A. J. Foyt's phone number right here." He pulls out a pocket address book and hands it across the table. "Here, you want to talk to A. J.? There's his number."

When he returned to Calgary in late middle age, Frank's involvement in racing still wasn't over. He continued to help various racers with car preparation, but in 1994 received a different kind of offer. Ben Docktor, owner of Calgary's Race City Speedway, wanted to bring outlaw-style sprint cars to his oval. He needed a race steward or pit boss who was knowledgable about racing and had the strength of personality to deal effectively and authoritatively with the often vocal, strong-willed men who drive sprint cars. Frank was Ben's choice, and to the credit of both men, the sprint cars, designed and built to compete on dirt tracks, staged an exciting show on asphalt at Calgary for two seasons.

Frank lives alone in his house just around the corner from the bodyshop he and his son Paul operate. Frank is now over 80, but it is only in the past few years that he has begun to distance himself from the day-to-day business of body repair. He still keeps his racing contacts warm. He flew to Toronto recently to witness his old friend Eldon Rasmussen's induction into the Motorsport Hall of Fame, and makes regular visits to Race City Speedway.

When asked if he would change anything if he had his life to live over again, Frank's often-rheumy eyes suddenly brighten. "Damn right I would. " He pauses for effect. "I'd be twice as wild!" He chuckles. "Don't you think that'd be fun?"

CHAPTER 6

MEN IN DRAG

*Never again will I use the hackneyed term
"neck-snapping acceleration" in one of my road test columns.*
—Calgary *Herald* automotive columnist
Art Suderman, 1986, after taking his first
ride as a passenger in a drag-race car

In road racing, no Albertan has ever won a Formula One race. On asphalt oval tracks, no Albertan has taken first place in a NASCAR Winston Cup or Grand National race, nor in an Indy car race. In sprint car racing, Tim Gee earned two World of Outlaws feature-race wins in his six-plus years on that tour.

In light of that sparse harvest, it is remarkable that Alberta drag racers have, at the time this is being written in early 2004, won no less than 34 National Hot Rod Association (NHRA) nationals. Of the thirteen Albertans in the Canadian Motorsport Hall of Fame, all but four are drag racers.

The cynic might suggest that because drag racing involves driving in a straight line, and most of Alberta is flat, there is not much chance to learn how to go around corners fast. That convenient line of reasoning would have to ignore the frightening reality that many an Alberta wanna-be boy-racer first practised his craft on the curves of Highway 1A, Groat Road, or Edmonton's infamous traffic circles. In truth, there are probably as many reasons for the province's drag racing achievements as there are successful racers.

Richard Chevalier explains the workings of his car to drag racing's biggest fan, Highways Minister Hon. Gordon Taylor, at Highway 14X racing site in 1960. Mechanic Orie Bazan is at left. *(Richard Chevalier collection)*

Namao: Geoff Goodwin in the dragster goes against the coupe of Verne Massey from Davenport, Washington. *(Richard Chevalier collection)*

Acrobatic starter John Chalmers flags off this race at Namao.
(Richard Chevalier collection)

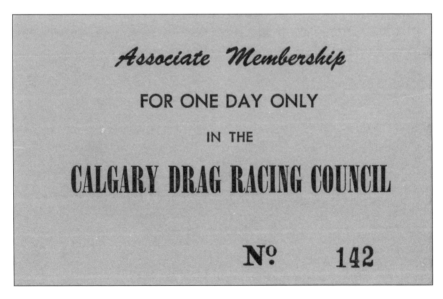

One of Gene McMahon's numerous attempts to circumvent the Lord's Day Act
at Shephard (1963). One dollar and you were part of the club.
(Gene McMahon collection)

The first drag race in Alberta was held in 1953, on Princess Elizabeth Avenue in Edmonton, and involved two Mercuries, driven by Orv Bambush and Art Delmar. The starter for the race was the youngest member of the Roadents Car Club, Geoff Goodwin, who, being legally unable to drive anything, was given the job of flagging. Geoff recalls that the race was sanctioned by the City and was the Edmonton hot-rod community's salute to the coronation of Queen Elizabeth II. The event was not timed and covered only 200 feet or so. The first proper quarter-mile race would not take place until 1955, when Calgary hot rodders gained permission to run on the abandoned British Commonwealth Air Training Program airstrip at DeWinton, south of Calgary.

Calgary hot rodders were able to race fairly regularly in the 1950s, using the airstrips at DeWinton, Airdrie, Claresholm, Lincoln Park, and Shepard, but through a curious sequence of events, the sport never would have succeeded in Alberta as it did if Edmonton racers, who were reduced to running ice drags on Cooking Lake, had not found themselves without a track.

Edmontonian Jim Martin went to California on a holiday in early 1958 and friends there took him to several drag races. Jim was quickly caught up by the power and excitement of the sport, and on his return home joined the Rebels Car Club, a local hot-rod club. His enthusiasm for organized drag racing was infectious, and the club began to consider how it could find a strip of pavement to enable the sport to get started locally. One member, Terry Badger, originally from Drumheller, was acquainted with the Member of the Legislative Assembly for that area, the Honourable Gordon E. Taylor. By happy coincidence, Mr. Taylor was also minister of highways for the province. Terry thought that perhaps his MLA could be of help and arranged an appointment to see him. Terry, Jim Martin, and Ed Carrol of the Rebels met Taylor in his office, described their sport to him, and explained how it provided a safe opportunity for hot-rodders to test their home-built cars against others. Gordon Taylor was not the hardest sell the three could have had, as he had a long record of working with youth, both as a school teacher and as a volunteer organizer of a summer camp for underprivileged children. He liked what he heard from these "fine young men" as he called them, and offered to help.

The racers then boldly offered to escort the minister to the nearest permanent drag strip, at Deer Park, Washington, north of Spokane. They compared calendars and discovered that there was a highways conference in Spokane on the Friday and Saturday prior to an upcoming race meet at Deer Park. So one Thursday in June, Taylor, Badger, Carrol, and Martin all piled into the older man's Chrysler and headed south.

They were delayed more than an hour in Wetaskiwin when the transmission failed, but Taylor quickly got on the phone and commandeered a government car. When they finally arrived in Spokane, the minister handed the keys to the Chevrolet to his new friends and asked them to pick him up at his hotel Sunday morning—he wouldn't need a car while in conference.

If Taylor liked what he had heard about drag racing, he liked what he saw even more. Like Jim Martin before him, Taylor was hooked; so much so that at one point in the day, officials chased him off the track as he and his 8-millimetre movie camera got too close to the action for his safety and their comfort. He told the Edmonton rodders he would be happy to help them in any way he could, although he did warn them he was concerned that the Rebels were only one small car club, and there were other similar organizations out there. If he helped the Rebels, certainly the others would expect the same. Could they get together? In short order, the Rebels joined with the Sultans and the West Edmonton Drifters to form the Northern Alberta Drag Racing Council (N.A.D.R.C.), and it was on behalf of that body that Taylor contacted Group Captain Carr, commanding officer of the Royal Canadian Air Force base at Namao, just north of the city. Did the base have any pavement it didn't need? Arrangements were quickly made to close off the access road to the Number 7 Supply Depot, and that is where Edmonton drag racing began.

As happy as the racers were to finally have a facility, only a few drag meets were held before they realized the limitations of the site. Parking and access were problematic, but most importantly, the road was too narrow for two cars to race safely side-by-side. With deep ditches on either side, any high-speed accident could, and probably would be, catastrophic. They had promised the minister safe sport, and this wasn't it.

Another approach was made to Taylor, and this time he made the decision that above all else he did as minister of highways, gave legend to his term of office. The Honourable Gordon E. Taylor ordered that Highway 14X east of Edmonton, and the newly constructed Barlow Trail in Calgary, be closed on Sundays, as needed, for drag racing.

Public reaction was strongly negative. People relied on these roads for their day-to-day transportation. Why should they have to give them up so a bunch of kids could race their noisy cars? But Taylor was a veteran of political battles and equal to the challenge. When golfers at a course near Highway 14X publicly complained about being forced to take a detour around the drag strip to get to their club house, the minister stood at the roadblock and stopped their cars long enough to apologize for the inconvenience, explaining the need to provide a facility for his "fine young men" to practise their sport.

The public outrage he had to face for his decision was only temporary. The anger of golfers and acreage owners has long since disappeared, but the reverence with which the drag racing community views the man continues to grow as the young hot rodders of 1959 have matured and now more fully understand the political, and indeed, moral courage required to take the stand Taylor did.

Jim Martin: "You name me any politician today that would stand out on a highway just to talk to people who were pissed off with him. Or hand the keys to a government car to a bunch of hot-rodders."

Gene McMahon: "Gordon Taylor's a very special human being. He took a lot of flak over this. Big-time flak. Imagine today if you went out and closed down 22X for a day and let a bunch of people race on it. You know how much static you'd be getting?"

Richard Chevalier: "He legitimized the sport in Alberta because of his prominence in public life. When he said, 'These young men need a place to race their cars,' people listened. He also educated us on what we had to do to gain respect in the community. He got us started delivering gifts for Santas Anonymous, and even doing volunteer valet parking at a university fund-raising dinner."

Gordon Jenner: "Just look at what he gave us."

Just as he had earlier feared would happen, Taylor was approached in 1959 by a new group, the Edmonton Timing Association. The ETA was a joint effort of the Roadents Car Club and a number of independent drag racers. The group had just bought $10,000 worth of timing equipment and was looking for the same highway access N.A.D.R.C. had been given. Rather than say yes or no, Taylor invited both associations to meet in his conference room to determine how they could work together for the betterment of their sport. The gathering, with the minister mediating, resulted in the amalgamation of the two groups to form the Capital City Hot Rod Association (C.C.H.R.A.), or "Cha-cha hurrah" as it was quickly dubbed. C.C.H.R.A. still conducts drag races in the Edmonton area, and did so on Highway 14X for four years.

Public roads are not race tracks—they were never designed with that in mind. No highway engineer ever planned that crowds of people would stand on the road allowance, or that a car would accelerate so quickly as to cause the clutch to explode. But that's what happened in 1963 on 14X. The Tony Allison–Bill Sherman Chrysler-powered Messerschmidt sent shrapnel flying into the crowd, destroying the eye of a high-school girl.[1] C.C.H.R.A., which had no money to speak of, was sued.

At the time, the Government of Alberta had in place the Unsatisfied Judgement Fund. If a motorist involved in an accident was uninsured—which was then legal—the Unsatisfied Judgment Fund would pay the claim, but the motorist would be indebted to the fund and would have to repay the amount of the judgment or settlement, plus interest. The fund was never intended to cover claims arising from sporting events, but again Gordon Taylor stepped in on behalf of the drag racers. He arranged for the fund to

---

1. By the start of the 1964 season, drag-racing rules had been amended to require steel "scattershields" to surround the clutches of all standard-transmission, V-8–equipped cars.

Pioneer drag racer Orv Bambush works at modifying the body of his Mercury. Orv and this car competed in what is believed to be the first-ever drag race in Alberta. *(Provincial Archives of Alberta, A-8113)*

Alberta's first proper quarter-mile drag meet: DeWinton, 1955. *(Photo from Vern Scholz collection)*

Car clubs were the basis of much of early drag racing. Typical are these four members of the White Lightening Car Club wearing matching jackets, showing off their modified 30-year-old car in the 1960 Dominion Day parade at Smoky Lake. One wonders if the spelling of Lightening, written across a drawing of a lightning bolt, was simply a spelling error, or if it referred to the lightening that took place when they removed the car's roof. *(Provincial Archives of Alberta, G-2626)*

pay the settlement amount of $24,000.[2] A note in that amount was signed by C.C.H.R.A. President Geoff Goodwin and Treasurer Boots Cooper. All well and good, but where was a group of young men, most of whom had their life savings tied up in their cars, going to come up with the money to pay off a debt the equivalent of the cost of two Edmonton bungalows?

Racing on Sundays, C.C.H.R.A. had little revenue. The Alberta Lord's Day Act authorized municipalities to enact Sunday Closing bylaws prohibiting, among other things, admission charges to sporting events on the Sabbath. Voluntary payment—"silver collection" as it was called—barely covered expenses. The Unsatisfied Judgement Fund's note matured, and while payments had been made, there still remained a substantial balance. Goodwin and Cooper signed what would be the first of a series of renewals. Over time and with public pressure, the Sunday-closing bylaws were watered down, and eventu-

2. Hon. Gordon E. Taylor died in Drumheller on July 26, 2003, at the age of 93.

ally disappeared. C.C.H.R.A. was able to charge admission and raise enough cash from races to retire the debt.

In Calgary, Gene McMahon, operator of Shephard[3] Raceway, was having his own problems with the Lord's Day Act. Sunday was the day he wanted for drag racing, and the method he used to get around the Act was not to sell tickets, but rather sell one-day "associate memberships" in the Calgary Drag Racing Council for $1. In 1964, no longer associated with the C.D.R.C., McMahon simply asked each spectator for $1. For this he was charged under the Act. In court, he protested to Magistrate Quigley that people really didn't have to pay—they were merely asked for $1—to which His Honour responded that if McMahon was selling something for a dollar that he himself admitted could be had for free, perhaps he should be charged with fraud. Gene quickly rested his defence and paid the $25 fine.

The following year, McMahon went back to the "associate membership" system, and again was charged. In fining him $40 the judge ruled that, "The whole thing was a scheme devised to circumvent the Lord's Day Act."[4] Undeterred, the resourceful promoter then fenced off his grandstand area and rented seats to those who had already been admitted to the event on a silver-collection basis. Once more he was charged and fined, but not before he had sold out his grandstand twice in one day. After most of the seats had been sold, a wasp nest, apparently attached to the underside of the seating planks, released its many inhabitants, chasing away the paying customers. Once the bugs had been dealt with, McMahon sold the now-empty seats a second time.

Drag racing was not the only sport troubled by the Lord's Day Act. In Lethbridge, the Southern Alberta Auto Racing Association (SAARA) found it could sell out the 7,000 seats at the fairgrounds oval if they ran on Sundays. After being charged several times, association president Leonard Vaselenak and local sports car racer Harold Brown arranged a meeting with then-Premier Ernest

---

3. The sharp-eyed reader will have noticed that two spellings have been used to describe this location. The proper name of the original community is Shepard. When Gene McMahon was registering the holding company for his track, the name was inadvertently spelled Shephard on the documents, and that became the name of the racing facility.

4. Calgary *Herald.*

Manning in Edmonton. Manning was sympathetic, and for reasons Vaselenak can't fully explain,[5] SAARA was never charged again, although it would be 1985 before the unloved, and by-then unused, Lord's Day Act was repealed.

Back in Edmonton, C.C.H.R.A. raced at Namao through 1964–65, but in 1966 that facility too became unavailable, and for a year Northern Alberta drag racers had to either haul south to Calgary or sit patiently waiting for the completion of the long-promised Edmonton International Speedway. The drag strip was finally paved in the fall of 1966, but no organized races were held that year.

In the late 1960s, drag racing, particularly the amateur level, began a period of major change. Much like sports car racing, the number of classes of cars continued to increase. Policing the cars for compliance with the restrictions of a plethora of classes became a major challenge. But without the variety of classes, there couldn't be fair racing. Why race a car with the ability to cover the ¼ mile in 15 seconds if you knew the other guy could do it in 13? The answer was bracket racing.

Bracket racing involves each competitor declaring, or "dialling-in," the time he feels is the best his car can do. The difference between the dialled-in times of two cars is effectively the slower car's handicap. The timing of the green starting lights is staggered by the difference, and whoever crosses the finish line first is the winner. To prevent drivers from dialling-in a slow time to give themselves a bigger handicap, the rule is if you finish faster than your dial-in, you are disqualified. The end result is a sport that has room for every car, no matter how fast or slow. But again, like amateur sports car racing, it's not terribly exciting to watch. A well-promoted local drag meet can expect to have hundreds of cars show up to compete, but have few paying spectators. Entry fees and pit-pass sales are the bread and butter of the track owner. Only match races and major professional competitions draw large paying crowds.

---

5. The fact that one of Manning's own cabinet ministers, Calgarian Bill Dickie, had an interest in a Junior A hockey team and wanted to stage games on Sundays, may possibly have had a bearing.

With the opening of Edmonton International Speedway in 1967, drag racing began a growth spurt that would carry it from a simple pastime for teenagers to a major-league sport in Alberta. The great success of Armstrong, Beck, Bonin, Capp, Fedderly, Jenner, Peets, and others is detailed further along in this book, but it is worth noting here that the accomplishments of Albertans in the sport continue over three decades later. On several occasions, N.H.R.A. Top Fuel Funny Car titles have been settled between two cars, those of John Force and Cruz Pedregon, both having Albertans—Rob Flynn and Bernie Fedderly from Edmonton—as the crew chiefs. (A reasonable comparison would be to imagine the two teams in the National Hockey League Stanley Cup final being coached by people from Nebraska or Switzerland). The Lee brothers of Red Deer continue to set new N.H.R.A. records in Super Stock class. Calgary racer Les Davenport is involved in world land-speed record attempts at the Bonneville Salt Flats.

There is any number of theories as to why drag racing has been so successful. Gene McMahon gives much credit to Seattle racer Jerry Ruth. "I could always get Jerry to come up here, and he'd run at both Edmonton and Calgary. He was one of the very top drivers in the sport, and if the local guys wanted to compete in Top Fuel, or AA Fuel like they used to call it, they had to deal with Jerry. With Jerry coming up here, it wasn't hard to get people like Don ["Big Daddy"] Garlits, Don ["The Snake"] Prudhomme, and Shirley ["Cha Cha"] Muldowney to come too. And our guys got better until they could run with them. But Jerry Ruth started it."

Ron Hodgson says it was simply a fact that Edmonton had always been a centre of hot-rodding activity. Geoff Goodwin agrees, "There were all the car and hot rod clubs, and a lot of guys were learning how to build good cars."

Richard Chevalier credits the success in part to the availability of good equipment. When Richard left high school in 1957 and went to work in his father Bill's business, one of the first things he did was drive to California to visit all the speed part manufacturers located there and bring back the latest equipment to sell through Pioneer Automotive. Others followed suit, and racers could obtain locally what they had previously only been able to order by mail.

Sadly, the days of the world's very best drag racers making regular treks to Edmonton and Calgary seem behind us. Today, all professional sport is appallingly expensive, and motor racing is worse than most. The economic realities of our time are that so-called "small-market centres" cannot support major-league sport, and in this context, Alberta's cities are small-market. Only the stars of drag racing's second-tier series, the International Hot Rod Association (I.H.R.A.), pay visits to our two major centres. Having said that, their performance, with speeds exceeding 300 miles per hour (483 kmh), is close enough to that of the N.H.R.A. superstars to provide a spectacular show for spectators.

Alberta has contributed a wildly disproportionate amount of talent to major-league drag racing, but those contributions have been, and will continue to be, one way. Much like we do with wheat and oil, we send our best racers to other, bigger markets. Ron Hodgson, who has as much experience in the running of race teams as anyone, calculates that it costs a minimum of $3 million (U.S.) to field a single competitive N.H.R.A. Top Fuel car for a full season. Sponsors with that kind of money are not commonly found in "small-market" cities.

The sport has gone through countless changes over a half century, but the beautiful simplicity of two cars and two drivers racing in a straight line for a quarter mile, often at breathtaking speed, remains. The sport continues as the most popular form of participant auto racing, and one of the most popular for spectators.

CHAPTER 7

ARRIVAL OF THE SPORTS CARS

Funny little furrin cars.
—Remark attributed to any number of stock car drivers
in the early days of sports car racing

T he first examples of the breed of vehicle we came to know as the sports car arrived in North America shortly after World War II, imported by returning military personnel. These cars not only brought with them a different concept of motoring—an emphasis on light weight rather than comfort, and performance defined by handling instead of straight-line speed—but they also introduced new forms of motorsport to a part of the world where racing had rarely taken place anywhere other than oval tracks.

While there were enough of these cars in the heavily populated areas of Ontario, Quebec, BC's Lower Mainland, and both coasts of the United States to organize clubs and stage competitions prior to 1950, it would be the mid '50s before Alberta saw such a critical mass. The impetus in the West came not so much from army veterans as from the flood of European immigrants Canada witnessed post–WW II. When the time came for the new Canadians to buy cars, many opted for the imported models of their homelands. Once the first cars arrived, the novelty, the appearance, the economy, and the promise of performance of this new kind of automobile quickly attracted a following of native-born Canadians. Most of the first imports were such pedestrian vehicles as the Hillman Minx and the Austin A-40, but these were soon joined by the MG T-series sports cars, the early Porsches, and the XK-model Jaguars.

The original idea of the sports car was that of a car that could be used for day-to-day transport during the week, and then, by simply removing the top and the windshield and perhaps putting a few more pounds of air in the tires, become a race car on the weekend. This might seem a naive notion when viewed from the early 21st century, but it had a basis in reality, and was in fact[1] how the sport was commonly conducted for a decade after the arrival of the first sports cars.

European-style motorsport held many attractions for people who enjoyed speed and the opportunity to compete, but weren't drawn to existing forms of racing. For one thing, there was the road course rather than the oval track. In a road race, every corner was different. Instead of the two roughly-identical 180-degree turns that form a typical oval, road racing offered variety: lefts, rights, hairpins, tight corners, fast curves, and s-bends. The straights could be long and fast, and ideally there were hills. Aside from the variety, the larger playing field also meant that racing was conducted without the shoving, bumping, and destruction that had become the norm on oval tracks once stock cars displaced open-wheel racers.

Another appealing aspect of road courses was the foreign mystique built in large part around the fact that the roads on which the Europeans raced actually went somewhere. At Monaco, the cars went past and around the famous buildings of Monte Carlo. At Spa, the competitors drove at enormous speed through the mountainous forests of Eastern Belgium; and in the famous Mille Miglia, racers drove a 1,000-mile lap of Italy—Brescia-Pescara-Rome-Brescia—on everything from mountain switchbacks to village streets. Speeds

---

1. A 1954 book about sports car racing aimed at the teen-age market, *The Red Car* by Don Stanford, describes a sports car as "Not a specially bred racing machine, useless for any other purpose, but a car you could race all day and win with, and then wash a little bit and proudly take your mother to dinner or your girl to the movies that night . . . the best of all possible luxuries to own."

Calgary Sports Car Club's first ice race, 1954. *(Calgary Sports Car Club archives).*

Airdrie, 1954: Pat Brennan's MG at the limit. *(Calgary Sports Car Club archives)*

Airdrie, 1954: A Jaguar XK-120 leads Franz Pados's Porsche 356.
(Calgary Sports Car Club archives)

LeMans, France, 1960: Olivier Gendebien, wearing his Calgary gift hat, celebrates his win with co-driver Paul Frère. *(Calgary Sports Car Club archives)*

varied from first gear to as fast as the car could go. For sports car *aficionados* (as some enthusiasts liked to call themselves) there was something infinitely more romantic about the vision of driving an Alfa Romeo or a Jaguar at high speed through medieval villages with the Adriatic Sea glistening on their flank than there was of being rammed out of the way at 40 miles per hour by an armoured Ford on a track small enough to fit inside the boundaries of a football park. While the reality may have been somewhat different, the vision prevailed, and the sport grew.

Racing was not the only competition for sports cars. Rallies took place on public roads and required two-man teams of driver and navigator to follow a set route at a precise average speed, with equal penalties for being late and early. Gymkhanas, time trials, and slaloms involved racing against the clock on a course laid out with pylons on a paved surface, usually a parking lot or airport. And if you had a sports car, you didn't necessarily have to compete, as clubs commonly organized weekend tours on scenic roads.

A final unfortunate, but not insignificant, attraction for some was a sense of elitism. This is best illustrated by a 1954 entry in the Calgary Sports Car Club's archival scrapbook:

"A sports car will do or try to do anything asked of it the instant it is asked, and to the purist, driving a sports car is a form of self-expression equalled only by the ballerina's approach to dancing. To him it is an art. Like the car, the aficionado expresses the tempo and aesthetics of our time and considers himself a concise understatement of disciplined sophistication, a sleek symbol of movement entitled to look down on people from below. Togetherness is the cult that keeps sports car people out of the house with an instinct as irresistible as that which draws salmon upriver to spawn, sports car owners are drawn together in clubs and associations [sic]."

A social schism quickly developed between sports car racers and oval track racers. On one hand the stock car drivers were the heirs to the traditions of North American racing; they prided themselves on being tough men, following the customs of their sport dating back to the era of Barney Oldfield. No women were allowed in their pits, and brawling at races, if not as common as at hockey games, was an occasional reality. They were generally blue-collar workers: tradesmen and farmers who did most of their own mechanical work, often with a level of skill and imagination far greater than the appearance of their cars would indicate. They expected to receive prize money at the end of each racing day, and knew what they had to do to earn it—each day's racing was called a "show," and that's what they aimed to provide to their paying public.

By contrast, the sports car drivers tended to be white-collar workers, often from academia and the professions (although as the pretentious drivel in the quoted paragraph above illustrates, intelligence and literacy were not prerequisites to participation). Their cars cost much more than the decades-old Fords and Chevs found on oval tracks, and they viewed themselves as amateur sportsmen. Many became skilled back-yard mechanics. Each group tended to stereotype the other, oval trackers seeing the "sporty car drivers" as wealthy, effeminate playboys, while the view from the opposite direction was one of crude, uneducated ruffians. It is not unfair to say that many in both groups carried with them an attitude of self-superiority, a sense that their racing was the only real racing. Happily, time would demonstrate that both sides of the sport had much to offer the whole.

In 1953, Calgary became the first Alberta city to have a sports car club. The Calgary Sports Car Club (C.S.C.C.) was formed under the presidency of Ken Lord and held regular meetings in Pogue's Health Clinic. The club held its first competition the same year: a speed trial on the Airdrie airport. In 1954, in addition to taking care of the details expected of a sports car club such as approving the design of car badges and lapel pins and striking a building committee, C.S.C.C. organized their first ice event: a speed trial, or "ice dice," in January on a nearby lake. On May 22 at the Airdrie Airport, the club held its first proper race, featuring Eric Bland and Louie Tortorelli in Jaguar XK-120s, Franz Pados in a Porsche 356, and Tony Ball, Pat Brennan, Eric Festor, Rod Gaunt, and Les Johnson in MGs. Safety equipment consisted of goggles and lightweight helmets for the drivers, and hay-bale barriers to protect the spectators. Entry fees, ticket sales, and a $50 anonymous donation left the club with a $225 profit for the day.

There is, regrettably, a gap in the early history of the sport in Northern Alberta. Richard Chevalier recalls the formation of the Northern Light and Sports Car Club around 1954. The group organized at least one race at the Namao air force base with a field of roughly half cars and half motorcycles. Richard himself competed in a Morris Minor convertible. The Edmonton Light Car Club (E.L.C.C.) split away as a rally-only club, and the N.L.S.C.C. disappeared, and with it, apparently, any records of its activities.

In 1956, the Calgary Sports Car Club was formally incorporated. It also organized the first "Loop Rally," an event that would become one of the longest-running motorsport competitions in Canada. The rally was won by an MGA, but second place was taken by a Ford Thunderbird, one of the first successes by an American-made car. C.S.C.C. also ran a gymkhana on the Lincoln Park airfield, approximately where Mount Royal College stands today. This was a novelty event with a normal round-the-pylons time trial, but with each car carrying a passenger who in turn had to carry a bag of water without spilling any. Time was added for any loss of water.

In September of 1957 a new general-interest sports car club was formed when fourteen enthusiasts showed up for the first meeting of the "Edmonton Sports Car Club." The following month, after a recruiting campaign consisting of word-of-mouth and leaving invitations on the windshields of parked sports cars, over 60 attendees decided the name should be changed to "Sports Car Club of Edmonton" to avoid confusion with E.L.C.C. By December, another name change had been made, this time to Northern Alberta Sports Car Club (N.A.S.C.C.), and that is the name by which the club was finally incorporated, under the presidency of Ken Finnigan.

Some Edmonton drivers hadn't waited for a club to be formed before entering competition. Ken Finnigan and Jim Milligan had travelled to Davidson, Saskatchewan, midway between Saskatoon and Regina, to compete on the airport track there in the summer of 1957. Both men had MGAs, but Finnigan had put his on the chassis dynamometer at Loveseth's automotive tuning shop before leaving, and discovered extra power by first advancing the ignition timing, then enriching the fuel mixture. He drove the MG to the race and finished second in the feature behind an Austin-Healey.

The lack of a permanent road racing facility meant that the clubs had to be imaginative in devising competition events. Hill climbs were tried for the first time in 1957. Calgary ran a dirt-track hill-climb on the Groenveld farm property near High River, but seemed to have difficulty distancing itself from novelty events. Their climb had each competitor take four separate runs at the half-mile course. The first run was standing start, flying finish; the second was a LeMans start; and the third required the drivers to stop their cars half-way up the hill and inflate a balloon to bursting before completing the run. The final run was a standing start and standing finish, with penalty time added for stopping before or beyond the finish line. Later Groeneveld events would mercifully drop the silliness. Edmonton ran a straightforward hill climb with just two classes: over and under 1,500-cc engine capacity. Calgary also set up a dirt-track road course in the yard of their clubhouse and ran a one-time-only time trial. Edmonton ended the year with their first ice dice, won by E. Bordeaux in a Citroen DS 19.

Canadian Automobile Sport Clubs (C.A.S.C.), imperiously calling itself "Governing Body of Motorsport in Canada," had been formed in 1951 to coordinate the activities and the rules of competition of the sports car clubs that had begun springing up around the country, mostly in central Canada and BC's Lower Mainland. In 1958, the Calgary Sports Car Club, followed in 1960 by N.A.S.C.C., joined C.A.S.C. The benefits of membership in C.A.S.C. were, first, the standardization of the rules of the sport; second, the coordination of competition schedules; and finally, the ease and economy of insuring their events under a group policy rather than shopping locally for coverage.

Under C.A.S.C., a competitor could travel to a distant track knowing that the rules would be the same as they were at his home track. The more ambitious drivers were already taking advantage of this system by travelling to the airport tracks at Abbotsford, BC,

Claresholm, 1960: A Triumph TR-3, having done what TR-3s were wont to do: flip. Note the exhaust-tube roll bar—flimsy, but on this occasion it got the job done, and was more than what the rules called for. *(Calgary Sports Car Club archives)*

Helmet of the driver of the TR-3. *(Calgary Sports Car Club archives)*

Davidson, Saskachewan, 1964: Dr. Gordon Deane (front) on the starting grid in his home-built Canada Class. Note air intake for side radiator behind front wheel. Was this home-built the precursor of modern formula car design? Saskatchewan driver Ivan Johnson is in MGA #117, Tom Johnston has the #4H Austin-Healey Sprite, while Edmontonian Vince Ciochetti drives the MGA on the right of the photo. *(Tom Johnston collection)*

Davidson, Saskatchewan, and Deer Park, Washington to race. Sanctioning and scheduling of the individual events by C.A.S.C. assured the local club that it would not be competing with other clubs for entries.

With C.A.S.C. affiliation came the end of the era of Mickey Rooney-esque "let's have a race" quality of planning. The national organization demanded certain minimum standards of drivers and organizers, and to that end held a Race Theory Class on March 28, 1958.

The clubs were finding out, however, that taking a weekend course on how to race and actually staging a race were not the same thing. N.A.S.C.C. tried to put together a cooperative venture with C.S.C.C. to hold a race meet at Innisfail Airport south of Red Deer,

and that fell through. Attempts to put on events at Namao, north of
Edmonton, and at Airdrie met a similar fate. N.A.S.C.C. member
Gene McMahon recalls the frustration of the Edmonton racers over
the lack of activity out of Calgary. "They had all those abandoned
airfields around Calgary—Airdrie, Shepard, Claresholm, DeWinton,
Fort MacLeod, and they could hardly ever get a race organized. All
we had was Namao, and that was air force property." Nevertheless,
by midsummer the Calgary club had prevailed, and Alberta's first
C.A.S.C.-sanctioned race was set for August 16, 1958, at the Shepard
Airport on the southeast edge of the city.

The event drew entries from all over Western Canada and as far
east as Ottawa to race on a 1¼-mile (2-km) track. A program of
seven races was set, and spectators were invited at $1 each (children
under 13 free). In addition to the usual sports cars and small sedans,
The Thing, a sports-racing special owned and driven by Arley Pilkey
of Vancouver, appeared. While *The Thing*'s[2] combination of
Triumph TR-3 chassis components and Coventry-Climax engine
attracted much attention, at the end of the day it was the Alberta-
based MGs, Triumphs, DKWs, and Porsches that took home the trophies. Edmonton drivers won five of six individual races, and participated in the winning three-car relay race team. For the record, the
winner of the first-ever C.A.S.C. race in Alberta was Hans Seigerst in
a three-cylinder, two-stroke DKW competing in the under-1,300-cc
Touring Car class. The LeMans-start feature was won by Jim
Rideout in a Triumph TR-3. This was also the first race and first trophy for young Edmontonian Bob Stokowski, who would still be
winning four and half decades later.

A year later, N.A.S.C.C., through Ken Finnigan's connections
with the construction manager of the new Edmonton International
Airport, managed to organize a race on the new, and as yet unused,
asphalt. For all his efforts, Finnigan ended up on the sidelines as his
MGA Twin-Cam blew its engine at the August 16 event. Bob
Stokowski kept his two-race trophy streak alive by winning one of

2. Vancouver racing historian Tom Johnston maintains that it was only on the Prairies that
Pilkey's car was known as *The Thing*. At home on the west coast, it was simply *The Pilkey
Special*.

the two novice races. Jim Milligan won the feature in an Austin-Healey after Gene McMahon's over-powered, under-braked, and appropriately-named special, *The Beast,* went sailing off the track at the end of a long straight.

While *The Beast*[3], with its bizarre name and spectacular horse-power (Oldsmobile, and then later Chevrolet V-8), is probably the best remembered of the home-built specials, it was neither the first nor the last of these in Alberta. As early as 1956, C.S.C.C. club president Bob McDonald had begun construction of a sports-racing special, which he ultimately sold, incomplete, to Rolf Armbruster—a fate that was to befall many a home-built.

The impetus for the development of specials was the realization that do-it-yourself represented a significantly less expensive way to achieve tremendous performance. For the cost of an entry-level sports car such as an MGA or a Triumph TR-3, an imaginative racer with some decent engineering and shop skills could build a car that would go as fast or faster than a Corvette or a Jaguar. A small passenger-car engine can push a formula car weighing 500 kilograms just as fast as a 6- or 8-cylinder engine can a 1,400-kilogram sports car.

C.A.S.C. understood this and brought out "Canada Class" for small-engined, home-built cars costing less than $2,500. Phil Goodhall and Cappy Thompson of Calgary had such cars prior to 1960, the former a front-engined formula car with a wooden body, while the latter had a transverse-mounted English Ford engine in the rear, driving swing axles through a motorcycle gearbox and chain. In 1962, Dr. Gordon Deane of Edmonton built a rear-engined, Skoda-powered Canada Class, which in at least one respect was ahead of its time. Deane took the stock Skoda radiator, and rather than put it in the conventional position at the front where it would do nothing to help either the balance or the aerodynamics of the car, split it in two and installed one half on each side of the cockpit, just behind the driver's seat. Almost a decade would pass before Formula One and Indianapolis car builders adopted this layout, but since the early

---

3. McMahon seemed to have an affinity for cars with eccentric names. When he sold *The Beast* to Wendell Hoover, he bought *The Thing* from Arley Pilkey.

1970s it has been the standard for rear-engined race cars.[4] Jim Land of Edmonton built a beautiful, but conventional, rear-engined Canada Class—later called Formula C—car in 1963, and followed that with a sports car patterned after the Lotus 23. Aside from Canada Class, John Barnaschone and Mike Day took an NSU Sport Prinz sports car, removed the drive train, and replaced it with the front-engine, front-wheel-drive mechanism of an Austin Mini—in the rear. After buying Gene McMahon's *The Beast,* Wendell Hoover sold it and improved on the design with his own *The Beast II.*

The topic of locally-built road racers could fill a book in itself; Vancouver historian Tom Johnston estimates that there have been close to 200 of these machines built in Western Canada since the sport began.[5]

In late May 1960, Calgary Sports Car Club was honoured with a visit by one of the greatest sports car racers of all time, Belgian Olivier Gendebien. It being Calgary, the club presented Gendebien with a white cowboy hat, in which he posed for photographers. A reporter from the Calgary *Herald* asked the debonair racer whether he would ever wear it again. He said he would be proud to wear it in the pits when he returned to Europe. Three weeks later, partnering with fellow Belgian Paul Frère, he won the LeMans 24-hour race, and photos of the two smiling racers celebrating their win were flashed around the world, with Gendebien proudly wearing his white Calgary hat.

In 1960, racing safety was roughly as high on the perception scale of the typical sports car driver as was cigarette smoking. Race cars and cigarettes were both understood to be dangerous, but precious little preventative action seemed warranted in either case. Drivers, the majority of whom probably smoked,[6] were required to

---

4. There are records of a Cooper Formula Jr. car in England trying such an arrangement, albeit unsuccessfully, in 1962. After a few races, the car was rebuilt in conventional form, apparently leaving Dr. Deane's as the only one of this design on the planet.

5. Tom Johnston, *Sports Car Road Racing in Western Canada.* Vancouver: Granville Island Publishing, 2004.

6. At a 1967 meeting of N.A.S.C.C., Diane Connolly moved that the club purchase an exhaust fan to remove cigarette smoke from the clubrooms. Club records show that "the motion was laughed off the floor."

wear lap belts and crash helmets. Any other safety equipment was optional. But even at that minimal level, the amateur sports car racers were ahead of their heroes in Formula One, who would wait until the late '60s before consenting to being strapped into their cars.

Formula One had come out with a requirement for roll bars in 1961, but without any minimum specifications that could be relied on to ensure the safety of the driver.[7] Roll bars were a topic of hot discussion in the N.A.S.C.C. clubrooms in February of 1962. In the absence of any regulations from C.A.S.C., a motion was proposed that would have required them in all club speed events. The motion was defeated, but to little effect, as C.A.S.C. took the decision out of the hands of its member clubs before the end of the year and made roll-over protection mandatory in open cars. The C.A.S.C. rule allowed roll bars to be as much as 2 inches (5 cm) below the top of the driver's helmet and required no lateral or longitudinal bracing. Promising young Calgary driver Paul Moffat paid a horrible price for those lax standards in 1963. He was critically injured in a race near North Battleford, Saskatchewan when his Triumph Spitfire flipped. Subsequent enquiries revealed that not only had Moffatt's roll bar failed, but also that he was driving with sight in only one eye, a fact that may have contributed to his driving up and over the rear of an open-wheeled Formula Junior, causing his flip.[8] Because of incidents such as Moffat's, in 1964 C.A.S.C. mandated driver medicals, including vision tests. Roll-bar rules did not change for several years, and in fact cars with steel roofs—even hardtops with minimal vertical support—were exempt from any roll-over protection requirements until 1968.

Despite Gene McMahon's earlier complaints that Southern Alberta racers were letting perfectly good airports go to waste, the

---

7. Formula One and sports car star Stirling Moss once bragged that when he found the roll bar in one of his cars to be uncomfortably close to his helmet, he bent it back out of the way with his bare hands.

8. Calgary *Albertan*, August 31, 1963.

9. The Claresholm newspaper carried a front-page story on the 1960 race, featuring one of the first—if not the first—female sports car racers in the province. "Mrs. Richard Draper" is described as a petite 19-year-old who drives in her bare feet.

races did come. Claresholm's airport[9], which had only been abandoned by the military in 1957, hosted its first race in 1959. Fort
MacLeod's airfield was taken over by the Lethbridge Sports Car Club
in 1964 and renamed Sundance Speedway. C.S.C.C. used Dewinton
for race driving schools.

Edmonton was still the poor sister in terms of places to race, the
International Airport race of 1959 being a one-time event. Dirt track
racing was tried with racing-only club Scuderia Carro Tiro organizing an event at the Rimbey Fairgrounds and N.A.S.C.C. ploughing a
road course out of Jim Milligan's grain fields near Bon Accord. Both
courses proved to be car-breakers. In the absence of a road course,
ice racing became the staple event for N.A.S.C.C.. Beginning in 1961
races were staged at Alberta Beach, west of the city. The first year featured a four-hour endurance race, with Calgarian Stan Johnson
driving solo for the feature win at a 57-mile-per-hour (92-kmh)
average, beating the Lethbridge Triumph TR-3 of Bob Copp by three
laps. The local team of Mel Gregory and Allan Howard claimed 3rd
after having to push their dead Austin-Healey across the finish line.
A crowd estimated at 10,000 caused problems for the local police,
who found themselves dealing with a major traffic jam on an otherwise dull Sunday in mid-January.

In 1964, N.A.S.C.C. staged a race meet on the paved oval at
Speedway Park. While it didn't provide the style of racing the sports
car men preferred, it was easier on their machinery than were the dirt
tracks and provided greater public exposure than Rimbey and Bon
Accord. The experiment was repeated in June 1965 as part of the regular weekly Wednesday stock car card, but a major wreck involving
an Austin-Healey Sprite and a DKW, and a second that heavily damaged a Triumph, cooled N.A.S.C.C.'s enthusiasm for the oval.

The image of sports car drivers as gentlemen amateur sportsmen
was important to C.A.S.C. and its clubs—N.A.S.C.C. even instituted
a jacket-and-tie rule for the clubhouse in 1960—but as more and
younger members joined the sport, that image became harder to
maintain. N.A.S.C.C. in particular seemed to have had problems
with unruly members who were in the sport for a good time and had
little empathy towards its upper-class European traditions. Gene

McMahon was expelled from the club in 1960, but invited to meet with the executive and give reason why he should be reinstated. As this is written over 40 years later, he is unable to recall with certainty how he got into such trouble with the club, but his friend Jack Ondrack remembers the problem beginning when Gene, competing in a rally, drove his convertible to a checkpoint while perched on the backrest of the front seat, steering with his bare feet and operating the throttle and brake with a hockey stick. The checkpoint officials might also have seen the empty beer bottle McMahon threw in the ditch a hundred or so yards earlier. Gene guesses it might have had something to do with him, along with friends Bob and Teddy Toupin, giving Ondrack the benefit of 600 pounds of illegal ballast by hiding in the trunk of Ondrack's Buick during an ice race. Ondrack disputes that, firmly maintaining they were never caught. He then wonders aloud if he is safely past the Racing Statute of Limitations.

Jack Ondrack later incurred the wrath of C.S.C.C. when he won that club's hill climb on the site of the West Calgary television transmission tower, driving his girlfriend's Jaguar XK-150. This was the first C.S.C.C. event that had been televised, and as winner, Jack was interviewed live. He explained to the Calgary TV audience that his win was no big deal as there were probably a half dozen drivers back in Edmonton who could have gone even faster than he had. Another driver who found himself living on the edge of sports car respectability was Bob Stokowski, who was fined $5 by N.A.S.C.C. in 1968 for driving on the newly-paved Edmonton International Speedway without permission.

Sports car racing would continue as a slightly eccentric fringe activity until the opening of Edmonton International Speedway in 1968 threw open the doors of the sport to the larger world of Alberta society. The sport quickly became—for a while at least—the dominant genre of motor racing. It attracted both fans and participants from every walk of life. People with no direct ties to Europe, no particular bias towards European cars and no wish for dress codes, people who would be happy to see advertisements on their cars if someone paid cash, all flocked to this exciting, glamorous sport. The new kid on the block was suddenly the big kid on the block.

CHAPTER 8

ELDON RASMUSSEN

Mokokit-ki-ackamimat.
(Be wise and persevere.)
—Blackfoot proverb

It's hard not to like Eldon Rasmussen, the first Albertan to race in the Indianapolis 500. He combines the charm of the successful car salesman and the straight-talking drawl of the Southern Alberta farm boy—both of which he once was—with the quick, analytical mind of the master fabricator and mechanical designer he has been since his early youth. Put these characteristics together with just a touch of the physical frailties that enter the lives of all humans as they pass through their seventh decade, and you have every movie director's image of a favourite uncle.

Eldon Rasmussen has spent his entire life in racing. Encouraged by his first hero, elder brother Gordon, who himself was a successful competitor in the mid-century Model T races, Eldon built his first race car, a soapbox derby special, at the age of eight. The car was hauled to a race in Calgary in 1944, where it proved itself to be quite uncompetitive. Undeterred, the younger Rasmussen spent the next year building a new, more sophisticated soapbox complete with 13-inch wheels taken from an English baby carriage, turning on spindles custom lathed by the machinist at the local General Motors dealership. The new car was a vast improvement over its predecessor and finished third overall in the 1945 Derby.

Encouraged by this early success, Eldon decided that his future mounts must have engines. Over the next year, using a grain-auger motor, a homemade frame, and the narrowed rear end of a Model A Ford, he built a crude garden tractor capable on at least one occasion of transporting him to school.

Given that the average ten-year-old is at his mechanical limit in adjusting the brakes or oiling the chain of his bicycle, it's interesting to explore the background of the precocious young Master Rasmussen. Eldon Rasmussen's grandfather moved to the unbroken land that would become the family farm near the village of Standard in 1911. Shortly after arriving, he apparently decided that the breaking of the hard prairie soil would happen much quicker if he used steam rather than equine power. An Avery steam tractor was ordered, and subsequently delivered to the nearest rail point, at Gleichen. All that remained to be done was drive the 52-ton behemoth 20 miles to the farm; a simple enough task, except for the crossing of two streams on the way. The second stream proved the machine's downfall—literally—as the creek bed collapsed under the weight. All efforts to move the tractor proved futile until the prairie summer dried the stream and a log path could be built under the massive 42-inch by 7-foot steel wheels. Six weeks after leaving Gleichen, the tractor arrived at the Rasmussen farm. Once there, it could pull 14 ploughs—12 more than a team of horses—as long as it was fed its daily ration of one half-wagon-load of coal.

As the Rasmussens were the first in their area to have mechanical power, it was natural that they would develop the skills and acquire the tools needed to maintain their own equipment. By the time Eldon was a child, the farm had a well-equipped repair and machine shop that not only took care of the farm machinery, but also brother Gordon's Model T race cars. Father, grandfather, and older brothers encouraged Eldon to involve himself in the mechanical side of farming.

The benefits of this early education have stayed with Eldon throughout his life. In 1959 he fashioned what may well have been the world's first pick-up truck gooseneck trailer, and he has the dated photograph to prove it. In 1961, tired of constantly having to

Eldon in his 1959 Modified, sitting on the gooseneck trailer he designed and built. If only he had patented it! The truck is a home-built, too, constructed from parts of three different wrecks. *(Eldon Rasmussen collection)*

1961: World's first downtube roadster? *(Eldon Rasmussen collection)*

Beating the dragsters at their own game, at RCAF Number 7 Supply Depot, October 1965. *(Eldon Rasmussen collection)*

The SAAB Sonnett ice-racing special, designed and built by Eldon Rasmussen and driven by Tom Jones. *(Donald MacKay collection)*

adjust and readjust the ride heights and wedge on his modified racer, he decided that the problem was not in the springs, but in the twisting of the car's frame under cornering loads. He came up with the then-novel idea of building diagonal struts from the top of the roll cage to the front suspension pick-up points on the frame. The system worked well, but, surprisingly, it would be twenty years before the idea, known today as the down-tube frame, gained broad acceptance in sprint car construction. Regrettably, Eldon patented neither of these ideas.

The accomplished mechanic at age 10 waited until he was 15 before starting his driving career. In 1951, using his brother Gordon's Model T, he drove his first car race at the Gleichen fairgrounds. Because of his inexperience, Eldon started at the rear of the grid. By the time he reached the start line, the dust from the other cars rendered the track virtually invisible. He drove on, believing that he was in the middle of the track. When the dust cleared, he found to his horror that he was about to run over the legs of the spectators who sat along the corral-style outer fence. He turned the car to safety just in time and, somewhat shaken, finished the race, which was won by fellow Standard resident Tommy Fraser.

Eldon drove only one more race that summer, on the fairgrounds at Red Deer, but he had the racing bug, and, whether he knew it then or not, he had found his career.

Modified stock cars, or "jalopies"—stock cars with the fenders removed, and crash bars built in place of the grille—soon followed. A two-year stint in the Royal Canadian Air Force in the mid '50s didn't interrupt his racing, and by the end of the decade he was successfully racing modifieds out of Hinton, Alberta, where he had an interest in a car dealership. He was also building his own cars and fabricating parts for other drivers. As a consistent winner at Speedway Park in Edmonton, he was known as the "Hinton Hornet"; certainly a catchy moniker, but not one that could last long. The commute from Hinton to Edmonton coupled with all his other activities became too much of a burden, and he moved to the capital city, taking a job first at Edmonton Motors, and then Stedelbauer Chev Olds.

Racing modifieds all over Western Canada and the northwest United States in the early 1960s, Eldon was one of many racers who wished there were standardized rules of racing from track to track. They wanted to know that when they hauled to tracks in other cities their cars would be accepted as legal, and there would be at least minimal safety standards in place. While the initiative to create the Canadian American Modified Racing Association (CAMRA) came primarily from the track operators, Eldon and many other drivers immediately bought into the concept. Being part of an organized professional racing circuit was a clear benefit for promoters and drivers. Working together, they created the most successful oval-track circuit the area had ever seen, with clean, fast cars, highly skilled drivers, and intensely close competition. Many people believe that CAMRA was second only to the United States Auto Club's Championship circuit in North American open-wheel racing.

In CAMRA's first season, 1963, Eldon Rasmussen finished 7th in the circuit's final standings, behind such notables as Billy Foster and Jim Malloy.

Racing at the CAMRA level was proving expensive, and in 1964, Eldon was unable to complete the full season, and finished out of the top 10. The year was not totally uneventful though, as he had made contact with Dale Smith, head of development with General Motors in Lansing, Michigan. Eldon, like many others, had been racing with modified small-block Chevrolet V-8 engines. This was problematic for GM, as Chevrolet had publicly forsworn racing in the late 1950s in the wake of numerous tragedies. The company preferred that racers use engines other than Chev. A new Oldsmobile engine had been developed, scheduled for introduction with the 1966 model year— would Eldon test it for them? He did some testing in Lansing, then put the new motor in his racer. With no more power than his Chev, and weighing almost 100 pounds (45 kg) more, it wasn't competitive. The fact that there was no readily available speed equipment for the new engine only compounded the problem. In the end, he went back to the Chev, but GM asked him to use the new Olds as his tow car, and report to them on how well the engine dealt with heavy loads on mountain roads. For this, he received a small fee.

To cover the costs of a racing and travel, not to mention supporting a young family at home, a driver, no matter how skilled, needs financial backing. Large sponsors were rare in the 1960s, and Eldon never had one—a little help from Edmonton Motors, and then Stedelbauer Chev Olds, coupled with his GM testing fee, was the limit of his sponsorship. He did, however, have a supportive family. Dianne, whom he married in 1959, was patient; and his brother Arnold was often there for him, pitting, driving the tow car—sometimes supplying it—and occasionally even chipping in financially. When asked if he has photos of his CAMRA days, Eldon says he has very few. "I couldn't afford a camera back then."

Out of those financially trying times came remarkable friendships. One of Eldon's toughest competitors was Billy Foster of Victoria, the 1963 CAMRA champion. Competitors or not, the two drivers often cooperated in the preparation of their cars; Foster was the better mechanic and Rasmussen the skilled fabricator.

In 1965 Eldon came back to CAMRA full time and ended the season second only to Jim Malloy. In October, when most serious racing is over for the year, Eldon was invited, on one day's notice, to take part in a season-end drag race at the No. 7 Supply Depot road at the Namao air base. The organizers asked Eldon if he would like to see how his oval-track modified stacked up against the local dragsters. Always up for a challenge, he agreed. Despite running on staggered rear tires, having no transmission, and having to manipulate an awkward hand clutch, he beat the dragsters at their own game. Not that his best quarter-mile result of 12.64 seconds and 113.35 miles per hour (184 kmh) was a serious drag-racing performance, but in their determination to beat the oval-track man, the dragsters—four in a row—red-lighted (jumped the start) and were disqualified. "Those guys weren't happy," he recalls with a laugh. "They gave me about a three-dollar trophy, and I had to phone them just to get that."

The year 1966 was one of transition, as Eldon began his move to the Indianapolis area. He left his car in the care of Edmonton racer John McEachran, but he still came back West often enough to finish 6th on the CAMRA circuit.

The move to Indianapolis was a huge step. In Edmonton Eldon had a young family, a good job with Stedelbauer, and access to great racing. With no guarantee of a living in Indianapolis, he couldn't take Dianne and the children with him, so the family lived separate lives 3,000 kilometres apart. Only when Eldon was sure he could make a living driving and building in the racing capital was the family reunited, after two years of occasional visits.

Once he got to Indianapolis, Eldon became a regular competitor in USAC sprint car races and picked up occasional rides in "champ cars" (cars competing in the United States Automobile Club National Championship series) on short tracks such as the one-mile ovals at Trenton and Phoenix, and on the super-speedways of Ontario, California, and Pocono, Pennsylvania. All the while he continued to design and build chassis and components. His skills as a fabricator actually took him inside the walls of the famed Motor Speedway before his driving talent did. In 1970, he built updated suspensions for the otherwise year-old cars of Al Unser, Sr and Johnny Rutherford, and to this day he expresses pride in the fact that those two cars qualified first and second for the 500, a mere eight one-thousands of a mile per hour apart.

But being known as a skilled fabricator doesn't translate into a ride at Indianapolis, and it was to be five more years before Eldon finally qualified for the 500. He did it in 1975 in his own used race car. His minimal expenses for the month of May were $25,000, and at one point his friend and erstwhile competitor back in Edmonton, Ray Peets, started a public fund-raising campaign to keep Eldon on the track. He had difficulty getting the local media on his side, and in the end raised only $800.

"It was pretty rough," Eldon recalls. "I only had one engine, and it wasn't new, so I couldn't risk putting on the same practice miles as the bigger teams. But I couldn't take it easy either, because there were more than 60 cars trying to qualify." Not surprisingly, he rates qualifying for and competing in his first Indianapolis 500 as the high point and biggest thrill of his driving career.

Competing at that level did not disrupt Eldon's designing and building work. Over the winter of 1975–76 he accepted a commission

Eldon and crew, having just qualified for the 1975 Indianapolis 500. Frank Weiss is standing, third from left. *(Indianapolis Motor Speedway photo from Eldon Rasmussen collection)*

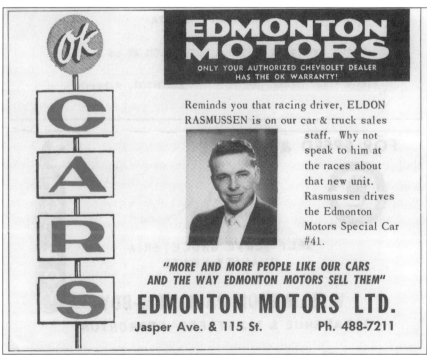

Prize money doesn't always pay the bills. Here's Eldon making a living, 1962. *(Donald MacKay collection, with permission of Edmonton Motors)*

from Ontario ice-racing star Tom Jones to build a car suited to that particular type of racing. Under the body of a SAAB Sonnett, he built a tube spaceframe and fitted it with a modified small-block Ford V-8. A Hewland model DG 300 transaxle provided drive to the front wheels, and a huge, hydraulically adjustable wing mounted high above the hood made sure there was plenty of traction, particularly in fast turns. With this ungainly looking monster, Jones won 34 of 35 races in a two-year span.

Two years later in 1977, Eldon was again in the 500, again in his own car, and again qualifying in the last row of starters. By the end of the race he had moved up to 13th place, but apparently not far enough to catch the attention of any major sponsors. In 1978, he couldn't put together the resources to make an attempt at the big race.

Eldon's final ride in the Indianapolis 500 was 1979, when he qualified 33rd (but not last, as qualifying irregularities that year forced the organizers to start 35 cars) and moved up ten places by the finish.

Later that season, on the high-banked oval at Pocono, Pennsylvania, Eldon's right front tire cut down entering a corner and he slammed into the wall at full speed. The right side of the car was smashed, along with Eldon's right leg, ankle and foot. A tire ricocheted back into his helmet, and he remained unconscious for over four hours. Eldon's broken leg was set and cast in a local hospital, but in recovery he noticed that his right foot seemed to toe-out more than his left. He mentioned it to the surgeon, who assured him that it would heal properly. After two days he was certain something was wrong, and telephoned Henry Banks, the head of United States Auto Club, and asked if he could have USAC's famed surgeon, Dr. Terry Trammel, look into his case. Trammel arranged to have Eldon flown to hospital in Indianapolis, where he found that the leg had been set while still misaligned. He rebroke and reset the leg properly, then reported the Pennsylvania surgeon to his professional association. Eldon's health problems still weren't over, though. While his injuries healed, doctors discovered that he had diabetes, a disease that tended to run in his family. In his case, the disease was controllable, but its known presence ensured that he would never pass a driver medical again. His 28-year career as a race driver was over.

No longer racing, Eldon carried on with his repair and manufacturing trade. He created the high wing on the Beck-Peets championship-winning dragster, and until the advent of carbon-fibre construction, built many of the wings seen on Championship Auto Racing Team (CART) cars. He contracted with Mario Andretti to build miniature racing cars to be driven by customers on tracks franchised under the banners of Mario Andretti Grand Prix International, and Rent-a-Racer.

By the early 1990s Eldon was spending much of his time doing work for Dick Simon Racing. When Simon decided he needed a new, larger shop, he had Eldon design it. Eldon subsequently moved his own tools and equipment in to become part of Simon's organization, and gave up his freelance work to concentrate on the Simon team cars. He became a partner in some of Simon's property holdings, and his future looked secure. But in the fall of 1994, Dick Simon Racing suddenly lost both its major sponsors, Duracell and Panasonic. In anticipation of the continuation of the sponsorship, Simon had made large cash deposits on four new Lola cars and 17 Cosworth engines for the 1995 season. The team was now effectively broke. Simon brought in a new investor and reinvented the team as Scandia Racing, but Eldon was left out. A series of suits and countersuits between Rasmussen, Simon, and the two sponsors followed, with Eldon ultimately accepting a settlement of $75,000 for his losses.

Since 1995, Eldon has worked out of a small shop adjacent to his home on a suburban Indianapolis acreage. Racers from all branches of the sport seek him out to build or repair the parts for their cars. During practice for the 2002 Indianapolis 500, a team brought him a magnesium bell housing that had shattered into four pieces. His price to put it back together was $2,500 (U.S.). His reputation as a craftsman has reached beyond racing, and he has, among other assignments, undertaken extensive modifications to pill-manufacturing equipment for an Indianapolis-area pharmaceutical company.

In 2002, Eldon Rasmussen was inducted into the Canadian Motorsport Hall of Fame. A measure of the man's stature is that not only was his entire family present for the ceremony, coming from as far away as Oklahoma, but old racing friends from Edmonton and Calgary also made their way there to pay tribute.

CHAPTER 9

EDMONTON INTERNATIONAL SPEEDWAY

Build it, and they will come.
—W. P. Kinsella, *Shoeless Joe*

In the 1940s, Gavin Breckenridge operated a farm just north of Edmonton on 127 Street. In 1943 he became caught up in the Model T Ford racing that had developed tremendous popularity over the past two summers. From then, as often as farm work and finances permitted, he ran his old Ford in the series until 1951, when he won the last-ever race of that class run in Edmonton.

With the end of Model T racing and the growing reluctance of fairground operators to permit continued racing on their horse tracks, Gavin was without a car, and even if he had one, a place to run it. But he did have land. Edmonton was obviously in need of a purpose-built motor speedway, so who better to provide it?

Working together with his brother-in-law, Oscar Green, he ploughed a ½-mile dirt track on the farm, just north of 137 Avenue. A small grandstand was built, and Edmonton had its first speedway.

The opening-day race card in 1951 featured stock cars and a field of approximately eight Alberta Auto Racing Association sprint cars. The sprint car drivers told Breckenridge that they would require a fee to perform at future events. That made no sense to

Gavin, and the first time was the last time the sprints took to his track. Model T racing was gone, so Breckenridge Speedway was a strictly a stock car track.

The ½-mile track was soon shortened to ¼ mile. "People wanted more action," recalls Gavin.

Racing now had a foothold in Edmonton, but Gavin and Oscar realized that they lacked the resources to nurture the speedway and develop it to properly serve its market. When the Booth brothers, Percy, Reg, and Russell, who had already built a paved track in Calgary, came calling in 1953, the Edmonton promoters were ready to deal. Gavin leased to the Booths a piece of land immediately adjacent to the dirt track, and the brothers wasted little time in building a ¼-mile paved oval.[1] The new track, named Speedway Park, opened for business in 1954.

While Breckenridge and Green had operated the track, one of the regular drivers—a quite successful one—was known only as "Mr. X." When the track was sold, Mr. X's true identity was revealed. He was really Gavin Breckenridge. Gavin had preferred to remain anonymous while he owned the track, believing that having one competitor owning the track and paying the officials would not reflect well upon the professional image of the sport in Edmonton. Once the disguise was removed, Gavin continued racing, perhaps even more successfully than before, winning the 1955 Gold Cup among numerous other races.

The Booth brothers were businessmen, and they weren't afraid to get their hands dirty to make their business work. At one point during construction, Percy Booth decided some additional grading was needed. Rather than go to the expense of hiring a contractor, he decided to rent a grader himself. He had the track's public relations and advertising director, Donald MacKay, drive him to a rental company shop and then follow him back to the track as he drove the grader. When the little convoy arrived at the track, MacKay casually

---

1. While the track was advertised as being a quarter mile in length (402 metres), it appeared much smaller. Most people agreed that the quarter-mile measurement was the outside circumference, but veteran racer Reg Kostash believes it was even smaller than that, with a true inside circumference of just 910 feet (277 metres). The author has been unable to verify this.

asked Percy when he had learned to operate such a machine. "In the past half-hour," was the reply. Later, when faced with a shortage of racers, the Booths went shopping for suitable used cars and converted them to stockers themselves. The cars were then sold or rented to aspiring drivers who lacked the skills and tools to build their own.

The Booths ran the track with a close eye on the profit-and-loss statement, and they didn't seem to care who they offended. At the 1966 CAMRA Gold Cup race, Percy Booth overruled timer Bob Derval and lap counter Sid Ashley, both of whom had scored Norm Ellefson as winner, and declared Al Smith of Victoria to be the champion. As Ellefson, a Canadian, was then racing out of Washington State, American drivers, who had been competing in the Gold Cup since the mid-1950s, threatened to boycott any future Edmonton races. The Booths didn't flinch, and Ellefson and the Americans kept coming to Edmonton. On another occasion, Calgary racer Ron Harris recalls threatening Percy Booth with physical harm after the second or third time the purse at the end of the day came out substantially less than the amount advertised. In this age prior to that of political correctness, Frank Janett remembers Percy Booth telling George Lemay that his name when racing in Edmonton would be "Frenchy." Lemay protested that he couldn't speak French and didn't even know how many generations he was removed from France—his parents had immigrated to Alberta from the United States. Booth told him that didn't matter, but they needed him as an attraction to draw "those frogs from St. Albert."

In 1960 the Booths dug their heels in on an issue they probably later wished they hadn't. At the annual Gold Cup in 1960, American driver Cliff Spaulding bumped into several other cars during practice. Flagman Don Sharp, a former midget racer who had been with the Booths since their track first opened, waved the black flag on Spaulding. The driver stayed on the track, ignoring repeated efforts by Sharp to get him off. When the practice session ended, Sharp told Spaulding he was disqualified from the day's racing, although not for rough driving—that in itself would have brought only a reprimand—but for ignoring the flagman's signals. Reg and Percy Booth, who had paid Spaulding tow money to make the long trek from the

Breckenridge Speedway: The original ½-mile oval has been shortened to ¼ mile, as can be seen in this 1952 aerial photo. *(Tim Erlam collection)*

Typical early Speedway Park action: The ever-happy-just-to-be-racing John McEachran extricates himself from this c. 1953 wreck.
(Raffant Studios photo from the Paulette McEachran collection)

More early Speedway Park action: Jack Freeborn (#28) speeds by a spinning Duke Foster. *(Don Sharp collection)*

U.S. west coast, overruled Sharp. With his authority suddenly removed, Sharp prepared to quit, at which point the Edmonton drivers, who had enormous respect for their flagman, told the Booths that if Sharp left, they would do likewise.

The Booths capitulated, but the relationship between track management and its star employee—Sharp enjoyed great popularity and a high profile in the community—was poisoned. His one-year contract with the track was not renewed at season's end. Speedway Park carried on for the next two seasons with other flagmen, but fans and drivers, and ultimately the Booths, recognized that Sharp's unique combination of fairness, firmness, racing knowledge, people skills, flair, and athleticism (he typically leapt three feet in the air while waving his flags) was not easily replaced. Prior to the start of the 1963 season, Speedway Park held a press conference to announce that Sharp had been re-signed. Percy Booth's statement to the media was: "We had to get him back simply because he's the best flagman we know."

In spite of all its problems, Speedway Park for a decade and a half would be the hub of auto racing in Northern Alberta, hosting everything from demolition derbies to future Indianapolis stars competing in their Super-modifieds. Every Wednesday evening a minimum crowd of 1,000 people, and often many more, would file past the bust of Eddie "Tiger" Matan[2] that stood at the east gate, to be entertained by a line-up of Early-Late Stock cars and A and B Modifieds. If the evening air was still, the sound of the racing cars could be heard over much of north Edmonton. The little track was so successful that it would later become the basis for the largest, most complete auto racing facility ever in Western Canada, and arguably all of the country.

Sports car and drag racing had first appeared in Western Canada in the mid 1950s and, much to the credit of the pioneers of these two disciplines, grew and thrived in the absence of any decent facilities. Airports were the favoured venue but, with the exception of the Namao military air base north of Edmonton, were all rapidly deteriorating World War II training facilities. The lack of any topographical contour made for monotonous road racing, and the crumbling asphalt and concrete surfaces destroyed the tires of road and drag race cars alike. With the active support of Alberta Minister of Highways Gordon Taylor, drag cars were able to run on closed public roads, but that effectively ended with a tragic accident in 1963 in which a young Edmonton girl lost an eye.

An attempt had been made to develop a complete racing facility. In late 1961, Jim Rideout, a founding member of Northern Alberta Sports Car Club, tried to raise money to build a track near Bon Accord, but at $200 a share, received little response.

The Booths knew there was a need for more than just an oval, but they also understood that this would be a far bigger undertaking than anything they had previously done. Consider land, for instance. Speedway Park, with track, grandstands, concessions, and parking covered just over 20 acres. A ¼-mile drag strip, with another ¼-mile braking area, all tied into a 2 ½-mile road course and a ½-mile banked oval, along with reasonable parking area, would require

2. Eddie "Tiger" Matan reigned as the star driver of Speedway Park for a short time in the early to mid 1950s, winning the first Gold Cup in 1954. Tragically, he was killed in a boating accident in 1958.

a quarter section, or 160 acres. The land would have to be bought or leased in Edmonton's booming, and therefore expensive, market, and three miles of asphalt paving wouldn't be cheap either. Some research was called for, and in 1964, while attending the Indianapolis 500, Percy Booth and Don MacKay invited United States Auto Club director and two-time 500 winner Rodger Ward to Edmonton to act as honourary starter for the Gold Cup race. After touring the city and seeing the level of support for good racing, Ward told the Booths that he felt Edmonton could indeed sustain a larger facility. Not that the Booths ever needed much encouragement to build race tracks, but Ward's assessment was the nudge they needed to begin planning. They began with a tour of North American tracks: Daytona Beach, Florida; Riverside, California; Mosport near Toronto; and Westwood near Vancouver. Back from their tour, they decided to proceed with the project and enlisted the services of St. Albert sports car racer, chassis designer, and most importantly, architect, John Barnaschone.

Barnaschone's preliminary plan, drawn in late 1964, envisioned a drag strip forming the front straight of a road course that would work its way onto a new half-mile oval to be constructed immediately to the west of the existing track. Road course cars would exit the drag strip at the west end and work their way to the new oval, which they would enter turning right onto the west turn, complete roughly three-quarters of a lap, then exit by making a left turn off the back straight. From there they would go through a series of curves and rejoin the drag-strip at its east end. The new ½-mile oval would have a motorcycle flat-track on its infield, and the old ¼-mile track would be converted to a kart track, with an infield road course. There would be a control tower, pit garages, and grandstands for 4,000 at the drag strip and 6,000 at the oval.

Don MacKay scheduled an official announcement and scale-model display to take place the evening of January 25, 1965, at Stedelbauer Chev Olds. New cars were removed from Stedelbauer's showroom, but there still wasn't enough room for the crowd that showed up. An estimated 10,000 attended, and a second night's showing was scheduled. Public reaction was overwhelmingly enthusiastic,

January 25, 1965: Unveiling of the model that would become Edmonton International Speedway. Far left is Richard Chevalier, third from left Roy Scott, fourth from left Mike Atkin. Russell Booth is second from right, architect John Barnaschone fifth from right, Percy Booth seventh from right, Grover Compton eighth from right. Others are unknown to the writer.
(Provincial Archives of Alberta, WS 683/2)

Announcement Night, January 25, 1965: Thousands crowd into the Stedelbauer Chev Olds showroom to view a mockup of the new Edmonton International Speedway, and a display of some of the cars that will use it.
(Wells Studios photo from Richard Chevalier collection)

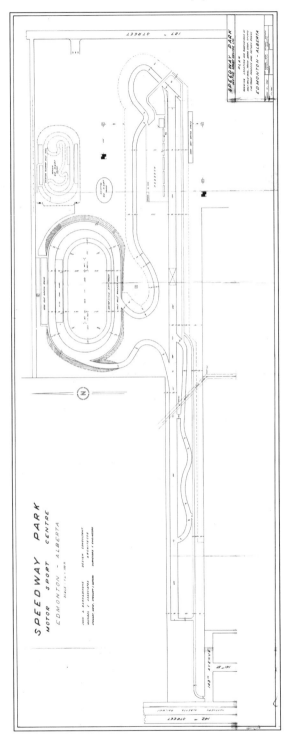

Architect's drawing of the original layout. *(Credit: John Barnaschone)*

February 1967: A DKW leads a mixed bag of sedans and sports cars out of the snow and onto the new drag strip in an N.A.S.C.C. race that was the first official use of Edmonton International Speedway's new facilities. The Speedway Park oval is in the background. *(Author's collection)*

although there was the inevitable nit-picking. For instance, some sports car drivers expressed reservations about the idea of entering the oval midway through an 18-degree banked turn. Barnaschone was confident, however, that with the drivers already being in a curve as they approached the oval the transition could be made smoothly.

It's one thing to develop enthusiasm among the racing crowd, but quite another to get serious investors on side. Racers, as a group, typically have little spare money to invest—racing is expensive. The hunt was on for financing, and sometimes it didn't go all that quickly. When it became obvious that a small group of investors was not going to be able to finance the project itself, they had to go public. In May 1966 Speedway Motor Sport Centre Ltd. received regulatory approval to raise capital by selling shares to the public. Directors of the new corporation were:

Russell Booth, *President*
Darrell Bennett, *Vice President*
Reg Booth, *Secretary*
George Stedelbauer, *Treasurer*
Howard Melchin, *Director*
Thomas Fox, *Director*
George Becker, *Director*

The subsequent sale of stock did not set any market records, but it did raise enough money to restart construction, and gradually the project began to take shape. By the fall of 1966, the developers were able to build the drag strip, which hosted an informal meet in October. Four months later, a sports car race was held using a track ploughed through the snow-covered fields and onto the drag strip, but there was no sign of a permanent sports car track, a control tower or pit garages.

In the spring of 1967, a temporary wood tower was built at the start line of the drag strip, and arrangements were made with the Capital City Hot Rod Association to stage a race the weekend of May 21. Not only would this be the official opening of the "Most Northerly Drag Strip in the World," it would also be the first time C.C.H.R.A. started its races with a Christmas-tree light standard rather than flags. Race day was warm and sunny, and an estimated 15,000 fans—the greatest attendance at an auto race in the province since the Model T era—and National Hot Rod Association director Terrell Poage showed up to watch the politician who had done so much for Alberta racing, Honourable Gordon Taylor, Minister of Highways, cut the ceremonial ribbon. The track was officially open and the racing began.

Prior to the weekend, there had been talk of 200-mile-per-hour (325 kmh) speeds, as three of the entrants had already done that, but it wasn't to happen this time. By early afternoon, the temperature reached 77 degrees Fahrenheit (25°C) when suddenly what had appeared to be a perfect day for racing was literally blown apart by an unexpected squall. A wind strong enough to knock over the new $9,000 Christmas tree came across the track, dropping temperatures, laying a film of dust on the racing surface, and finally blowing in a brief rainstorm. Competitors, officials, and fans rushed for cover. A half-hour later, the wind and the rain died and the reconstruction started. The Christmas tree was repaired, the start line was swept reasonably clean, and racing resumed; but the 200-mile-per-hour speeds were not to be seen. The new track surface covered in a thin layer of mud would not support record speeds. Fastest run of the day went to Frank Rupert of Spokane, Washington, with an 8.25-second

May 21, 1967: Opening day of the Edmonton International Speedway drag strip. Two street stocks launch from in front of the temporary control tower. *(Richard Chevalier collection)*

Aerial view of the final layout. Heavy black line shows shortcut for 1.5-mile road course. *(City of Edmonton Archives, EA340-516)*

elapsed time and 188-miles-per-hour (306-kmh) top speed. In the Top Fuel Eliminator final, the Gord Jenner–Nick Kozak *Royal Canadian* took top prize, as Rupert red-lighted. The final race took place almost nine and a half hours after the spectator gates opened.

The tower was built, the drag strip completed, and the winter-spring of 1967–68 saw the road course, the pit garages, and an access bridge over the final turn constructed. For now, the idea of a half-mile oval was abandoned. In a gracious gesture, the developers named the various landmarks on the new track after pioneers of the sport in the Edmonton area. The front straight / drag strip was Chevalier Straight after J. G. (Bill) Chevalier who, with his sons, Richard and Ross, helped so many racers through their Pioneer Automotive speed shop / foreign car dealership. The 180-degree series at the west end was named Parker's End for Wally Parker, president of Edmonton Auto Racing Association. The quick left-right sequence before the first left became Smalian Chicane, to acknowledge the years of help in advertising by Edmonton *Journal* employee Ernie Smalian. The left turn was Breckenridge Bend, in honour of the man who first set land aside for a race track. The following right was Meldau after Emil Meldau, long-time executive on the Edmonton Auto Racing Association and founding vice president of Canadian American Modified Racing Association. A steeply banked, almost-180-degree turn was named Green Bank[3] for Oscar Green, who worked so hard with Gavin Breckenridge in the development of the original track. A tight left-hander was Taylor Turn, out of respect for the contributions to the sport made by Hon. Gordon Taylor.

The layout was based on Barnaschone's 1965 plans, but he had left the project earlier over differences with the Booths, and the final design work was done by the project's engineers. An added touch to the final product was a right-turn shortcut off the main straight to enable road-race organizers to reduce the length of the course by almost a mile. While use of the shortcut would render the circuit too

---

3. While the new oval track planned by Barnaschone was left out of the final construction, Green Bank was just where that track's east turn would have been and was configured as one might expect to find a turn on a ½-mile oval.

short for major races, it was a benefit to regional races—the cars remained in view of the spectators for a longer portion of each lap.

The first sports car race, called "The Alberta Cup" and organized by the Northern Alberta Sports Car Club, took place July 27 and 28, 1968. For a large group of novice Edmonton drivers, the new track was nothing more than what they expected, but for the weather-beaten veterans of the sport, the men who had for years hauled, and in many cases driven, their MGs, Triumphs, home-built specials, Austin-Healeys, and Porsches across the Prairies to race on feature-less, abandoned slabs of asphalt in places like Davidson, Saskatchewan, Macdonald, Manitoba, and Fort MacLeod and Claresholm, Alberta, not to mention dirt tracks, this was pure luxu-ry. Here they drove over a bridge to get from outside the track to the paddock—the paddock with new pavement. Coming off the bridge, a four-storey, concrete-block control tower sat on their left, and beyond that, locking garages, if they were lucky enough to be assigned one. Indoor plumbing, a steel pit wall (no more hay bales), permanent grandstands, V.I.P seating atop the garages, a public-address system that could be heard and understood—was there no end to it? And beyond all that, a real city with more than one place to eat! Sports car racing had arrived in Alberta.

For the record, the first heat on the new track was a six-lap race for novice drivers, won by Barry Fox of Edmonton in a Lotus 51. There were seven races altogether, with the 30-lap feature won by Edmonton's Mike Atkin in a Merlyn Formula Ford.

In two months, these same drivers would be back, but only as a warm-up show to the greatest sports car racing on the planet, as the Canadian American (Can-Am) Challenge Cup was about to come to Edmonton.

CHAPTER 10

RAY PEETS

If racing is part of a really good life, it's a really good thing,
but if racing is your life, you don't have a life.
—Paraphrase of a comment by professional
hockey-player agent Ritch Winter,
substituting "racing" for "hockey"

Ray Peets is well past most people's idea of retirement age, but he still puts in a full day, every day, at Reliable Engine Services, the Edmonton company he founded in 1965. The level of energy that brought him success as an oval track driver in the 1950s and '60s, and even greater triumph as a drag racing builder in the 1970s, is still part of him.

Ray Peets is initially reluctant to take time to talk about his racing career. He claims to be "up to my ass in alligators" and working harder and longer than the "retired guys" a historian should really be interviewing. Once he begins talking, though, the anecdotes and the memories flow easily. And no visit is complete without a tour of his pride and joy, the 80,000-square-foot shop that is headquarters to Reliable Engine.

The Reliable plant is a remarkable facility. This huge descendant of the 2,500-square-foot shop Peets opened almost four decades earlier not only does machine work on automotive engines, as it always has done, but also rebuilds engines and parts for trucks, oilfield equipment, earthmovers, military vehicles, and railway locomotives.

For Reliable, nothing is too big. There is a honing machine that required holes to be made in the floor and the roof to accommodate its mass. The monster will machine cylinders up to a 56 centimetre (22-inch) bore and is worth $1.5 million. Ray the businessman is proud that he acquired it, only slightly used, for $100,000.

Evidence of Reliable's size and reputation is the fact that its largest customer is CP Rail, and its second largest is the Canadian Army.

While racing engines haven't been a major part of the business for many years, Ray still does the specialty machining that racers need, such as opening up bearing passages to allow the installation of needle bearings. Surprisingly, there is little racing memorabilia visible at the plant. A "Thank you" photo of Al Green's sprint car and a framed montage commemorating the induction of Ray Peets and Gary Beck into the Canadian Motorsport Hall of Fame is all. Everything else is business.

Ray Peets was a teen-aged high-school dropout and apprentice mechanic when, encouraged by Southern Alberta Institute of Technology classmate Don Tupper, and by memories of watching World War II–era Model T races from a makeshift grandstand in the back of his father's dump truck, he decided to get involved in racing in 1952. By 1953 he was a regular competitor at the dirt track of Breckenridge Speedway on the north outskirts of Edmonton. His career began with a 1933 Ford coupe, which served him well until he managed to create enough horsepower to shear a hub free of its wire wheel. The resultant rollover prompted him to switch to a Chev, with steel wheels.

He raced the Chev through the mid 1950s, competing mainly on the new Speedway Park, asphalt successor to the dirt Breckenridge facility. He was successful, too, winning among other races Speedway Park's Bronze Cup, Silver Cup, and Gold Cup races in 1956.

By 1958, Ray was developing other plans and became engaged to Marlene, a young schoolteacher. At the time, he was a Gold Cup Champion. He had been voted "Most Popular Driver" by the fans. His smiling face, framed by helmet and goggles, was the image most commonly used in ads and promotions for upcoming races. Edmonton *Journal* headlines referred to "Ramblin' Ray" and stated "Ray Peets Is Big Noise In Stock Car Racing." Even the Calgary *Albertan* identified him, at age 21, as "The King of Western Canada stock car racing." But through all that, and as young as he was, he understood that in the grand scheme of life racing was only a hobby. He also understood that marriage takes money, and he didn't have much, so he set aside his racing and all the attention it brought with it and went north to work on the construction of the Distant Early Warning (DEW) line radar system. When he returned to Edmonton in 1960, he and Marlene married and bought their first house. Then he went back racing.

Ray's old Chev chassis was still a competitive way to race, but Ray, the mechanical tinkerer, knew there were better ideas to be found. He had heard about the tremendous handling characteristics found in the chassis of European sports and formula cars, but he didn't have enough information to build one for himself. Some enquiries among local sports car drivers turned up the name of John Barnaschone, an English architect and sports car builder who had recently moved to Canada. Barnaschone had no experience with oval track cars, but he did have a solid understanding of modern chassis and suspension design. He convinced Ray that a lightweight structure constructed of many small, mild steel tubes brazed together to form a space frame would be lighter and just as strong as the traditional arc-welded assembly of large-diameter tubing that was the standard of the day. Attached to the frame would be a four-wheel independent suspension system with its pick-up points, alignment, and anti-roll bars all being fully adjustable.

The design was a complete change of direction in oval track car design, and many drivers of the era would not have been at all interested. But Ray Peets, who so many years earlier had painfully found out that wire wheels were obsolete, and who had been the first racer in Edmonton to use a Chevrolet V-8, and who was now devising a way to put one more four-barrel carburetor on an engine than anyone else, was game to try the new chassis technology. The car was built in 1962. Ray's crew member Geoff Goodwin recalls, "It seemed

Ray climbing into his then state-of-the-art, dual-wheeled stock car at Edmonton's Speedway Park, 1953. *(Ray Peets collection)*

Ray poses with his first car powered by an overhead-valve engine, a Pontiac V-8, 1955. *(Ray Peets collection)*

Ray, the happy racer, c. 1956.
(Ray Peets collection)

Ray Peets in his new John Barnaschone–designed, Ray Peets–and–Geoff Goodwin–built Weldangrind Special, 1963. *(Ray Peets collection)*

like we spent the whole winter just cutting, fitting, grinding, and welding a thousand little tubes." Initially the design was not effective, but with everything being adjustable, it was only a matter of time before it began to work. When the car was finally properly set up, it was competitive with anything else in the Canadian American Modified Racing Association.

Ray was able to race on the expensive CAMRA circuit by doing most of his own work and by always having at least a bit of sponsorship. He raced with the likes of Eldon Rasmussen, Billy Foster, Art Pollard, and Jim Malloy, all of whom made it to the Indianapolis 500. Did he ever have any aspirations of following them to the major leagues of racing? "No." he states flatly. "I never wanted to go fast enough to kill myself. You just named four guys. Three of them are dead.[1] Racing for me was a hobby."

The relationship between oval racer Peets and his crew man Geoff Goodwin worked both ways. In 1963, while still actively racing his modified, Ray formed a team with Geoff and his C-class dragster. With Geoff driving and Ray building the engines, they went undefeated through the complete 1963 season. In a way, it was a portent of what was to happen in the 1970s.

Since beginning his career as an apprentice mechanic at Maurice Carter's dealership in Edmonton in 1952, Ray Peets had honed his mechanical skills operating a Shell service station, running his own speed shop, working for Engine Rebuilders and for Weldangrind, and even spending six months with Howard Racing Cams in California. By 1965 it was time to put his collected experience to work and, not coincidentally, his racing on hold again while he opened a new business, Reliable Engine Services, in a rented shop. With a solid reputation in both the automotive business and the racing community, Ray's little machine shop grew. Reliable was able to give the automotive trade the service it needed and keep its racing customers happy too.

---

1. Jim Malloy of Colorado and Art Pollard of Oregon were both killed practising for the Indianapolis 500. Billy Foster, of Victoria, BC, was killed in a stock car race at Riverside, California.

While no longer part of the CAMRA circuit in the late 1960s, Ray still kept in touch with his racing roots, building engines, and even buying a Formula Ford and competing on the new Edmonton International Speedway road course.

He was also part of a group of Edmonton businessmen and racing enthusiasts who became involved in the *Spirit of Edmonton* Can-Am racer in 1970. After the 1969 Can-Am race that drew some 42,000 people, local stock car racer Grant Armstrong and public relations executive Bob Russell decided that Edmonton could not only support a race, but also a race car too. The two managed to get Reg Booth involved, and before long the "race-ready" M-12 McLaren of Toronto's George Eaton had been purchased. Actually getting the car to Edmonton was a comedy of errors as the new race team almost immediately found its car being evicted from Eaton's Toronto garage. Arrangements were quickly made to put the car on a westbound moving van, and that worked fine until the moving company went bankrupt and their van, with all its cargo, including the race car, was placed under seizure by a sheriff's bailiff. When the car was finally freed and it arrived in Edmonton, two Australian mechanics who were in town waiting for a Continental Formula A race agreed to take a look at it. They found it to be far short of race-ready, but they happily went to work restoring it. Ray Peets was called in to look at the engine and quickly pronounced it to be "junk," a statement he later tempered to "a little loose." While the Australians worked on the chassis, Ray rebuilt the engine. An 18-man committee, including Peets, was struck to raise money for a proper Can-Am campaign, and no one in Edmonton was immune from their efforts. Even the mayor was hit up for $100 at a ceremony at City Hall, where the car was christened *The Spirit of Edmonton*.

Sadly, their season was a classic case of the *Spirit* was willing, but …

With journeyman New Zealand driver Graeme Lawrence, the team finished the year in 27th place in the Can-Am standings, their best race yielding only an 8th place, at Elkhart Lake.

In the early 1970s, Ray began working with a drag racer named Gary Beck. Beck, a bricklayer originally from the Seattle area, had moved to Edmonton, married a local girl and was campaigning an

Gary Beck launches the Beck & Peets Export A Top Fuel dragster, 1973.
(Ray Peets collection)

alcohol dragster with partner Ken McLean. He needed an engine, and asked if Reliable could help. In short order, Ray Peets had created one of the early racing 426 Chrysler hemis. The car did well, and even better when Ray custom-built a crankshaft offering an extra half-inch of stroke.

In 1972, Peets formally joined forces with Beck and McLean. The intent was to form a strong Canadian team to campaign a Top Fuel dragster, the fastest class of car in drag racing. Little did anyone know just how strong that team would become.

Their first National Hot Rod Association (N.H.R.A.) national was in Montreal. It was soon apparent that they had, if not the fastest, certainly one of the fastest cars there. The only problem was that Ken McLean as driver was not getting off the line as fast as the competition. "He left too late," says Ray, commenting on McLean's slow starts. The team was eliminated in the first round and Beck and Peets decided that the driving duties should be turned over to Beck.

N.H.R.A. requires a special licence to race fuel cars and Gary was only licensed for alcohol, so the following weekend they went to a meet in Michigan and took a few runs under the supervision of N.H.R.A. officials, who quickly issued the licence.

The next race was the biggest and most important race on the N.H.R.A. calendar, the Indianapolis Nationals, and the Edmontonians headed south. Because of a dispute between many of the top drivers and N.H.R.A., the field at Indy that year was thinner than usual, but there were enough name drivers—notably Jerry Ruth, Don Prudhomme, and Tom "Mongoose" McEwan—that Beck and Peets, an unknown team from somewhere in Canada, whose driver had held his Fuel Licence for two weeks, were given little chance of success. Ignoring the odds, Beck drove as fast as he could, and after each run Peets pulled the oil pan and quickly changed the bearings. This routine got them through the qualifying rounds, and despite damaging the supercharger in the semifinal, they made it to the final round. Working frantically, Ray got the car repaired in time to race against one of the titans of the sport, Jerry Ruth. At the start, Ruth pushed too hard and smoked his tires, while Beck ran away from him with a clean run. The nascent team from Edmonton, Alberta, Canada had won the biggest event in drag racing!

With a record of success behind them, they were able to get a good sponsor, Export A cigarettes, for the 1973 season. "In a year, we went from having one motor, to two, and then three!" recalls Ray with obvious pride.

It was a different N.H.R.A. Indianapolis National they went to in 1973. The previous year they were unknown; this year they were the defending champions. In 1972 many top drivers had been absent; now everyone who mattered was present and ready to be counted.

With their new sponsor in place, Peets and Beck were intent on making a good impression, and they hosted one of the first cocktail receptions drag racing had seen. They also had Beck & Peets T-shirts and halter tops made and sold them off the back of the team truck. This level of promotion was a large step beyond what most racers practised at that time, and N.H.R.A. founding president Wally Parks complimented them on their professionalism.

Life was good, but could they really race?

They wasted little time in providing the answer. In the first round, they drew the biggest name in drag racing, Don "Big Daddy" Garlits, and beat him. Now everyone knew the team from Canada was for real. But no matter, they kept on winning, reaching the final against Carl Olson. With a 5.96-second, 243.9-mile-per-hour run they achieved their second consecutive N.H.R.A. Indianapolis National title.

For Ray Peets, that single weekend is the fondest memory of his racing career. "The second win at Indy, I understood the significance of it. The first year, I hadn't realized how important that race is. I didn't know enough about drag racing then."

The team's success continued. In 1974 they won three N.H.R.A. Nationals and capped their season with Beck being named Top Fuel World Champion.

Gary Beck and Ray Peets raced as a team until the end of the 1975 season. By then, the strain of running a growing business, raising a young family, staying in daily contact with Beck, who by then had moved to California, and flying to a different track every weekend was wearing on Ray, and he left the team. "It wasn't fun anymore."

Since then the focus of Ray Peets' energy has been his family of Marlene, their two daughters and one son, the family's equestrian hobby, and of course Reliable Engine. Racing was again in the background until 2000 when Ray Peets, the man for whom racing was "just a hobby," together with Gary Beck, was invited to Toronto to be inducted into the Canadian Motorsport Hall of Fame.

THE BOYS

My father would be proud of me.
—Jacques Villeneuve, 1997

The accident that broke the arm of a teen-aged boy in Saskatoon in 1946 might seem unrelated to an attempt in 2003 to take another teenager from Calgary to the biggest league in stock car racing, but there is a connection.

The unfortunate lad in 1946 was a friend of 13-year-old Buddie Boys of Moose Jaw. The two were in Saskatoon for a car race in which the friend was entered. The broken arm meant he would not be able to wheel his 1939 Ford around the Saskatoon Fairgrounds oval. A replacement driver was needed and young Mr. Boys offered his services.

Most 13-year-olds have never driven a car, and to put someone that young into a dirt track race with full-sized cars might seem injudicious at best, and criminally negligent at worst. But Buddie Boys was no ordinary 13-year-old learning to drive. His father was a trucker who had put Buddie behind the wheel for the first time at the age of ten. By the time he was 12, the youngster was driving a tanker truck on the highway. One time he was pulled over by the police and asked for identification. Having none, he tried lying about his age. The constable didn't buy the story, but he agreed to give the neophyte trucker and his rig a police escort to the nearest town, where he was told to park the truck.

In Saskatoon, much to his own delight, young Buddie found himself leading the race. But just as visions of victory began to dance in his head, the overheating Ford blew a radiator hose, and Buddie's race was over.

Rather than being discouraged by this setback, Buddie had found his life's passion. For the next four decades, Buddie Boys would race. He would drive stock cars, sprint cars, midgets, modifieds, and super-modifieds all over North America on dirt tracks, paved tracks, and road courses. And his son and grandson would follow him.

Jump ahead to 2003, and Buddie Boys's driving days are now behind him. His grandson Wheeler Boys, at age 19 already a veteran of mini-stock, sports car, I.M.C.A. modified, and CASCAR racing, is being groomed to join the big league of stock car racing, the NASCAR Winston Cup.[1] In the coming year, Wheeler plans to compete in NASCAR races at Pocono, Pennsylvania; Phoenix, Arizona; and Dover, Delaware. A car has been purchased, and an experienced crew chief contracted. Buddie's son and Wheeler's father, Trevor Boys, is putting to work the many contacts he made in his own racing career to pave his son's way to a professional career.

"He's going to be a star in Winston Cup," says Trevor.

"Or we'll kill him," adds Buddie.

Wheeler listens, expressionless.

Trevor Boys, like his father, has driven just about every type of race car. In the 1970s he drove a Formula Vee car on road courses well enough to win the Prairie Region championship. On ovals he raced stock cars, midgets and sprint cars, at times living in California and Washington State to be closer to more racing. In 1980 he was West Coast Midget champion, and in the same year managed to win a Canadian American Modified Racing Association race. In 1983 he got the proverbial big break when Calgary businessman and sports car racer Maurice McCaig agreed to back a NASCAR Winston Cup entry, with Trevor as driver and Frank Janett as mechanic. Trevor had earlier driven the final Winston Cup Race of 1982 on the

---

1. The name of the series was changed in 2004 to "Nextel Cup."

road course at Riverside, California, and while he didn't win, the experience gave him the confidence that he was capable of running in the major league of stock car racing.

Trevor had no problem adapting to the higher speeds of some of the huge NASCAR ovals. By the end of the 1983 season he was 25th overall in the final Winston Cup points standings and runner-up to Sterling Marlin for Rookie-of-the-Year honours, well ahead of the other two rookie contenders, Ronnie Hopkins in 31st position and Bobby Hillin, Jr in 37th. A good start, and even more impressive when one considers that Trevor earned more points than either Cale Yarborough, Benny Parsons, David Pearson, or Mark Martin.

But he feels he deserved better. To this day Trevor believes that he, not Sterling Marlin, rightfully should have won Rookie of the Year. "Points were changed," he says unequivocally, citing the desire of the management of NASCAR in the mid 1980s to raise their public profile and image. "The image they wanted was guys wearing $100 slacks flying in to races, while their car and everything was hauled to the track with brand-new semis," he states. "They didn't want truck drivers, and that's what I was."

The next year, 1984, building on their success rather than dwelling on their loss, the team from Canada moved up to 17th place overall—solidly in the top half of the NASCAR hierarchy. 1984 also gave Trevor a momentary flash of fame as his speeding car, high on the banking at Daytona, appeared around the world in a remarkable Associated Press photograph. Like much of his Winston Cup career, though, Trevor was overshadowed by one of the bigger names in racing. The photograph was shot on July 4, and immediately above Trevor's car in the photo was the United States President's private jet, Air Force One, in its final approach for landing at Daytona Airport. President Ronald Reagan was arriving as guest of honour at the Firecracker 400. The ultimate star of the day was Richard Petty, who won his 200th, and last, major race, and many papers identified the car in the AP picture as his number 43. Close inspection reveals that the car really was Trevor's number 48 (see photo page 121).

With an unsympathetic administration, no factory backing, and having to constantly scramble for sponsorships, 17th was to be as

Winston Cup Rookie-of-the-Year contenders, 1983: L to R, Bobby Hillin, Jr, Trevor Boys, Sterling Marlin, Ronnie Hopkins, Jr. *(Trevor Boys collection)*

July 1984, Daytona, Florida: Trevor running wheel-to-wheel with United States President Ronald Reagan in Air Force One during the Firecracker 400. *(AP Wide World Photos)*

Daytona, 1985: Trevor with Benfield-McCaig Racing Monte Carlo.
(Dorsey Patrick Photography)

Trevor Boys, c. 1984, with son Wheeler. *(Trevor Boys collection)*

high as Trevor would ever finish in the points. He continued to compete and to be competitive, but from 1985 on, the number of races he was able to run steadily dropped.

In spite of his reduced schedule, the fans continued to notice and appreciate Trevor. In 1985, NASCAR polled its fans to find the most popular drivers. The top 20 would be asked to compete in a special invitational race at Atlanta. Much to his own surprise, particularly since he ran in only ten Winston Cup races that year, Trevor was 11th on the list. That recognition by the fans, against the background of his struggles to stay in the game, remains his fondest memory of his time in the south.

In 1985, Trevor was involved in a major wreck at Talladega Superspeedway. At 200 miles per hour, he touched fenders with another car and ended up sitting in a completely destroyed car against the wall. What he prefers to remember about that day is not the wreck, however, but the fact that early in the race he set the fastest race lap that had been driven in NASCAR history to that point.

In 1989, Trevor devoted his energies primarily to the NASCAR Northwest Tour, but he still managed to make it back to the big-league Winston Cup circuit for selected races, driving for Earl Sadler. At the 1989 Daytona race, the Sadler team took two battered race cars and mixed and matched parts until they had one operable car. Once on the track with the hybrid, Trevor found himself three or four miles per hour too slow to qualify. Their engine simply couldn't keep up.

Trevor canvassed the other teams, looking for anyone who might have a competitive engine for sale, and found what he needed at Cale Yarborough's pit. A deal was quickly struck between Cale and Trevor, and a low-mileage motor changed hands for $18,000. Just as the engine was on its way to Trevor's pit, Cale's team owner intercepted the crew members and told everyone that the deal was off. The engine was strictly a qualifying unit, he said, and wouldn't last more than a few laps into a 500-mile race—a "grenade" in stock-car parlance. Sadler and Boys insisted that a deal had been made, and they were sticking to it. Yarborough's team owner offered another engine: a race motor rather than a qualifying motor. But the harder he pushed for a return of the original engine, the more Trevor and Sadler sensed they had probably bought an awful lot of horsepower. Trevor also understood that he had no reasonable chance of winning the race, but if this motor could help him qualify and then possibly get near the front of the pack, even temporarily, the exposure and publicity would do nothing but good for his profile and that of his team. The Sadler team installed the engine in their race car, and the hopelessly slow team of a day earlier suddenly found itself qualified in 14th position on a 43-car grid.

By lap 40 in the race, Trevor had moved up from fourteenth to fourth place, and the engine was still running well. At that point, Richard Petty drove into the most spectacular wreck of his career, cartwheeling and pirouetting down Daytona's front straight, bouncing off the wall and high into the fence as he went. Under the ensuing yellow flag, most of the front-runners headed for the pits, and Trevor realized that he would soon be leading the Daytona 500. But Earl Sadler's crew chief Bobby King had other ideas and demanded that Trevor pit with the leaders. Against everything he had planned to do and hoped for, Trevor followed team orders and came in for tires and fuel. He returned to the race in mid-pack, a lap down. Amazingly, the fragile "grenade" lasted to the end, but Trevor was never able to gain his lost lap back.

After that, Trevor's time in Winston Cup began winding down. His last fleeting moment of success in the big league came in 1993, when he briefly led the Pocono race. Daytona in 1994 was more frustration as he spent most of his qualifying time trying to scrape up $5,000 to pay a fine he was assessed on the first day of practice for running without a restrictor plate. By the end of 1994, Trevor Boys had competed in 118 NASCAR Winston Cup races. In that time, he had not won but had proved to himself, and to anyone else who cared, that he could keep pace with the superstars of stock car racing, and had he enjoyed the level of support of the major teams, he probably would have won.

Given the frustrations he endured during his time with the Winston Cup tour, it seems natural to ask why Trevor is so determined to see his son follow the same path. "It's totally different with

The coming generation: Wheeler Boys gets set for a 2001 CASCAR race.
(Trevor Boys collection)

Wheeler. He's much more marketable than I ever was, and that's what counts. I was just another truck driver to them."

"Why put him into Winston Cup so young...so soon? Wouldn't a year or two more in CASCAR, or perhaps some time in the NASCAR Truck or Busch series be good for him?"

Trevor is adamant. "It's a lot easier to finish dead last in a Winston Cup race than it is to win in any of the other series, but it gives a driver a lot more exposure and credibility. Why waste time in the other series?"

None of the three generations of Boys racers talk readily about themselves. Wheeler seems naturally quiet, seated between his ebullient father and grandfather. Buddie says there is nothing in his past worth chronicling: the real story is Wheeler. Trevor brushes off his own successes and says that Buddie is the "toughest, most dedicated racer" he has ever known. "If Dad thought there was a race in Seattle tomorrow night worth going to, he'd hook up and leave right now."

Buddie agrees, but only to a point, insisting that any Canadian who races professionally deserves the same credit. "Nobody sacrifices as much as a Canadian does to race as a professional. Hell, you got ten million people in Florida—a third the population of Canada. And all of them are an easy drive to Daytona. Us Canadians have to haul thousands of miles."

Buddie says that when he raced, you had to be tough, but not just on the track. He snaps out a false front incisor and holds it up proudly, like a war wound. "This happened in the pits. After a race." Trevor recalls that his dad had an arm almost torn off in a racing wreck.

Is racing still fun?

"Fun?" asks Trevor rhetorically. "We don't race for fun. Racing isn't what we do for fun. Racing is what we do. Racing is what we are. We are racers."

CHAPTER 12

A RACER AND A GENTLEMAN: BUCK HEBERLING

Buck was well known for his love of life, his family,
and being the best he could be at all he did.
—Ron Doherty, January 25, 2002

No one paid much attention to Buck Heberling one Saturday in June 1990 when he pulled into the pits of the ⅓-mile oval in Saskatoon. The 51-year-old car builder, mechanic, crew chief, and former driver was always attached to someone's car. Renowned for his expertise at chassis set-up, his services were constantly in demand. Only a few people bothered to ask who the driver was of this apparently new International Motor Contest Association (I.M.C.A.) modified he hauled to the infield.

As he had done a thousand times before over the past thirty-plus years, Buck unloaded the race car and began readying it for the track. Shortly before practice was to begin he picked up a kit bag and asked the owner of a van if he could use the vehicle for a few minutes. "Sure, what do you need it for?"

"Gotta change into my driving suit."

Minutes later the long-retired driver emerged, his crisp new Nomex suit in distinct contrast to his weather-beaten farmer's face. He walked past the shocked stares of the pit population, climbed into the car, fastened the belts, and took to the race track for the first time in eight years—the first time in 21 years on asphalt. It didn't take long for the rust to show. On his first quick lap, the car spun out in a cloud of rubber smoke. "Crazy old fart—what's he trying to prove?" was one comment. Others were less polite.

Buck turned the car around and returned slowly to the pits. He got out and, apparently undaunted, went to work adjusting tire pressures, ride height, stagger, and the other esoteric minutiae that dictate how well a race car handles. Back out on the track he drove a few more laps, this time staying out of trouble. He returned to his pit and parked, apparently satisfied with the adjustments he had made.

Twenty I.M.C.A. cars did qualifying laps that night. When they had finished, the fastest lap of all belonged to Buck Heberling.

Duane Spurrier Heberling, called Buck by everyone but his wife, Stella, was born in 1939 to Rosebud, Alberta farmers Bob and Mildred Heberling. Buck came by his racing heritage honestly—Bob was a successful chuckwagon race driver who in 1950 won the Calgary Stampede Championship. Bob was also a fast automobile driver and, for a few years, had his young son afraid of cars. "I white-knuckled myself to death as he was driving around, and I vowed I would overcome that. I guess I did," recalled Buck years later.

The younger Heberling briefly dabbled with the chuckwagons, competing as an outrider on his father's team one season. But having grown up with horses, he had no love for them and was far more drawn to things mechanical. In his late teens he left the farm to take up an automotive mechanic apprenticeship in Calgary, and he quickly became part of the local stock car racing scene. In 1958 or 1959—various people's memories differ—he put a roll bar in a 1937 Ford and drove his first race. By 1961 he had moved up to a modi-fied and won his first track championship.

There was never any doubt about Buck Heberling's driving abil-ity, but in the eyes of most people, his real strength was on the tech-nical side of racing, particularly chassis setup. His mechanical train-ing—he completed his apprenticeship and gained his automotive ticket—combined with his intuitive understanding of what happens

Circa 1960: Buck Heberling in his first modified. *(Stella Heberling collection)*

1967: President, Alberta Modified Racing Association.
(Stella Heberling collection)

1994, Race City Speedway: Buck Heberling (#49) leads the author (#20) in this International Motor Contest Association race. Note precise driving line—also typical of the man. *(Dan Frederickson photo from author's collection)*

July 15, 2000: Buck Heberling preparing to come out of retirement—again. *(Photo by the author)*

to each component of a car's suspension under braking, cornering, and acceleration loads, enabled him to take cars that other racers found to be pigs and turn them into competitive rides.

For a time in the early 1960s, Buck raced with Dale Armstrong, who would go on to fame as one of the great drag racers of all time and create the car that would run the first-ever 300-mile-per-hour ¼ mile. It is hard to imagine that other racers knew what they were up against when they put their cars on the track against one prepared by Armstrong and Heberling.

Throughout the 1960s, '70s and early '80s, Buck was a consistent winner wherever he ran: sometimes as driver, but often as owner-mechanic for the talented Lloyd Eby. Calgary, Edmonton, Olds, Brooks, Didsbury, Lethbridge, Standard and Red Deer were all on his circuit and all of them yielded feature race wins, and often track championships, to the man from Rosebud. At one time, wanting to race closer to home, he talked the local Lions Club into building a race track on the outskirts of Rosebud. With the help of his father, a ¼-mile dirt oval was graded. The facility only lasted a short time, there being a certain critical mass of population needed to support a track—something Rosebud lacked.

In 1964, Buck moved back to the farm upon the death of his father. While he proved himself to be a successful farmer, the real focus of his attention on the homestead was the large quonset shop. There he maintained his race cars and farm machinery, built new race cars for himself and others, and acted as unofficial guru for most of the oval-track racing population of Southern Alberta. And if a neighbouring farmer needed a broken plough blade welded, Buck could take care of that too.

In the early 1980s, Buck quit driving race cars to concentrate on mechanical work. The Hampton brothers of Youngstown were entering a car in the NASCAR North West Tour and needed a crew chief. Buck was the obvious choice, and for three seasons he took care of the Hampton cars, housing them in his by-now famous quonset. This was happening at the same time Trevor Boys of Calgary was competing on the NASCAR Winston Cup circuit in the Southern U.S., and Buck would find time to travel down there and lend a hand. "When Buck came to help us, he was there to learn," recalls Trevor. "He didn't come knowing all the answers. Buck isn't set in his ways; he'll experiment and ask for advice."

Buck didn't limit his Winston Cup involvement to Trevor Boys' team. By the time Boys returned to Canada, Buck was well enough known in the South to be able to pick up work with any of a number of the smaller teams. James Hylton, D. K. Eldridge and Dick Trickle are some of the drivers he crewed for.

At the race track, whether it was Winston Cup or a dirt track near home, Buck would begin every day with a walk the full length of pit row, both sides, stopping at each car. Many of the teams would have questions for him. His answers would be succinct, and inevitably the other racer would come away smarter, but the learning process was always working both ways. Buck would snoop. There would be new cars to be examined, and there would be drivers trying out different ideas and modifications. Those facts would be tucked into the computer that was Buck Heberling's mind, and in the course of the races that followed, he would watch and learn how well they worked.

The night Buck Heberling ended his retirement in Saskatoon in 1990, he didn't win, and he took home few trophies over the entire season. But he was consistently quick and, more often than not, a threat to the winning cars. In 1991, he put it all together and won the Race City (Calgary) track championship for I.M.C.A. cars. Then, as if to prove it wasn't just luck, he repeated as champion in 1992 and 1993, by this time competing against drivers half his age. While he stayed with the same basic car over those years, he continually tinkered with it, trying to find ways to improve it, even running most of the '91 season with the radiator mounted in the rear of the car— unheard of for a stock-based oval track car.[1]

When Buck retired as a driver at the end of the 1995 racing season, many people asked him if he really meant it this time,

---

1. In the end he decided that the benefit gained from having the weight of the radiator concentrated at the rear of the chassis was offset by having it on the right-hand side—necessary to provide adequate airflow. By the end of 1991, the rad was again at the front of the car.

remembering that he had previously retired in the 1980s. He never gave a perfectly straight answer, but at age 56, what would be the point of once again taking up what was a very physical sport? He busied himself instead working as mechanic and crew chief for Don Mossman's I.M.C.A. car. Together they won the 1997, 1998, and 1999 Race City championships, although there were times when Mossman thought Buck was trying to give it away. The sight of Buck making his morning walk through the pits, dispensing free advice to any competitors who asked, unnerved the driver. "They're already fast enough without you helping," Mossman would complain.

In 2000, Buck took a little time for himself and built a new race car. On the 15th of July, at the Race City oval, he became one of the first—perhaps the first—drivers in Canada to race in six different decades. It wasn't a particularly auspicious race—the new car had teething troubles all evening and Buck wasn't able to finish the feature. Nevertheless he had made his record. And he had a car that only needed some sorting out to be competitive. Who was to know what he might accomplish?

Sadly, we will never know what might have been because shortly after his first race of the 21st century, Buck Heberling was diagnosed with cancer. Over the months of hospitalization and chemotherapy that followed, Buck never lost his enthusiasm for cars, nor his curiosity of how and why things worked and how they could be made to work better. Six weeks before his death, lying in his hospital bed, he busied himself sketching plans to install American V-8s in Japanese four-wheel-drive trucks.

Buck Heberling died on January 22, 2002, leaving behind to grieve Stella, his wife of 39 years, and their children, Jeff and Brenda Lee. Also grieving were the hundreds who in a driving blizzard on a weekday morning overflowed the chapel at his memorial service. Racers from all over Southern Alberta joined farmers from Rosebud in braving treacherous roads to pay their respects—surely an accurate measure of the respect those who knew him had for the man.

CHAPTER 13

CALGARY TRACKS

Those who build it, labour in vain.
—Psalms 127:01

The city of Edmonton enjoyed uninterrupted racing from 1951 through to the early 1980s, mainly on the same piece of land. Calgary's story, however, from the end of the fairgrounds events in the early 1950s until the opening of Race City Speedway in the mid 1980s, was, with the exception of drag racing, one of short-term successes, quick failures, false starts, and racing droughts.

In 1952, when he came to Calgary from Toronto, Charley Greenley already had five years' experience in the relatively new sport of stock car racing. What he found in Alberta was dirt-track sprint car racing on the fairgrounds, and midget cars running on the perimeter tracks at football parks. To be sure, local stock car racing had been tried as early as 1950, but it had not caught on with drivers or spectators. Travelling American shows of full-bodied late-model stock cars took place on the fairground ovals beginning in Edmonton in June 1951, but like the I.M.C.A. races of the early part of the century, there was little local participation.

Shortly after arriving, Greenley announced that he had taken a five-year lease on the dormant Chinook Jockey Club horse-race track, thirteen kilometres south of the city centre, and that he would replace the track with a ¼-mile (.4 km) paved circuit and rebuild the various structures. Fellow Ontarians Percy, Reg, and Russell Booth, small-time building contractors and big-time optimists from Sault Ste Marie, were assigned the construction work.

Greenley and the Booths felt that a purpose-built car race track could be a viable entertainment business, and they saw its future on asphalt, not dirt. They also felt that stock car racing, not open wheel, was where the growth potential lay. Sprint cars were dangerous, and midgets only slightly less so. When un-fendered wheels became entangled, it was easy for a car to get flipped over, and with open cockpits, there was no protection for the driver when that happened. Stock cars, on the other hand, encouraged contact. With full steel bodies and built-in roll bars, a collision or a rollover generally had little consequence beyond a trip to the auto wreckers the next day for parts. The fans were assured of lots of excitement—and lots of cars too, as it was much cheaper and easier for a young racer to find a '39 Ford than to build or buy a sprint car. Ads were placed in the newspapers stating, "Wanted: Men With Cars For Stock Car Racing," and inviting those interested to meet at "Chinook Raceway." By the time the track held its opening show on Labour Day, September 1, the promoters had changed the name to Springbank Speedway. For seven years it would provide Calgarians with continuous stock car racing and hone the talents of such drivers as George Lemay, Frank Janett, Kelly Save, Jim Ward, Roy Sharratt, and Ron Harris. By 1958 the land had more value as a gravel pit, and the track was torn up.

For stock cars, what followed could be considered the racing equivalent of the biblical seven years of drought. While there were attempts to restart racing, any tracks that were built, such as Roy Sharratt's dirt track near Midnapore, lasted only a short time before failing. If a Calgarian wanted to race, he went to Edmonton to run on the ¼-mile paved oval, or to places like Lethbridge, Olds, and Didsbury, which had dirt tracks.

Drag racing had begun in Southern Alberta in 1955 and had taken place more or less continuously through the remainder of the decade. The abundance of World War II airports in the south ensured that the sport could carry on. Dewinton, Airdrie, Claresholm, and Shepard were all used until the new Barlow Trail came available. When Barlow could no longer be used, ex-sports car driver Gene McMahon saw an opportunity to establish a permanent racing facility for both drag and sports car racing. Of the airports, Shepard, with its close proximity to Calgary, was the preferred site. McMahon approached landowner Arthur Grobe and was initially rebuffed. Grobe complained that when he had rented his airstrip to drag race associations in the past, he found broken beer bottles in his fields and people using his granaries as toilets. McMahon persisted, presenting himself as a professional businessman and promoter who would build proper facilities and police his events. In the end, the two men agreed to a five-year lease beginning with the 1963 racing season, with McMahon as tenant holding an option to purchase the land for $80,000.

Both the road course and the drag strip were immediately successful. Drag racing started in May under the Calgary Drag Racing Council, with the strip officially opened by Alberta Highways Minister Gordon Taylor. Calgarian Keith Wood set an opening track record of 150 miles per hour, and Shephard Raceway was in business.

The climax of the first season came on Labour Day weekend, when McMahon scheduled both a provincial points drag meet and a round of the Canadian sports car racing championship. Richard Chevalier took drag honours at 144 miles per hour (233 kmh) in a new car that had just been completed at 2 a.m. the same day. Keith Wood, who had earlier cleared 170 miles per hour (275 kmh) in Edmonton, blew his engine on his first run of the day. Dennis Coad in a Lotus 19 beat fellow Torontonian Ludwig Heimrath in a Porsche RS-60 for the sports car title. Top Albertan was Jon Karkar of Edmonton in an Austin-Healey, finishing third.

The Labour Day weekend clearly showed McMahon where the strength of his market lay—the dragsters had drawn 6,000 spectators and the sports cars only 2,500.

The following spring, the Calgary Drag Racing Council looked at its options and decided that a better deal was to be had racing on the old airport at Airdrie. In May, a deal was struck with the owner of that property, Mr. Bower. Gene McMahon in the meantime still had four years to go on his lease at Shephard. He decided to continue operations and run races in head-to-head competition with C.D.R.C. under the auspices of the Calgary Timing Association.

What happened next borders on the bizarre. On the day of C.D.R.C.'s first Airdrie race, Mr. Bower dropped dead. By midsummer, his heirs had decided they wanted no part of drag racing and terminated the agreement he had made. "Can you believe it?" asks Gene McMahon rhetorically. "The day they opened! I took that as a sign."

By late summer of 1964, C.D.R.C. was looking for a place to race. McMahon welcomed back the individual drivers, but he would not deal with C.D.R.C.

Tragedy hit the new strip in August of the same year when popular veteran driver Paul Linderman of Crows Nest Pass inadvertently shifted the automatic transmission of his super stock into reverse at the end of a run. The rear wheels locked up, the car spun, then rolled and cartwheeled, and a seat-belt buckle broke. Linderman was killed instantly. It was the only fatality the track would see in over 20 years of operation.

Racing continued at Shephard, and in 1966 McMahon brought Californian Frank Pedregon to Calgary in what would be the first of many guest appearances by top-ranked racers. Pedregon's visit ended when a gust of wind at the end of a 196 mile-per-hour run flipped his car. He suffered only minor injuries.

The drag strip was successful, but the continuing lack of an oval track in Calgary was frustrating for stock car racers. It made little sense to them that Edmonton and any number of smaller towns could support tracks, but Calgary couldn't. Finally in 1965 racers Ron Ferworn and Terry Graham obtained a lease on land just north of Calgary on Symons Valley Road. With the help of friends in the Stampede City Auto Racing Association, they built a ¼-mile dirt oval, and by 1966, Calgary had racing again. In its first season Stampede Speedway drew a total of 19,000 spectators to watch Early-Late Stock cars and B-Modifieds. For the 1967 season, Ferworn and Graham paved the track and, as evidence of the clarity of the vision of Charley Greenley and the Booth Brothers back in 1952, attendance jumped to 50,000 for the season. With Lethbridge having a paved track at the same time, ambitious drivers could race three times a week: Edmonton on Wednesday evening, Calgary on Saturday, and Lethbridge on Sunday.

On August 26, 1968, Stampede Speedway hosted a Canadian American Modified Racing Association event. While the CAMRA cars with their V-8s were more powerful than the 6-cylinder B-Modifieds of the Calgary drivers, some locals, particularly Frank Weiss who finished fourth, reminded the CAMRA regulars that, on a small oval, horsepower isn't everything. Over 3,000 fans watched the show, and while CAMRA would return many times to Calgary, the level of fan support it saw there never rivalled that of Edmonton.

If the early '60s had been a drought for racing, 1969 brought a flood. Seven rain-outs, including a CAMRA date, left Ferworn and Graham unable to maintain their lease payments, and they lost the track.

Ferworn had by now, in spite of the inglorious end of his Calgary venture, developed a love of running a track and promoting races. He estimates that over the next several years he visited 117 race tracks all across North America, learning why some succeed and others fail. From that experience he built a dirt track in Grande Prairie in 1974, and, after proving it could be profitable, sold it in 1976 to Sandy McDonald. "I sold this one—I didn't lose it."

Back in Calgary, Gene McMahon bought Stampede Speedway from the wreckage of receivership, along with a ten-year land lease. Taking control of Stampede Speedway, McMahon realized that running an oval track profitably was not the same as operating a drag strip. He knew that the Booth brothers had for many years made a good living with their Speedway Park in Edmonton and he went to Reg Booth for advice. He came away impressed with the older man's knowledge and willingness to share it.

McMahon's track reopened in 1971 under the name Circle 8 Speedway, in deference to the new promoter's plan to feature figure-8 racing. While McMahon's sometimes abrasive personality did not win him many friends among the drivers, he was respected for the fact that he kept racing alive in Calgary and stood behind whatever he promised. Veteran racer Steve Morros recalls, "A lot of guys didn't like Gene, but I'll tell you, whatever purse he advertised, you knew it was going to be there."

Shephard, 1966: Frank Pedregon's "world's fastest coupe" just prior to a high-speed rollover. *(Gene McMahon collection).*

Circle 8 Speedway: Late '70s racing featuring a mixed group of CAMRA super-modifieds and converted dirt-track sprint cars. White car on inside is Tim Gee. *(Ron Doherty collection)*

Late '70s Hobby-Stock action at Circle 8 Speedway. *(Ron Doherty collection)*

One thing Gene McMahon learned from the Booths was that three was the optimum number of classes of race car. Fewer than that, and there was no natural ladder of progression for drivers to follow. More, and the fields tended to thin out, with their drivers becoming less identifiable to the fans. Circle 8 would have B-Modifieds, Super Stocks, and Hobby Stocks. By the end of his first year, McMahon was beginning to think he could get by with two classes as the number of modifieds declined, and the fans were showing a clear preference for the Super Stocks. "The sprint cars (modifieds) were fine, and I know the people in Edmonton loved them, but this was Calgary, and people wanted to see cars they could identify with—Fords and Chevs," he would later recall.

A decline in the previous high level of close competition in CAMRA events presented an additional problem with Modifieds. Tom Sneva of Spokane had come out with a rear-engined, four-wheel-drive Super-modified that annihilated the competition. In Calgary on June 26, 1971, as had been the case for a full season, only yellow flags prevented the Spokane school teacher and future Indianapolis 500 winner from lapping the entire field. This did not happen with Gene McMahon's Super Stocks. In future, when CAMRA wanted a show in Calgary, he would simply rent his track to that group. As a promoter, his interest was stock cars.

Meanwhile, at Shephard, track conditions were not getting any better. The 25-year old asphalt was becoming badly grooved by the drag cars. As a sports car course, it was boring for both drivers and spectators—the former because it was flat, and the latter because they saw the cars only briefly each lap. While his drag-race business was still fairly successful, Gene McMahon, whose racing career ironically began with sports cars, could not justify any reinvestment on the road course. "The sport was all screwed up with too many classes. You never knew who was racing against who, and they let anything run out there. Who was going to pay to see stuff with 50 horsepower piddling around a two-mile track?" Then, answering his own question, he goes on, "Let me tell you about sports car racing: it's like masturbation—it's a lot of fun for the guy doing it, but no one's going to pay to watch." After his successful 1967 Player's Prairie national championship race, for which he rented the track to the Calgary Sports Car Club, he held no more sports car events, but he left the track open for others to rent for their own events. There were no takers.

Into this void came Happy Valley, an entertainment park west of the city. It offered families the use of picnic and barbecue facilities, playgrounds, rides, and a swimming pool at reasonable cost. In early 1964, owner Ernest Lutz invited the Calgary Sports Car Club to stage a hillclimb on the roads in the park. Thirty-seven cars showed up to run on a combination of snow, mud, and ice. Paul Dyson took first place in a Volvo, followed by Henry Acteson in an MGB, with Cappy Thompson and Werner Wenzel tied for third. Mr. Lutz must have liked what he saw because shortly afterward he announced that with the support of C.S.C.C. he would add a 2 ½-mile (4-km) road circuit, a drag strip, and a ¾-mile (1.2-km) oval to his attractions. Preliminary planning and surveying were carried out, and C.S.C.C. applied for and was granted a Canadian Automobile Sport Clubs race date for the 1965 season. All this was done in advance of any approval from the Municipal District of Rocky View within whose jurisdiction the land lay. When Lutz finally applied to the district for permits, he ran into a wall of opposition. Not only were the usual race track concerns over noise raised, but also the fact that cars would be racing within view of Highway 1, and this was cited as a traffic hazard. Further complicating matters was the anticipated increase in traffic volume that would hit that same, already-over-loaded, Banff highway with cars entering and leaving the track on weekends. At this point, there was no chance C.S.C.C. would be able to fulfil its 1965 race date.

In February 1965, citing the "grudging manner"[1] in which Rocky View had dealt with his application, Lutz asked Calgary City Council either to apply to the Government of Alberta's Local Authorities Board for annexation of his land, or to instruct its members on the Calgary Regional Planning Commission to press for annexation. The C.S.C.C.'s Geoff Fairs, speaking for his own club, for the Calgary Drag Racing Council, and for the Calgary Motor Cycle Club, pointed out the economic benefits of having such a facility in the city. In this he was supported by a number of Calgary aldermen, but not by Mayor Grant MacEwan or the city planner.

In the end, Lutz's application failed, and the estimated $250,000 invested in the track was lost. Calgary was back to having an old drag strip, a small oval, and occasionally a sports car course.

Gene McMahon guided Circle 8 Speedway through a decade of continuous operation, but by the time the lease ended in 1980, the track was within the rapidly expanding boundaries of Calgary, and the money to be made by using 20 acres of land for racing was insignificant in light of real estate prices in the booming Alberta market. The lease was not renewed, and the life of the little track that had nurtured the talents of George Blumenschein, Reg Bowett, Harold Browne, Lloyd Eby, Wayne Desebrais, Randy Green, Del Kornelson, Gary Miller, Fred Pinder, Brian Skaalrud, Frank Weiss, and a host of others, was ended. Gene McMahon personally arranged the demolition of the facility.

"If Circle 8 was a success, and I think it was," McMahon recalls, "the second most important reason for that success—after me—was

---

1. Calgary *Herald*.

Bill Powers." He goes on to recount how Powers, then a sports writer for the Calgary *Albertan* and broadcaster with radio station CKXL, regularly attended and covered the stock car races. One day, McMahon got into a heated argument with his track announcer and blows were exchanged, with McMahon getting the better of it. The announcer laid charges, and Gene was convicted and fined. "Which was OK, but now I didn't have an announcer." Powers was offered the job and accepted.

Bill Powers has a somewhat different recollection. "One day at the races the Fat Man walks up to me and says, 'You're my new announcer.' I told him no (bleeping) way. I'd never announced anything live in my life. Then he offers me $100 a day, so I told him to throw in two cases of beer and I'd do it. We kept that deal going for eight or nine years until the track closed. But I wouldn't start announcing until I saw the Fat Man coming across the infield with my two cases of Old Vienna."

Powers' greatest contribution to the track's success was not so much in announcing the races, but in teaching McMahon how to effectively deal with the news media. Bill would write the news releases—one for the press and another for radio—and Gene would personally deliver them to the sports editors. Circle 8's press conferences were changed too. "I'd just been asking these guys to come to a hotel room and I'd tell them what I was planning," recalls Gene. "Bill told me I had to make it worth it for them to come—feed them lunch or whatever."

Powers also told McMahon about his own philosophy of media relations: "You can't buy the media, but you have to buy the media. Just don't tell them you're buying them." Bill had Gene host an annual dinner at Hy's Steak House for the sports writers and broadcasters—order whatever you want. The first year's dinner cost McMahon $1,000—eight years later it was over $3,000. Bill recalls taking one CBC reporter aside and admonishing him for ordering a $200 bottle of wine. "Gene choked on that one, but he paid."

As much as McMahon credits Powers for his help and advice with the promotional side of running a race track, the "Fat Man" himself was not short on talent in that area. Whether by bringing in

Hell Driver stunt shows or making public pronouncements about the inequity of pari-mutuel betting being legal for horse racing but not for cars, Gene McMahon kept auto racing in the Calgary news. One year, he ran ads addressed to "Jim" in the personal columns of the *Herald* and the *Albertan*, explaining that "life was becoming a bore, and if you want to find me and excitement call me at…" The phone number was McMahon's answering machine with dates and times of upcoming races.

Bill Powers also worked as announcer at Shephard Raceway, albeit not as often as at Circle 8. He delights in recounting Gene McMahon's problems with drag racing's foremost female competitor. On one particular weekend, McMahon contracted Don Garlits and Shirley Muldowney to appear for a match race on promise of $2,500 each. Muldowney showed up, but with a broken wing on her car, and claimed she couldn't race. Garlits, who carried welding and fabricating equipment on his truck, offered to repair the wing, which he did. Muldowney then complained that the repaired part was not as sound as new equipment, and she wouldn't be able to safely drive flat out, but she would at least put in an appearance. The match race was no contest at all, Muldowney making no attempt to compete with Garlits. McMahon told her that as she had shown up with a broken car and hadn't put on any sort of a show for his paying customers, he didn't think she had earned the full $2,500 and offered her a reduced cheque. Muldowney cursed and swore at the promoter, screaming that she would tell every racer in the U.S. about how this Canadian had cheated her. In the end McMahon relented and gave her the full $2,500. Bill Powers[2] carries on with the story. "We're getting ready to leave and Gene starts in with this 'I can't afford to pay you $100' b.s. on me. I just did what Cha Cha did and told him what he could do with his announcing if I didn't get my $100. It worked for me too."

---

2. Bill Powers' contribution to the sport did not end with track announcing and media relations. In 1979, drag racers Geoff Goodwin and Gord Jenner had all their racing equipment stolen from their trailer while in Calgary. Powers mentioned the theft on every broadcast for two days, asking anyone with information to call the radio station. On the second day, an anonymous call was received, with directions to a building near the airport, where the goods were found.

Problems with Shirley Muldowney aside, the 1960s and '70s were notable for the regular appearances of front-rank drag racers at Shephard. Working together with Edmonton International Speedway, Gene was able to bring to Alberta on two-city tours not only Muldowney and Garlits, but also Don Prudhomme, Roland Leong, and Jerry Ruth. When the Americans arrived it wasn't always to match race each other, as Alberta had developed its own cadre of top drivers such as Gary Beck, Gordie Bonin, Terry Capp, Garry Egbert, Don Kohut, Graham Light, and Bob Papirnick, all of whom were perfectly capable of keeping up with the visitors.

In 1981, Calgary was again without an oval track, but this drought didn't last as long as that of the '50s and '60s. A land lease in southeast Calgary had been arranged by a promoter who ultimately found himself unable to finance the construction of a car racing track, although a motorcycle track was built. Stock car racer Terry Goyman and bodyshop operator Larry Weisgerber felt that drivers and the public would support a dirt track, and they offered to take over the lease. They knew construction would be expensive, but with $52,000 capital from the two partners and help from the racers in using their tools, skills, and contacts, it could be done. Goyman and Weisgerber pitched their idea to the Stampede City Auto Racing Association, and the membership of that group jumped at the proposal. The racers helped with construction of a 1,000-seat grandstand and, as a group, persuaded Kidco Construction to provide the use of two earthmovers to grade the track. The new facility opened in 1982, using the old "Stampede Speedway" name. It ran weekly cards featuring three levels of full-sized stock cars, plus mini stocks and sprint cars.

History had proven that Calgary fans preferred asphalt to dirt, so there was some concern that the new track wouldn't do well at the gate. Happily that fear proved groundless. The local sports media was generally positive, particularly Powers, who became so caught up in the excitement that he not only promoted the races on air, but also provided his services as track announcer, refusing any offer of payment. Over the next two years, grandstand seating was increased to over 2,500, and buildings were acquired. The racers—now collectively called Stampede Speedway Auto Racing Association—financed the improvements by running the 1983 season with no prize money.

Problems began when Goyman and Weisgerber decided to operate the facility year-round. A major snowmobile race was organized, with competitors invited from all over North America. Prize money was guaranteed by the track. The partners spent weeks preparing the track surface to professional standards by creating layers of ice, particularly on the banked turns. The weather was mild for midwinter, but nightly watering of the racing surface ensured a depth of ice that would withstand a weekend of hard traffic, no matter how warm it got. All that was needed was two days of decent weather. Instead, what the promoters got on the eve of the race was an overnight temperature of 40 degrees below zero Fahrenheit (-40 °C). The racers raced and collected their money, but the paying customers simply weren't there. The track lost $44,000 in one weekend.

Stampede Speedway needed operating capital to get started for the 1984 season, but Goyman was now broke. He had sold his house and still didn't have any cash. In the end he sold his 50 percent share to Weisgerber for just $5,000.

The track struggled on for one more season, but by that time Ben Docktor had begun construction on Race City Speedway, with its paved half-mile oval. There was no question where the drivers and spectators would go, and Stampede Speedway closed.

Shephard Raceway—Calgary International Raceway in its latter years—ran continuously for over 20 years, but after 1981, it was only as a ⅛-mile (.2-km) drag strip—half the regulation size. The expansion of Calgary's main north-south transportation corridor, Deerfoot Trail, necessitated the expropriation of much of the racetrack property. The portion of the land needed for the highway—the land on which Gene McMahon had once held an $80,000 option to purchase—was sold by its then-owners Shell Oil for $3,000,000.

Even at ⅛ mile, the land space was so restricted that it was necessary to build a nylon catch net at the end of the asphalt to stop any race cars from plunging onto Deerfoot Trail.

Just as six- and seven-year-old hockey players have games on a half sheet of ice, drag racing can take place on ⅛-mile strips. But in either case, that's not how the game is meant to be played, and those facilities are worthy neither of accomplished hockey players nor of the engineering, the power, and the sophistication of modern race cars. The days of regular visits by the sport's big names were over. Local bracket racers and slower classes would now dominate, and Gene McMahon would work to keep public interest by bringing in such quasi-race attractions as the Canadian Stuntmen's Championship, the Canadian Wheelstanders' Championship, and the Jet Car Nationals. These were more reminiscent of the driving-through-walls-of-fire circus acts that the exhibition associations had used as come-ons in the 1930s than of the real, great racing that had carried Shephard Raceway for almost two decades. Like Circle 8 Speedway, it was ultimately a victim of the economic growth that had fuelled its success, and it was swallowed by Calgary's urban sprawl.

For two decades, love him or hate him, Gene McMahon, "Gino," "The Pudgy Promoter," "#%@$*!," "The Fat Man"—call him what you will—almost single-handedly kept auto racing alive in Calgary. If not for his efforts, Stampede Speedway / Circle 8 would likely have been ploughed under a decade before it was. If he had lost the 1964 battle over drag racing to the Airdrie strip, where would that sport have gone? If McMahon had not been there, it is possible that someone else could have come to fill the void, but he was there, and ultimately he is the one who put his name on the leases and his cash on the line to make racing happen.

CHAPTER 14

SHELL 4000 AND THE EVOLUTION OF THE RALLY

I cannot find words to describe our condition at times.
We had to pass where no human being should venture.
—Explorer Simon Fraser, writing
on his cross-Canada journey, 1808

Sports car rallying in the early 1960s in Alberta, and the whole of North America for that matter, was anything but racing. Properly referred to as "Time, Speed and Distance" (TSD) rallies, these events put far more emphasis on mathematical and map-reading skills than on driving. Run on public roads, with the object being to follow the correct route at a precise average speed—mandated to be at least 10 percent below the posted speed limit—and measured to the ⅒th mile per hour, rallies were commonly won by dead-stock cars, perhaps equipped with snow tires and a couple of auxiliary driving or fog lights. Only if the road turned to thick mud or glare ice were the talents of the driver anywhere near as important for success as those of the navigator. In fairness, the organizers of some rallies in Canada such as the Quebec Rally, Ontario's Winter Rally, and Calgary's Loop Rally did provide at least a modicum of driving challenge by calling for relatively high speeds on terrible roads.

This was the basic format of the first cross-Canada rally, run in conjunction with the British Columbia International Trade Fair (BCITF) in 1961. "Cross-Canada" only if the Maritimes were no longer part of the country, the rally started in Montreal and ended seven days and 4,100 miles (6,598 km) later in Vancouver. Nevertheless the event was a success, drawing public attention to a form of motorsport largely unknown beyond the sports car community.

The 1961 event was in many ways a microcosm of the sports car movement of the time. There was whimsy represented by the entry of a 1937 Rolls Royce from Port Alberni, BC, but there were also practical commercial considerations, as seen in the factory sponsorship of the winning Studebaker Lark of Jack Young and Reg Hillary of Toronto. Shell Oil was the official fuel supplier, but their attempts at self-promotion were by today's standards, weak at best—the Montreal starting ramp was built on the lot of a Shell service station on Rue Jean Talon. While the rally drivers were not racers, there were, in deference to the great European tradition of "special sections," several speed tests included. A slalom at the new Mosport track outside Toronto, a "driving skill competition" in a grocery-store parking lot at Winnipeg, and a short hill climb near Regina were all apparently intended to add some European flair to the event.

Alberta entries did not enjoy great success. The Passmore Zephyr from Edmonton rolled over, and the Morgan MG of Calgary dropped out with mechanical troubles. In all, 93 of the original 105 starting teams finished the route.

For 1962, Shell Oil agreed to become title sponsor of a renewal of what had been originally planned as a one-time event. But without the BCITF tie-in, even $6,000 in prize money was not enough to attract the entries of a year earlier. Only 42 cars, including a 1951 Mercedes Benz, rolled down the ramp in Montreal on April 7. More driving skill tests were thrown in this year, but the real test was the Canadian spring weather. Fog, snow, and rain, brought on by a huge blizzard off Lake Superior were followed by the thick gumbo of a particularly wet Prairie spring. The three factory-backed Renaults won the Manufacturers' Team Prize not by brilliant individual effort, but by simply staying together so that there were six men to push rather than just two. The generally tougher roads the rally planners chose for the route left only 24 cars crossing the finish line in Vancouver on April 14. The most common mechanical failures were punctured gas tanks, except for the Chevy IIs, two of which lost their tanks completely. *Canada Track and Traffic* magazine said the rally had evolved to "somewhere between rugged European car breakers and American paper chases." The winning team was the Lalonde and Jones Studebaker from Ontario. There were no Alberta entrants.

In 1963, the start and finish points were reversed, with the 47 starters leaving from Vancouver. A more mixed bag of automobiles it would be hard to imagine, with a Bentley Mk VI, a DKW, two Skodas, and a Corvette Sting Ray competing against the usual batch of sports cars and compact sedans. Again there were no Alberta entrants, but there was the first glimmer of interest from Europe; four-time LeMans 24 Hour winner Olivier Gendebien of Belgium entered, with navigator Mike Kerry of Ontario in a Volvo Canadian; Swedish driver Gunnar Engillen and Quebec navigator Robin Edwardes ran another Volvo, and Czechoslovakian champion Vaclav Bobek with Quebecer Joe Mazuch appeared in a Skoda. This year the weather was milder and 42 cars arrived safely in Montreal, with Americans Doyen and Gibbs winning in their Chevy II. Gendebien and Kerry finished fourth, while the Bobek and Engillen cars dropped out.

The year 1964 was one of evolution. Supporters had been touting the rally as the finest in North America—and by now it probably was, being the longest rally in the world and the only event on the continent counting towards the Royal Automobile Club world championship—but it was still very much in the shadow of the great European rallies, and certainly of the infamous East African Safari. What it needed was real special sections: effectively open-road races on lengthy stretches of challenging road, closed for the day to allow the rally competitors to drive flat out, with the timed results of each section counting towards the final points. Organizers Jim Gunn and Peter Bone canvassed provincial parks, forestry reserves, and army camps, and the result of their effort was a network of special sections across the country. The change in format, coupled with an increase in prize money to $10,000, attracted more European professionals.

Shell 4000, 1964. Edmonton Light Car Club members happily service the half-million-mile Bentley Mk VI of McQuirk and McQuirk at a checkpoint. *(Photo by the author)*

Shell 4000, 1964. Blazer, white shirt, tie, and antique helmet—what the well-dressed rallyist wore in 1964. Volvo team navigator John Bird at Wainwright special stage. *(Photo by the author)*

A Datsun 510 tackles the Moose Wallow selective stage in the 1972 Harvest Night Rally—proof that fun can be had at 10 percent below the posted speed limit. *(Mike Dean photograph)*

The Hopkirk / Kerry Austin Mini-Cooper on the Calgary starting ramp in 1968. Note the handy wing nuts and electrical plug-in to facilitate quick removal and installation of the light bar / grille assembly. *(Mike Dean photograph)*

The invasion was led by Gendebien, back with Kerry and the Volvo, Bobek in the Skoda, and Swedish star Bo Ljungfeldt fresh off a second-place finish in the Monte Carlo Rally. Ljungfeldt provided one of the more spectacular moments of the rally when he lost control on the special section over the fast, winding, gravel roads of Wainwright army camp and barrel-rolled his Ford Falcon off the road and down a hill. The other Alberta special section, the Calgary hill climb, was uneventfully won by Ontarian Bert Rasmussen. Overall winners were Klaus Ross and John Bird of Ontario, followed by Mo Carter[1] and Ian Worth, the Merson / Davies Ford Falcon in third, and the Gendebien / Kerry Volvo in fourth. Bobek, with navigator Jim Luce, came 13th, a surprising seven places behind their Canadian teammates Blair Bunch and Robin Edwardes. There were three Alberta teams entered, with the Calgary team of Werner Wenzel and John Proctor bringing their Volkswagen 1500 home in 10th place, and the Morgan / Hartley Ford Falcon coming 28th. The Marchildon / Jackman Mini-Cooper S was 40th.

Now that special sections were a fixture of the event, 1965 saw more international name drivers. Henry Taylor of the U.K. entered in a Ford Cortina GT, Formula One driver Pedro Rodriguez of Mexico in a Studebaker Commander, and, as unlikely as it might seem, stock-car star David Pearson from South Carolina came with a 426 hemi–equipped Dodge. Supposedly long-retired Italian grand prix and sports car star Luigi Chinetti was entered for the second year with a Ferrari 330 (he missed the start in '64) and Olivier Gendebien was listed again with a Volvo, but withdrew when his wife was killed in a traffic accident days before the event. Top Ontario race drivers Craig Fisher, Al Pease, and Eppie Wietzes also entered. Alberta was represented by Werner Wenzel and John Proctor (Chevrolet Corsa), Ron Hughes and Harry Hartley (Mustang), Barry Fox and Dave Fowler (Corvair Monza), and Ewan Graham and Henry Acteson (Volvo Canadian).

---

1. At the time, Maurice (Mo) Carter was a resident of Hamilton, Ont. A decorated veteran of World War II, he had his start in business in Edmonton, operating South Park Motors. After a successful career, both in business and motor sport in Ontario, he retired to Pincher Creek, Alberta, where he died in 2002. Maurice Carter was inducted into the Canadian Motorsport Hall of Fame.

The overnight stop in Alberta was in Edmonton, where Pedro Rodriguez arrived at the parc fermé with smoke pouring from his knocking engine. By the time the car was released the following morning, Studebaker had arranged for major repairs at its Edmonton dealership. All available mechanics were put on the job, and Rodriguez and navigator Bill Leatham rejoined the chase in less than two hours. Arriving at a mid-morning checkpoint just before it was to close, Leatham said they had been travelling consistently at 100 miles per hour (162 kmh) since leaving Edmonton.

Weather again played a major role, particularly in Ontario where thick, wet mud rendered some roads virtually impassable. The Fox / Fowler Corvair became high-centred in the muck and took seven hours to extract, thus ending that team's rally. Particularly galling for the Edmontonians was the presence of a shallow, dry ditch on one side of the road. Following competitors avoided the Corvair by simply driving off the road, into the ditch, and safely past. Only 37 of the 64 starters finished, the Pearson Dodge (cooling problems) and the Chinetti Ferrari (disqualified for unsportsmanlike conduct after getting into a too-vigorous argument with a police officer) not among them. First overall, for the second year running, was the Klaus Ross and John Bird Volvo, followed by fellow Canadians Paul McLennan and John Wilson in their Mustang. The top-finishing European was in third place, as Henry Taylor and navigator Robin Edwardes brought their Cortina GT home, having "zeroed" the special sections by simply winning every one of them. Ewan Graham and Henry Acteson set a new high-water mark for Alberta entrants with a fourth-place finish. The still-ailing Rodriguez / Leatham Studebaker crossed the finish line in 28th.

For 1966, organizers changed the route to Vancouver–Quebec City, and the number of closed sections increased to eight. The route and the weather proved particularly tough, and only 26 of the 60 starters made it to Quebec. It was a banner year for Alberta rallying as Graham and Acteson finished second overall behind winners Paul MacLennan and John Wilson in a Lotus Cortina, but ahead of the second factory-backed Lotus Cortina of Englishman Roger Clarke and his navigator, Robin Edwardes. Calgarians Werner Wenzel and

Rocky Mountain Rally founder Ian McArthur trying to make a section of road passable for the 1973 event. The AMC Javelin is a Hertz rent-a-car loaned to the organizers by that firm. By the end of the rally, it was no longer rentable. *(Ian McArthur collection)*

The winning Boyce / Woods Toyota on the same stretch of road. Whatever McArthur and his shovel did, it seems to have worked. *(Ian McArthur collection)*

Harry Hartley came in 12th, Edmontonians Hunter Floyd and navigator/car owner George Stedelbauer came 16th, the Harry Baker / Mike Hogben MGB was 22nd, the Stiles / Skinner Mustang 25th. Not finishing the route were the Duimel / Jackman Cortina GT, the Allen / Sharpe Mustang, and the Dyer / Jackman Renault R-8 Gordini. The European contingent was brightened by the appearance of Rosemary Smith of Ireland, along with navigator Ann Coombe of Ontario, in a Sunbeam Imp. Smith, who would later go on to become the first woman to win a world-championship rally (1967 Tulip Rally, Holland), drove the Imp to 8th overall and first in class.

Canada's centennial year, 1967, was the greatest year for Alberta participation in the rally—if not results. Nine Alberta teams in a field of 93 left the starting ramp in Vancouver. The only Alberta finishers were Dick Bartels and Tom Stibbard, in 24th place in their Volvo, and Peter Allan and Ron Lynch, 41st in a Ford Falcon. In total, 42 cars crossed the finish line at the Expo 67 site, with Englishman Roger Clarke and Ontarian Jim Peters taking top prize in a Lotus Cortina.

The year 1968 would be the last for the Shell 4000. Interdepartmental bickering at Shell would kill the great event. It was also the only year the rally went east of Quebec, starting in Calgary and finishing in Halifax. Americans Scott Harvey and Ralph Beckman took top prize in a Plymouth Barracuda. Behind them, three of the top five positions were taken by Rambler Americans, including Albertan Hunter Floyd and Ontarian Lutz Eken in 5th. The remaining Albertans did not fare well, with the Pat Stiles and Doug Jackman Datsun 510 35th; the Geoff Howe / Kneal Johnson Sunbeam Arrow 50th; the Stratton / Petersen Mini-Cooper 53rd; and the Skinner / Skinner Volvo 123 GT 54th.

Prior to the 1968 rally, one of the cars favoured to win was the factory-entered Austin Mini-Cooper of Paddy Hopkirk and Mike Kerry. If the Minis had a weakness, it was engine cooling, and this one, with a solid skid-plate below and four huge driving lights blocking the grill, was worse than most. Team mechanics had designed a second radiator that could be quickly put in place behind the auxiliary light bar. Apparently it worked well, but it was quite illegal.

Edmonton newspaper photographer Mike Dean recounts how on assignment, he was following the rally route on the first night of the event south of Calgary in his own Mini-Cooper, equipped with the same-style light bar as Hopkirk's car. Suddenly, a coveralled Austin mechanic jumped out from behind a building in front of Dean, tools in hand. As Dean slowed down, the mechanic appeared to suddenly realize he had the wrong car, and casually walked back to his own vehicle behind the building. Given that Hopkirk was disqualified within two days for the illegal second radiator,[2] Mike Dean's very reasonable assumption is that the mechanic who leapt out to meet him was in fact intending to fit the radiator.

A renewal of the rally in honour of the British Columbia Centennial took place in 1971, but it was only intended to last one year.

Nine runnings of an event do not make a dynasty, but can create a legacy. The seed of the notion that in Canada, rallies could and should be high-speed contests of drivers and cars, rather than map-reading tests, had been planted.

By the late 1960s, some Canadian rallies, particularly the Outaouais Rally near Ottawa, included "selective" sections where competitors were not given an average speed they must maintain, but rather a target time that, while within the legal speed limit, was difficult to meet because of road conditions. In Alberta the rural speed limit, unless otherwise posted, was 50 miles per hour (80 kmh). With the 10-percent-below-speed-limit rule, this meant 45 miles per hour was the quickest speed the organizers could set. Selectives were typically set on short, winding stretches of little-used road, where even 45 miles per hour would be a challenge, if not an impossibility. Because the roads remained open to the public, the events carried with them a certain danger factor. Rallyists recognized this, and by the early '70s event organizers were thinking towards European-style rallying with special stages on closed roads. The Rocky Mountain Rally (RMR), which began in 1973 as a cooperative venture involving Edmonton Light Car Club, Northern

---

2. After being disqualified, Hopkirk's team appealed the ruling, and continued on to the end of the route, awaiting a final decision. In the end, the disqualification was upheld.

Alberta Sports Car Club, and Calgary Sports Car Club, all under the leadership of E.L.C.C.'s Ian McArthur, did not by itself immediately change the form of rallying, but because of the roads used and the speeds set, it awakened many to the new paths open to the sport.

In planning his rally, McArthur discovered that provincial forestry roads, being under the control of the Minister of Lands and Forests rather than the Vehicle Highway Traffic Act, had no speed limit, and these were where he set the majority of his event. But change can bring with it chaos, and the 1973 RMR was no exception. The rally, won by Ontario's Walter Boyce and Doug Woods, almost didn't happen when C.A.S.C. National Rally Steward Iain Tugwell arrived from Ontario the day before the rally was to begin and could not believe that there were roads in Canada without speed limits, or that there could be a 62-mile stretch of route with only two adjacent residences. Speed limits or no, Tugwell was horrified that one short stretch of the route called for an average speed of 100 miles per hour (162 kmh). McArthur pointed out that the 100-mph figure was just a target, and, given the nature of the road, no one would be able to reach that speed, but Tugwell remained worried that if there were an accident, police and media would focus on the 100-mph route instruction, and the sport would be irreparably damaged.

"Common sense was lacking," Tugwell later recalled. "You had these high speeds, and no safety equipment. There were no ambulances, brain buckets (helmets), or roll bars, and the roads were open." He demanded major changes in speeds only hours before the event was to begin. McArthur refused, pointing out that the rally instructions had been furnished to the Regional Rally Director some three weeks earlier and no complaints were received, and furthermore the route would be impossible to complete on the weekend if the speeds were cut. After much heated discussion, with McArthur at one point loading all the route books and maps into his car to take back home, the rally was allowed to proceed according to the original plan.

This did not end the rally's problems, as there followed months of acrimonious debate between the event organizers on one side and

C.A.S.C., both Regional and National, on the other. McArthur complained of Eastern arrogance and lack of local knowledge, while Tugwell pointed to McArthur's lack of national-level rally experience and to the hazards he had created and apparently couldn't recognize. McArthur countered by declaring that the greatest danger on the rally occurred when Tugwell drove his car against traffic on a selective stage. Threats were made to strike the event from the C.A.S.C. National calendar, but in the end it continued in 1974 and runs annually to this day.

McArthur's organizing committee had had the foresight to provide a competitor questionnaire form to each entrant, and these came back almost universally supportive of the event. Event winner and national champion Doug Woods described the Rocky Mountain as having "more potential than any other rally in Canada." The documented competitor response probably had as much as anything to do with the renewal. Whatever errors had been made in the 1973 event—and McArthur didn't deny there were a number—it remained that the rally had provided the competitors with something they liked: a relatively high-speed test of driving skills. In 1975 the Rocky Mountain ran a combination of selectives and special stages. The following year, C.A.S.C. restricted its national rally championship to staged events only, with race-like safety requirements, and the Rocky Mountain Rally complied. The organizers set one of the special stages at Blackfoot Motorcycle Park in Calgary, and this provided the opportunity for rare press and television coverage of the sport. Viewers were treated to the sight of airborne rally cars with the city skyline as a backdrop. 1976 also marked the year that C.S.C.C. took sole control of the event. The rally was won for the third consecutive time—of a total of six—by Taisto Heinenen of British Columbia.

The Rocky Mountain Rally was joined in 1983 by the Bighorn Rally as Alberta's second national championship event. The two rallies now run on consecutive weekends to ensure a full turnout of competitors from across the country. Time-speed-distance rallies continue as well, but with recognition as a separate genre of the sport.

CHAPTER 15

OVAL TRACK
FEATURE RACERS:
CAMRA AND BEYOND

He who cheats, eats.
—Alberta auto racer Leonard Vaselenak

By the early 1960s, most Alberta cities and large towns had permanent auto-racing ovals. Typically these tracks would have a weekly card of races featuring three classes of cars. Different areas had different names for the classes, but the idea was the same: provide various levels of cost and performance to attract the maximum number of competitors. The entry level was a stock car class for older sedans with roll cages and minimal modifications. It could be called C Class, Early-Late or Hobby Stock. Next would be some sort of modified class, ranging from stock cars with the fenders removed, all the way up to what were essentially sprint cars with 6-cylinder engines; these could be called B Class or B Modifieds. At the top of the hierarchy were the A Class Modifieds, often called Super-modifieds. These were purpose-built race cars with powerful V-8 engines.

While most tracks followed this same general format, the devil was always in the details. The rules applicable to each class were rarely the same from track to track, and many a driver visiting a track in a different town found himself unable to compete because his car didn't match their rules. This problem was particularly acute in the top modified classes, where the owners and drivers had often progressed beyond any meaningful competition on their home ground and had the resources needed to travel from track to track.

Track owners and promoters recognized this problem. They knew it was not much of a show for the paying customers if the same cars ran in the same races every week, and the same few cars always won. They wanted to be able to stage a few feature events every season, offering more and better cars and drivers. Reg and Percy Booth, operators of Edmonton's Speedway Park, felt that the answer was to have a cooperative organization, involving as many tracks as possible within a limited geographic area. The area they envisioned was Alberta, British Columbia and the American Pacific Northwest.

In 1962, Reg and Percy went to work contacting all track operators and racing associations within their chosen area. The result of their effort was to be able to announce on September 18, 1962, that representatives from 11 tracks had arranged to meet in Portland, Oregon, on October 6 to discuss the formation of a modified race circuit. The first meeting hammered out an agreement on the rules, with the participants committing to them for two years.

At a second meeting in Spokane, Washington on the weekend of January 18–19, 1963 the Canadian American Modified Racing Association (CAMRA) was formed. The founding executive consisted of President Bill Crow of Boise, Idaho; Vice President Emil Meldau of Edmonton; Secretary Manager Don MacKay, then of Vancouver; and Recording Secretary Sally Gorder of Spokane. The tracks signing on were Salt Lake City, Seattle, Spokane, Victoria, Vancouver, Nanaimo, Boise, and Edmonton. The first race was scheduled for Nanaimo on May 17, 1963.

A pocket-sized, 40-page rulebook was printed, and it covered the usual racing details such as engine size, qualifications, prize-money distribution, penalties, and licensing, but most importantly, it dealt with safety requirements. In an era when auto racing was arguably more dangerous than it ever had been, when great improvements in vehicle performance had far outstripped any in

vehicle safety, and when many sprint car associations actively discouraged, in the face of multiple fatalities, any talk of driver protection[1], CAMRA dared to be different. CAMRA modifieds might
resemble sprint cars, but they would have full roll cages, built to
stringent standards of tubing diameter, thickness, and bracing. In
1964, after watching in horror as two men were incinerated in a
massive fireball fuelled by 100 gallons of gasoline at the
Indianapolis 500, CAMRA quickly amended their rules to require
fuel tanks to be encased in either a fibreglass coating or a rubber
bladder.[2] Later, CAMRA would be among the first, if not the first,
racing organization to require full-face helmets. In over two
decades of fast, close auto racing, CAMRA had just two driver
fatalities[3]—if not exactly a ringing endorsement of safety standards when viewed from the perspective of the early 21st century,
certainly remarkable in light of other experiences of the era such
as USAC, which lost as many as six drivers a year through the '50s
and '60s.

CAMRA was now in business and would provide quality open-
wheel racing for the next 22 years. From its ranks, Alberta drivers
Norm Ellefson, Eldon Rasmussen, and Frank Weiss would join other
CAMRA graduates Billy Foster, Davey Hamilton, Cliff Hucul, Jim
Malloy, Art Pollard, Dick Simon, and Jerry and Tom Sneva in driv-
ing Indianapolis "champ car" roadsters. CAMRA was for many years
the foremost training ground for major-league open-wheel racers in
North America.

At the beginning of the 1963 season, the fledgling organization had only four race dates scheduled: Nanaimo on May 17,
followed by Victoria, Vancouver, and Salt Lake City. Other events
quickly signed on, with Edmonton making its annual Gold Cup—

---

1. In his book *The American Dirt Track Racer,* Joe Scalzo recounts the story of a driver who
showed up at a mid '60s race with a full roll cage on his sprint car. Officials told him to get
rid of the cage if he wanted to race. The driver did as he was told, and was killed in practice when the car flipped.

2. CAMRA Rule 1306 (d).

3. Babe Sneva, as detailed in Chapter 5, and Nanaimo driver Tony Slogar at Eugene, Oregon
in 1964.

Organizational meeting of CAMRA, Spokane, Washington, January 1963. Standing, L to R: Paul Creighton, Seattle; Ken Langston and Dick Midgley, Victoria; Moe Valliant, Vancouver; Reg Midgley, Nanaimo; Mac Morrison, Vancouver; Reg Booth, Edmonton; Arthur Green, Vancouver; Lloyd Cook, Vancouver. Seated, L to R: Sally Gorder, recording secretary; Donald MacKay, secretary-manager; Bill Crowe, president; Emil Meldau, vice president; Bud Gorder. *(Donald MacKay collection)*

This photo predates CAMRA by two years, but the view of the starting line-up for the 1961 Gold Cup perfectly captures what CAMRA was all about. Starter Duke Adzich gives final instructions to the driver of the Mercedes-Benz pace car in front of a packed grandstand. Behind are 22 crude-looking but powerful and very effective race cars, many driven by men who are already professional race drivers, or trying hard to get there. Pole car is Art Pollard, while outside pole is Norm Ellefson. *(A. Wallace photo from Don Sharp collection)*

Typical CAMRA action, Speedway Park, c. 1966. *(Richard Chevalier collection)*

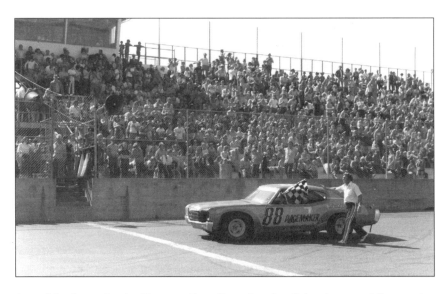

Age of the Super Stocks: Flagman Don Sharp hands off the chequered flag to winner Eric Dowler at Edmonton's Westwind Oval, c. 1975. *(Don Sharp collection)*

already a good draw for drivers from the coast and the U.S. Northwest[4]—a CAMRA points race. The winner that year was Billy Foster of Victoria.

Edmonton would continue to host CAMRA events—usually two or three—every season, and provide its fair share of drivers in Eldon Rasmussen, Ray Peets, Norm Ellefson, and later Ernie Fishbrook and Reg Kostash.

Of the Edmonton cadre, Ellefson, listed in CAMRA records as coming from Edmonton but sometimes living in Calgary, and other times Spokane—wherever there was a race car to drive—would enjoy the most success in the league. He won the CAMRA championship three times: 1966, 1967, and 1969. Only Doug Larson of Quesnel, BC, with four titles, would equal or better that. For whatever reasons, Ellefson's success in CAMRA would not translate into success when he moved up to USAC.

It would be several years before Calgary would become part of the circuit, and then with some reluctance. As previously detailed, Calgary promoter Gene McMahon felt that his crowds were more attracted to stock cars than sprint cars or modifieds. In that, he may have been ahead of a trend in oval track racing. As the simple front-engined, tube-framed modifieds of the 1960s evolved into ever more sophisticated and expensive race cars with wings, monocoque chassis, rear-mounted engines, four-wheel drive, and increasing power, fewer racers were able to financially keep pace. The inevitable result was smaller fields. In the 1960s, it was common to have over two dozen entries trying to qualify for only 16 or 20 available starting places, but by the mid 1970s many events were wanting for cars. Stock car regulations on the other hand prohibited many of the improvements seen in modifieds, and costs could be kept in check.

At the same time this was happening, the National Association of Stock Car Auto Racing (NASCAR) in the U.S. was surging in popularity, ultimately drawing more fans than open-wheel racing. With regular exposure on television, stock car racing was no longer a poor second cousin to sprint cars and modifieds.

---

4. The first out-of-town winner was Cec Hunt of Spokane in 1957.

A third reason for the trend away from open-wheel cars was safety. While CAMRA had earned an enviable record in that respect, the fact remained that tiny, fast, open-wheel race cars are more dangerous than stock cars. Regardless of safety measures, fuel is still flammable, and when its tank is built tight against the driver's seat, there is risk. This fact was driven home with horrifying reality in Lethbridge in 1970 when Calgarian Dwayne Feidler was killed in a fiery wreck at a non-CAMRA event. At speed, a drive-shaft universal joint broke in his 6-cylinder modified. The wildly flailing shaft threw the car out of control and punched a hole in the bottom of the fuel tank, triggering a huge fire. Feidler was pulled, still alive, from the burning wreck by fellow driver Bert Bath, but died 12 hours later. The courageous Bath suffered burns to his hands.

One of the first on the scene was Southern Alberta Auto Racing Association President Len Vaselenak, who tried to describe to the author what he saw at Feidler's car that day. But his voice trails off. He clears his throat, and changes the subject. "A lot of guys never came back after that. You just never saw them again."

Feidler was not helped by the fact he wore only jeans and a T-shirt, but nevertheless, had he been in a stock car, he would have had a metal firewall and over a metre of distance between himself and the blaze.

By the late 1960s quality stock cars—not just the aging Early-Lates and Hobby stocks—were beginning to appear in Alberta. Late-model mid-size cars had their interiors stripped, had roll cages installed, their engines modified within the scope of stringent rules, and their chassis altered only enough to make them somewhat adjustable and tough enough to endure hard driving on small tracks. These were promoted as either Super Stocks or Late Model Sportsmen. Not as fast, nor anywhere near as expensive as the modifieds, they nevertheless offered the public an excellent racing product. With close competition, more than a little "trading paint," recognizable brand names, and full starting grids, these cars developed a new audience and fan base.

The full-sized stock cars, with comparatively large areas of sheet metal, also appealed to sponsors, who saw the cars as bigger billboards for their messages. In 1974, as CAMRA began to lose its lustre, the MacDonald Tobacco Company, through its Export A and Mark 10 cigarette brands, signed on as title sponsor of a Late-Model series in Saskatchewan, Alberta and BC. The tour raced at Saskatoon, Regina, Calgary, Edmonton Westwind, Langley, Vernon, Victoria, Cranbrook, Penticton, and Prince George. The series road-raced—a new experience for most of the drivers—once at Westwood, near Vancouver, where a California car with disc brakes on all four wheels showed the local boys the way, mainly by outbraking them into the tight hairpin at the bottom of the course. The tour also paid a single visit to Edmonton International Speedway, creating an oval by linking the turn-off for the short road course directly to the bridge turn. This experiment was deemed a failure when Saskatoon's Bryce Mann was seriously injured as his car slammed into the earth embankment under the bridge.

The series later continued as NASCAR Canada West under the leadership of Leonard Vaselenak and later Ron Doherty, but when MacDonald's pulled its sponsorship, it struggled on for only two seasons before dying. The sport of late-model stock car racing survived, but on a track-by-track basis, with individual promoters working the phones to gather enough cars for a competitive field. In the 1980s, Garth Hazelhurst of Saskatoon organized the Western Speed Association (W.S.A.) and ran races throughout Western Canada for the stockers, but by the end of the decade the fields had grown unattractively thin. With the closing of both of Edmonton's paved tracks, that city was not part of what could have been a larger, more viable circuit. Instead, a dirt track was opened at Calmar, southwest of town, featuring, instead of stock cars, the always-exciting winged sprint cars.

In 1989 Wayne Bailey, Terry Gray, Bruce Hampton, Peter Jack, and Richard Lotnick acquired the International Motor Contest Association franchise for Canada. The brand name that had first staged races in Alberta in 1917 was back, this time with a fast, relatively inexpensive, highly cost-controlled class of modified. Quickly, a number of excellent late-model stock car drivers, notably Roger Bonneville and Steve Morros, switched to the new class. With a specified tire, a claiming rule on engines, and a requirement for mainly stock-based suspension components, operating costs were well under those of a W.S.A. car, with similar performance. A second attraction, particularly in light of the different tracks in the two major cities, was that with few relatively minor changes to the chassis, the same cars could be made to run well on both dirt and asphalt tracks. I.M.C.A. was soon running in Calgary, Calmar (later replaced by Capital City, Edmonton) Medicine Hat, Hythe, Smoky Lake, Regina, Saskatoon, Cranbrook, and Victoria. I.M.C.A. continues to operate in the three western provinces, run by Bruce and May Anne Hampton.

Canadian Association for Stock Car Racing (CASCAR) was formed in Ontario in 1981 by Tony Novotny, ostensibly to develop a nationwide stock car league. With echoes of C.A.S.C. three decades earlier, it humbly proclaimed itself to be "the governing body for amateur and professional stock car racing in Canada." In 1991 it made its first foray into Alberta, sending out a single car to run against the Calgary Hobby-Stocks. In 1992 it sanctioned Race City, Regina, and Saskatoon, and inaugurated the CASCAR West Super Series. In Calgary, it effectively took over the Hobby-Stock class, blending the existing cars into its own rule structure.

CASCAR's arrival in Alberta was timely, coinciding with the demise of the Player's-GM series. Kevin Dowler, Paul Gilgan, Carl Harr, and Wade Lee all moved over to the new series.

CASCAR quickly raised the standards for car preparation, public relations, and capital investment in the sport. In the past, stock cars had often shown up for August races still bearing the scars of June mishaps, but with CASCAR, cars with pre-existing damage were not permitted on the track. By offering clean cars and good promotion, Novotny's organization could get television coverage of national races. This in turn helped ambitious teams to attract major sponsorships, and those who could not find funding were quickly left behind as open trailers towed behind pickup trucks were soon replaced by semi-trailers. The public relations continued through the race weekend, as once cars were lined up in race-starting order for feature races, fans were invited down to the track for a half hour to meet the drivers and get autographs. The new level of profession-alism did not go unnoticed, and CASCAR soon took over Race City's annual 500 Race Weekend from A.S.A.

Both of Alberta's major cities are now served by exciting, well-presented, professional oval races several times a year, featuring local favourites competing on equal footing with imported stars. Unfortunately there is no opportunity for the traditional inter-city sporting rivalry to develop because the cars and the drivers are from two totally separate casts. Edmonton has the open-wheeled, high-winged, single-seat sprint cars running on dirt, and Calgary has the full-bodied CASCAR stockers racing on asphalt.

CHAPTER 16

LIFE AFTER RACING: FRANK WEISS

Every crisis is an opportunity.
—Harry Browne, 1974

Frank Weiss is a blunt, straight-talking man. He doesn't try to persuade anyone, least of all himself, that his driving career, capped by 13 Indy car starts, made much of an impression on the world of big-time racing. He knows the biggest impact he had as a driver was on the inside wall of the fourth turn of Indianapolis Motor Speedway in 1980. Great success at the local and regional level (he once simultaneously held four Canadian American Modified Racing Association track records) does not automatically translate into a lucrative career in racing's major leagues. Where Frank Weiss has made his presence felt is in building one of the largest and most respected manufacturing facilities of parts for Indy cars and NASCAR stock cars.

Frank Weiss's racing career began like those of thousands of other young men, driving a home-made stock car on tiny dirt and asphalt ovals. Growing up in Cardston, and later Calgary, Frank worked at his father's service stations, learning both the mechanical trade and the intricacies of running a small business. When he was 15, father and son collaborated on the construction of a stock car. By 1964 Frank had won his first championship, the Southern Alberta dirt-track stock car title, driving an Early-Late class car. In 1965 he bought a used Red Deer B Modified called *The Coke Machine,* and while not engaged in snowmobile racing over the following winter, stripped it down to its Ford Model A frame and rebuilt it. He renamed it *The Cowtown Special* and finished second in Calgary track standings the following summer. For 1967 he teamed with Terry Graham and Ron Ferworn and built a new B Modified. The car was sponsored by Metro Ford, and in keeping with that firm's sales slogan, carried the name *Little Profit Special.* With it, Frank won both the Calgary B Class and the Alberta Modified Racing championships in 1968.

Alberta Modified Racing Association rules called for 6-cylinder engines. To the south, north, and west of AMRA's Southern Alberta territory lay the mighty V-8s of the Canadian American Modified Racing Association. Their invasion of Calgary was inevitable and they arrived August 26, 1968. The local sixes weren't given much of a chance, but to everyone's surprise, Frank Weiss finished a very respectable 4th. Track owner Ron Ferworn commented at the time that Frank had "left about $24,000 worth of CAMRA V-8s in his dust." The young man from Cardston had shown he could run with the big boys.

Within a year, despite the responsibilities of marriage, children and a job as shop foreman at Jack Carter Chev Olds overseeing a staff of 45, Frank was part of the CAMRA circuit, driving a newer *Cowtown Special* with V-8 power. The car had been bought used, and he and Graham rebuilt it from the frame up. His success in CAMRA continued, as he finished fifth overall in point standings and was crowned Rookie of the Year. The following year he moved up to third place in points.

In 1971, Frank competed only occasionally and watched as the new technology of racing that was sweeping the world rendered older cars, including his, obsolete. If you can't lick 'em… In early 1972, he negotiated a ride in a Jim Tipke–built rear-engined car running out of Spokane, Washington. Sitting on tires over a foot wide, and standing only a fraction of the height of the *Cowtown Special,* this was one of the first rear-engined CAMRA cars. With a wing above the rear tires and the token roof no longer required, the

Evolution of
the oval track
modified: Frank
Weiss mounts
from 1965
through 1973.

(All photos from the Frank Weiss collection)

car bore more visual and driving resemblance to an Indianapolis roadster or a road-racing formula car than to its CAMRA ancestors of two or three years prior. Frank started, as by now was his habit, by stripping the car and refinishing the frame, then painstakingly reassembling each part. The car was not only beautiful but fast, and it took Frank to a 4th-place finish in the year-end CAMRA standings, and to a track championship at Spokane. In spite of his success, he was not getting along with the car owner and was without a ride by the end of the year. Nevertheless, his reputation as a driver ensured that by early 1973 he was back behind the wheel of another rear-engined car, this one a revolutionary Bob Katke creation. This car was a radical departure from conventional short-track car design because in place of the tube frame was a light-weight, monocoque tub. The massive wing that was the rear half of the body led to its nickname, "The Batmobile." The car was as fast as it was striking, but it could also be fragile. Crewman Peter Jack recalls that the car "would either win, or break a universal joint and back into the wall." With it, Frank drove to fourth place in the 1973 CAMRA standings, in spite of taking time off to race as far afield as New York. In 1974, with even more travel, he finished his CAMRA season in eighth place.

In 1975, Frank received a phone call from CAMRA graduate Eldon Rasmussen, who had by then been based in Indianapolis for nine years. Rasmussen needed a hand in his shop and thought Frank would not only be ideal for the job, but could at the same time further his driving career by being closer to the centre of North American racing. Frank jumped at the chance. Once he relocated, he was happy to be working with Eldon and quickly found that rides were indeed available for a qualified driver. Unfortunately, the owners who sought the services of unknown drivers often did so because the established men wanted nothing to do with their cars. At Milwaukee, at his first Indy-car event, Frank qualified for his United States Automobile Club (USAC) licence and made the field, only to have the car fail six miles into the race. The next stop was Trenton, New Jersey, where again he qualified for the race but snapped a half-shaft in the early laps.

Frank returned to Calgary, and from there went to Bremerton, Washington, where he worked, restoring from parts, an ex-Rolla Vollstedt Indy car powered by a formidable twin-cam Ford V-8. That job complete, it was back to Calgary, where he stayed until he got another call from Indianapolis in 1977. This time Eldon had entered an arrangement with Mario Andretti to manufacture and market small, inexpensive race cars under the trade name Rent-a-Racer. The idea was to provide a safe racing experience for first-time drivers. Rasmussen was in charge of production, and he felt that Frank, not only with his racing experience, but also his background in running a large automotive shop, would be the ideal foreman. And yes, Frank would still have time and opportunity to do some racing himself.

In 1979, after Frank had relocated his household to Indianapolis, fellow Calgarian Buddie Boys made a different kind of offer to Frank: Take two worn-out race cars that Buddie had acquired, fix them up, and run them in the Indianapolis 500. Frank accepted, sight unseen. When the cars arrived, they were in Frank's words "two trailer loads of old parts." Nevertheless, he persevered and got both of them running. But rather than drive them himself, he managed to find sponsorship from Vans by Bivouac for two other cars, one for each of himself and Eldon. At Indianapolis Eldon wrecked his car, then qualified for the race in Frank's, and Frank was left without a ride—but with the personal satisfaction of having had his 500 licence application endorsed by two of his fellow CAMRA alumni, Eldon Rasmussen and Tom Sneva.

The following year, in another Buddie Boys car, Frank finally got the opportunity to take his Indianapolis Rookie Test. In this test (which even world champions are obliged to take if they haven't run in the 500 before) the driver circles the track under the watchful eyes of experienced racers. All laps are recorded, and the veterans watch for smoothness and car control, rather than just great speed. Lap speeds should be consistently fast—a driver who clocks mediocre speeds, but with an occasional very fast lap, is probably not that good and is simply driving over his head occasionally to prove how fast he can go. In his rookie test, Frank Weiss drove laps of 132.4

mph, 170.7, 171.4, 170.8, 172.41, 172.08, 170.13, 171.1, 171.1, 169.9, 171.4, 170.5, 172.0, 172.0, 170.1, and 171.0. Not including his outbound warm-up lap, he drove 15 consecutive laps, carrying with him the pressure of knowing his every move was being carefully watched and analyzed, with a maximum speed variance of ¾ of a second—less than 1.5 percent. He had passed his Rookie Test.

Now he had to qualify for the race. For a week, Frank and the crew worked at the track, trying to find the formula that would move their used race car up into the low 180-mph range that would be needed to get into the 500 starting field. By the Wednesday before qualifying weekend, they had only succeeded in reaching 179. In midafternoon Frank was on the track, running laps in the 176 range, with the car badly oversteering. He decided to come into the pits for more adjustments, but he never got that far. The car drifted a little high in turn 3 and brushed the wall. Still pointed in the right direction, and having caused no more than superficial damage, Frank, by his own admission, overreacted in trying to bring the car down for turn 4 and the pit entrance, and spun. Missing the following car of Gordon Johncock by inches, he hit the outside wall just hard enough to shed some bodywork, become airborne, and ricochet down to the inside wall, which took the full brunt of his head-on trajectory.

By 1980, race cars had the radiators on the sides[1] and the engine, transmission, and fuel cell behind the driver, making him the furthest forward part of the assembly. The driver's feet were at or ahead of the front axle line.[2] When Frank Weiss hit the wall, he had no protection but a flimsy fibreglass nose cone and the bit of light tubing that supported it. Once the car stopped, Frank was trapped inside and in so much pain that the medical crew hooked him up to a morphine drip while they worked for half an hour to extract him

---

1. See Chapter 7.

2. Beginning with the Porsche 908 of 1969, positioning the driver as far forward as possible became standard race-car configuration. Only after a generation of drivers had been exposed to this high-risk design, and great competitors such as Frank Weiss, A. J. Foyt, Rick Mears, Johnny Herbert, and Danny Ongais had been crippled, did sanctioning bodies begin to mandate cockpits located completely behind the front axle line.

Frank collects his hardware at the 1968 Calgary awards banquet. *(Frank Weiss collection)*

Frank works his way into the cockpit of the Bivouac car at Pocono, 1979. The car is believed to have been seven years old at the time, as witness the antiquated front suspension. *(Photo by the late Dennis Torres; Frank Weiss collection)*

Indianapolis, May 1980: After spinning into the outside wall of turn 4, Frank caroms down toward a brutal stop against the inside wall. *(Frank Weiss collection)*

using hydraulic cutting and bending tools. When the Speedway's famed surgeon Dr. Terry Trammel went to work he found two broken hips, two broken legs, and two broken ankles—one with 19 separate, identifiable fractures. While Frank recuperated in hospital, Buddie Boys dispatched crew member Frank Janett to tell him that his services were no longer required.

There is a proverb: What doesn't kill us, makes us stronger. It certainly doesn't apply to everyone, but it applies to Frank Weiss. Crippled and unemployed, Frank moved his wheelchair out to his garage and began making custom race-car parts—the special little bits and pieces that can't be bought off the shelves of local auto-parts stores. He soon had several Indy car teams coming to him. A fellow might be able to make a living doing this, but the urge to drive was still there. In November 1980, he had his wheelchair pushed to the side of a sprint car, which he got into and drove.

More stable employment came along when Bill Smock, a manufacturer of materials handling equipment, offered Frank a contract to arrange and lay out his new manufacturing facility. Smock had no problem with Frank continuing to make race-car parts in his spare time, and in fact allowed him to build two complete sprint cars in his plant.

Gainfully employed and building a profitable sideline business, Frank continued to drive race cars, but that was becoming less and less acceptable to those around him. Wife Marilyn wasn't thrilled, nor was his banker, nor the insurers of his little business. Their unease reached a peak in July 1982 when he crashed in a sprint car race, suffered a concussion and re-broke a leg. His problems were compounded by the fact that he had been on an addictive prescription painkiller called Percaden since his Indianapolis crash, and now he had to come off. "That was the worst experience of my life— worse than the crash."

After the tribulations of 1982, Frank drove only occasionally, instead concentrating on the development of Frank Weiss Racing Components Inc. By 2002, his staff of 25 and their 17 computer-controlled machine tools had outgrown his shop on Gasoline Alley, a few blocks south of Indianapolis Motor Speedway. A mezzanine built above the back of the shop is not a permanent solution, and the search is on for larger premises. The former locations of both the Hemelgarn and the Pac West racing teams are in his neighbourhood, and they are vacant. Both buildings are larger than his present plant, and there might be a move in his future.

After over two decades in Indianapolis, Frank's voice has acquired an American accent, but he proudly retains his Canadian citizenship. "I think I'm the only shop in Indianapolis that closes every year for Boxing Day. The guys don't know what I'm talking about, but they sure take the day off."

By hiring only exceptional workers, keeping abreast of technology, demanding perfection, and thoroughly understanding what a race car needs in order to work properly, Frank Weiss has won the confidence of major race teams, both open-wheeled and stock car. His $1,200 to $1,400 (U.S.) wheel spindles are mandatory for cars in the Indy Racing League (I.R.L.). Most of the hand-held starters used to fire the engines on I.R.L. and Championship Auto Racing Team (CART) cars began life in his plant. He builds oil pans and pumps for Hendrick Motorsports and for Dale Earnhardt Enterprises. He builds the fuel injectors for Buick race engines, and exhaust systems for both stock and Indy cars. His threaded hose fittings, each milled from a solid block of aluminum, look more like fine jewellery than parts to be bolted to a racing car.

In the crammed and cramped front office—four people working in less than 300 square feet—son Wade uses computers to design the parts the factory makes. He uses a computer mouse to navigate through the three-dimensional graphics on a monitor screen the way his father once threaded his way around traffic on short tracks. Did Wade ever aspire to the driving side of racing? "No," says Frank, answering for his son. "He watched his old man get broke up too many times."

The importance of family to Frank Weiss is in plain view not only in his shop, where a son and a daughter-in-law work, but even in his racing scrapbooks. Among the usual newspaper clippings and posed snapshots of trophy presentations are supportive letters from his parents, photos of his father and his children sitting in his race cars, and lists of people who called, or visited, or took care of the children while Frank was recuperating from his Indianapolis crash. These days the shop is busy, but at midday, Frank will at times have to break away from his work to pick up an infant grandson at the house and return him to his mother. He doesn't appear to mind the interruption.

When a man's dreams of success are suddenly dashed against a concrete wall, the mental and emotional pain can be as great as the physical. A strong family and a strong will seem to have cushioned that part of the blow for Frank Weiss.

CHAPTER 17

300-MILE-PER-HOUR MAN DALE ARMSTRONG

Almost all great discoveries and inventions have been made
by men who united theoretical and practical knowledge.
—John Langton, Peterborough, Upper Canada, 1854

Dale Armstrong was the first crew chief to successfully install a computer in a dragster. He also developed the first two-stage clutch in the sport, and he is responsible for the magneto modifications that enable the spark plugs on modern drag race cars to maintain ignition to the end of the run. He will be forever remembered as the crew chief who engineered the first-ever 300-mile-per-hour ¼-mile run.

Not bad for a guy with no formal training or qualifications as an engineer, mechanic, welder, or machinist.

Dale Armstrong was born in Holden, east of Edmonton, in 1941. When he was eight years old the family moved to the BC Interior, living there until Dale was 11, then relocating to Forest Lawn, which was then a separate municipality on the eastern edge of Calgary. His interest in racing began early when he built his own soap-box racer, and when not busy with that project, he rode his bicycle on gravel roads to Shepard to watch drag races.

In high school, Dale hung around with an eclectic group of students ("not really a gang, but something like that") that included future mayor and premier Ralph Klein. "Ralph was a real cool guy, but if you had lined up one hundred of us and tried to pick who would be the premier of Alberta, Ralph wouldn't have been anywhere near the top of your list. He and I still keep in touch; not often, but occasionally."

While still a student Dale built his first hot rod, a 1936 Ford coupe with a 1951 Ford engine. On his first attempt at racing, on a section of Barlow Trail closed off for racing by authority of Highways Minister Gordon Taylor, he made his way through the elimination rounds to the final, where he was beaten by a Hudson Ambassador. Next he built a 1936 Ford to compete in oval track races, and there he met Buck Heberling, with whom he worked closely, the two brilliant young minds continually bouncing ideas off each other. While he found oval track racing interesting, he decided that his real love was drag racing: and over the next few years he built, modified, and traded his way through a multitude of cars: A 1951 Ford with a 1956 Ford Sunliner glass roof into which Dale crammed a 1957 Oldsmobile engine; a 1950 Chev called *Little Boy Blue* powered by a 1955 small-block Chevrolet V-8; a 1947 Ford coupe with a 1957 Oldsmobile engine; and a 1954 Olds with another 1957 engine, this time carrying a McCulloch supercharger. "There were a lot of other cars too, but I can't remember them all. We were always swapping and trading cars between us."

In those early days, all his work was done out of his parents' single-car garage behind the family home in Calgary, on 23 Avenue North, just east of Centre Street. Heat was by a 20-gallon oil drum that Dale converted to a furnace, with a chimney running out through the wall. "It's amazing we never had a fire," he recalls.

In December of 1962 Dale had a chance to buy a new Chevrolet with a rare 409-cubic-inch engine. The engine block had cracked in transit from Ontario (no antifreeze, in December), but the price for the car was still $2,400—as much as a regular Chev brand new. He felt he could fix the car and persuaded his parents to co-sign a loan for the purchase. Once he had the car in his garage, Dale welded the visible cracks on the outside of the block. It still leaked, so he bought a new block, then found that one of the heads was cracked too. At

Circa 1967: Dale Armstrong racing *The Canuck,* some time after he blew the roof off. *(Jere Alhadeff photo from Dale Armstrong collection)*

1975: Dale launches the Jim Foust funny car. *(Legends Racing Photos)*

All hands on deck: Dale (L, with hat and gloves) supervising quick repairs to Kenny Bernstein's funny car. *(Dale Armstrong collection)*

1986: Bernstein (L) and Armstrong work on the undressed funny car. Small figurines lined up above the cubicle are "Wallys," symbolic of NHRA National wins. *(Dale Armstrong collection)*.

the end of January, he finally had the car running. He built his own exhaust headers, and by spring the car was on the strip at Shephard. It was the fastest stock car there, but by mid-season an off-duty Calgary police officer showed up in a 1963 Plymouth with the new Maximum Wedge 426 engine. The Plymouth was fully competitive with Dale's Chev, so Dale figured it was time to upgrade. Chevrolet was offering a performance package, the Z-11. The kit included aluminum front-end body panels, reworked cylinder heads, hot camshaft, modified intake manifold, and heavy-duty valve springs. With this car, Dale got up to 115 miles per hour (185 kmh) in 11 seconds, enough to trounce the Plymouth, had it still been around.[1] The car had unfortunately disappeared from the racing scene when the policeman's superiors told him to either quit racing or forget about being a cop.

In 1962, Dale had taken his first trip to Southern California, an area that over the previous decade had developed as the epicentre of drag racing. He liked what he saw, and he returned in 1963 to race his 1962 Chev at the Winternationals at Pomona. He ended up staying three weeks, racing at as many drag strips as he could fit into a short visit. It was then he decided that if he wanted to be serious about drag racing, he should move permanently.

A 1961 marriage had collapsed and he was free of any personal ties, so he began the process of applying for a U.S. work visa. At the same time, he was having problems with civic authorities back in Calgary. He was doing enough work for other people out of his garage that he needed a business licence. That opened the door for the provincial labour inspectors to visit and tell him he couldn't operate an automotive shop without a journeyman mechanic in charge. Dale had briefly considered studying for his mechanic's certificate, but he "got so busy building things for me and for other people, that I never had time." He was on the verge of being shut down when his U.S. visa came through. In December 1964 he closed shop and moved south.

---

1. The Plymouth was gone, but its engine lived to enjoy a second racing life, this time under the unlikely hood of Arnie Gray's Volvo 544.

Once in California, Dale discovered that his lack of a journey-man's certificate was no barrier to employment, as the state had no laws covering trade qualifications. "Anybody could buy a box of tools at Sears and call himself a mechanic." He quickly landed work at a Chevrolet dealership in Redondo Beach, doing repairs to the used-car inventory. When management learned that the young Canadian had some genuine skills, he was promoted to the tune-up department, where he worked on commission, making substantially more money.

Dale's early racing in California was with a Chevy II, into which he later installed a supercharger and converted it to a funny car named *The Canuck*. When the transmission exploded and tore a hole in the roof, leaving Dale with painful bruises, he simply cut off the rest of the top and ran the car as a roadster. With this unlikely contraption, he got down to a best time of 8.89 seconds.

In 1969, fellow Calgarian Gary Crane moved to California, where he and Dale collaborated on the creation of a new funny car, the *Travelin' Javelin*. Quarter-mile times in the low six-second range were realized, with top speeds approaching 190 miles per hour (310 kmh). There is little resemblance between funny cars and the brand of passenger car they purport to be, but Armstrong and Crane evidently felt a little effort in that direction would be a good thing and built what is believed to be the last-ever car of the class to run with working tail lights and back-up lamps.

After the *Travelin' Javelin*, Dale ran his own '73 Plymouth Barracuda, then moved over to Tom Sturm's fleet of cars known as "Just for Chevy Lovers" before teaming with longtime friend Ken Veney to run a pair of Pro Comp dragsters. At the Pomona Winternationals in 1974, Dale reached the final, only to face Veney in the other team car. Dale won, and it would be the first of 12 N.H.R.A. Nationals. Later that season, driving Jim Foust's AA / Altered, he won the U.S. Nationals at Indianapolis. In 1975, with Foust's BB / Funny Car he won three Nationals and took the N.H.R.A. World Championship. In doing so, he became the first racer in his class to break the 6.7-, 6.6-, and 6.5-second barriers.

In 1980, Dale switched to Fuel Funny Cars, and while he never won a National in that class, he reached the final round three times;

Today: Dale Armstrong enjoying a day hanging out at the track.
(Dale Armstrong collection)

and in his last race of 1981, driving Mike Kase's car, he set a new Funny Car record of 5.891 seconds. Despite that success, it was becoming more and more difficult to keep pace with the wealthier teams. Budgets were rising dramatically, and Armstrong and Kase, with no major sponsors, were struggling. Midway through the 1981 season, Dale decided he would retire from driving at year-end. His decision was not intended to be public knowledge, but gossip travels quickly in the pits, and he received a phone call from Kenny Bernstein asking him if he would be interested in going to work as crew chief of Bernstein's Budweiser Racing team. Discussions followed over the next two months, and finally a deal was struck, with Dale starting to work immediately after his final race. Dale would have primary responsibility for Bernstein's funny car, and later the job description would be broadened to include advising on the preparation and set-up of the team's AA Fueler driven by Darrell Gwynn.

Despite his serious financial support from Budweiser, Kenny Bernstein had to that point only won two NHRA Nationals, and Dale's first three years with him were only modestly successful, resulting in a fourth-place finish in year-end Funny Car standings in 1982, and thirds the following two years. The team struggled, but in 1985 their perseverance began to pay off. The turnaround had begun in late 1983 when Dale took the body of Bernstein's *Tempo* funny car to the Lockheed wind tunnel in Georgia and used the data he gathered there to alter the car's aerodynamics. With the changes, Bernstein became the first funny car driver to clear 260 miles per hour (421 kmh). In 1985, Bernstein won 6 of 12 Nationals, broke two records, and won the season championship. In 1986, he became the first funny car driver to pass 270 miles per hour.

During this time, Dale was continually looking for ways to improve the car's performance. One thing he knew was that the car was not firing on all eight cylinders by the end of the run because spark plugs were burning up. He also suspected there was clutch slippage by the end of the strip, but he couldn't be sure. If anything was to be fixed, he had to have a way of positively identifying the problems. Computers were becoming common as people found more jobs for them to do, and this prompted Dale to work for six months at installing a telemetry system in Bernstein's car. First he had to decide what information he wanted, then determine how to pick up and record the data. He worked all that out, but then found the system wouldn't work because of electromagnetic waves coming off the magnetos. Once that problem was solved, the telemetry became a gold mine of information.

One of the first things he learned was that his hunch about clutch slippage was correct: the car was wasting 600 rpm by the end of the strip. Dragsters then typically had a two-speed transmission mated to the engine by a 12-finger, pressure-plate clutch. Dale reasoned that by adding three extra fingers, the slippage could be cured, but that would make starting difficult. As the slipping was only a problem near the end of each run, it made sense that activating the fingers only after the car was moving would solve the puzzle. He connected the three extra fingers to a switch on the steering wheel and had Bernstein trip it at around the one-eighth mile point. They tried the new clutch at an International Hot Rod Association meet, and found that while the revs momentarily dropped when the extra fingers were engaged, by the end of the run, they had gained 8 to 10 miles per hour (13 to 16 kmh).

Their next race was the N.H.R.A. National at Indianapolis. The team quite naturally wanted to keep this new device from their competitors, but that proved difficult. On their first practice run, they were the odd car out and had to run solo. Many in the pits thought they heard two gear changes rather than the usual one—could this be a three-speed transmission? Bernstein and Armstrong quite rightly denied that, but suspicions grew when on their first competitive run, their opponent car blew up on the start line, leaving only Bernstein accelerating down the strip. Again, people heard what sounded like a second shift. Whatever was in the car, it was obvious that the Budweiser team had something no one else did, and that something had resulted in a sudden jump in speed. Rival Joe Amato took the puzzle to his drive-train manufacturer, and a short time later had a device similar to that which Dale had designed. Within months, every serious fuel dragster had some form of a two-stage clutch and was going 8 to 10 miles per hour faster.

Today the two-stage clutch is still standard equipment on fuel dragsters, but it is now much more sophisticated, having 12 secondary fingers, and being computer, rather than driver, activated.

The next problem Dale addressed was the lack of spark near the end of each run. After every race weekend the magnetos would have to be returned to the manufacturer for an overhaul. Even then, spark plugs were burning up with the massive fuel load and compression. The telemetry told Dale that he was getting 3.8 amps at ignition. With more amperage, could he get spark right to the end of each run? The magneto manufacturer told him more amperage wasn't possible. Never one to take "not possible" for an answer, Dale started tinkering. The magneto used regular magnets, and apparently no one had ever tried rare-earth magnets. He managed to find some, and by shaving them down, shortening the lead wires and attaching large condensers to the magneto, he raised his output to 5.5 amps. Testing showed that with this design, spark plugs could live ten seconds at full throttle—twice as much time as was needed to win a drag race.

Dale's endless identifying and solving of problems continued to result in higher speeds and quicker elapsed times (e.t.). The climactic moment came in 1992, when Kenny Bernstein, who had by now switched from Funny Car to Top Fuel dragster, became the first man to reach 300 miles per hour (486 kmh) in a quarter mile. "We had run up around 296 a few times, so we really felt we could do it, it was just a matter of when," recalls Dale.

So what exactly does a crew chief have to do to create a car that travels over 300 miles per hour? Dale explains, "The chassis is store-bought, but once we get it we work on the bodywork aerodynamics a bit. I decide how the engine gets built. I choose the block, the crank, camshaft, rods and pistons. I choose the heads, and usually do some porting on them. I decide on the fuel flow, the ignition system and the cam and ignition timing. I also decide how I want the clutch set up. The crew chief is the most important piece of the team. The driver is important and has to be skilled, but there are lots of good drivers out there. You can have a great driver, but if his crew chief can't set up the car properly, he's not going to win anything."

Dale's value as a crew chief was brought home to him when some time after the Budweiser team began to rack up championships, he was approached by Top Fuel driver Larry Minor and a representative of his sponsor, Miller Breweries. They asked Dale if he was at all interested in moving over to their team. "I told them I was happy with Kenny, but they said they wanted to make me an offer. I figured I'd be crazy not to listen. We sat down, and they offered me a contract for three years at somewhere between seven and eight times what I was getting with Kenny. The Miller guy said he had the authority to sign on that."

Shocked, but still not wanting to leave the Budweiser team, Dale told Bernstein what he had been offered. "Kenny got on the phone to Budweiser and told them what was happening. They came back with a five-year contract, at the money I was asking for." One dragracing journalist commented that Dale Armstrong did for crew chiefs' incomes what Curt Flood (a baseball player who campaigned for free agency in that sport) did for his colleagues. No longer just "the mechanic"—or "grease-stained wretches" as one British writer put it—crew chiefs are now valued as highly as head coaches are in stick and ball sports, and at the top end can command salaries of $500,000 to $750,000 annually.

In 1997, Dale left Bernstein to work for Don Prudhomme's Miller Lite Top Fuel team. He was still getting along well with Bernstein, but "I was getting worn out. I'd had a two-year contract renewal sitting in my desk for months, and somehow I never got around to signing it. It was time for a change."

With Prudhomme, Dale was part of another record, as driver Larry Dixon was the first to cover the quarter mile in under 4.5 seconds. In 2000 he moved back to Funny Car with the Jerry Toliver World Wrestling–sponsored team.

Near the end of an illustrious career, Dale Armstrong's accomplishments began to be formally recognized. In celebration of its 50th anniversary, N.H.R.A. named the 50 greatest drag racers ever. Dale was selected number ten, ahead of such outstanding competitors as Mickey Thompson, Tom McEwan, Gary Beck, and Tommy Ivo. He has been voted into the Canadian Motorsport Hall of Fame, and then invited back to subsequent induction ceremonies as the keynote speaker. *Car Craft* magazine honoured him with its Lifetime Achievement Award.

Since 2002, Dale Armstrong has been retired from professional racing. But he has a 2,600-square-foot (242-square-metre) shop next to his home southeast of Los Angeles, and this is where he continues to make cars just a bit better than he found them. He has restored one 1958 Cadillac, which he sold to Funny Car champion John Force, and is now working on another '58 that is not only being restored but—somehow appropriately—also hot-rodded with the latest 32-valve Cadillac Northstar engine. You can take the boy out of the hot rod, but…

CHAPTER 18

EDMONTON INTERNATIONAL SPEEDWAY: TOO CLOSE TO TOWN

*We have overcome all our difficulties following
the collapse of Atlantic Acceptance Corporation
except for an inadequate supply of money.*
—C. F. Edgar, president, 1966

While the very best road and drag racers in the world were drawing large crowds to Edmonton International Speedway, their events were not alone sufficient to keep the facility in the financial black. The big races and the big names draw many people, but they are also very expensive to import. By 1971, Edmonton International Speedway was in trouble, and after three heart attacks, General Manager Reg Booth was in no position to provide the needed leadership. General Racing Inc., an American company operated by former Sports Car Club of America head Jim Kaiser, was brought in to operate the track over the second half of the 1971 season. Kaiser kept E.I.S. running, but outside management from thousands of kilometres away is expensive, and at year-end losses totalled $200,000.

Financial problems were not the only challenges facing the motorsport complex. The relationship between the Booth brothers and the stock car drivers, as is commonly the case with race tracks and drivers, had over many years often been an uneasy one. The drivers count the spectators, multiply by the price of a ticket, and wonder why they aren't being paid more. The promoter wonders what will be left for him after he pays land rent, insurance, staff, utilities, taxes, track and building maintenance, advertising, trophies, tow money for imported stars, and finally, prize money. In Edmonton, this perfectly normal friction was probably exacerbated by the oval's loss of star billing in the public's eye. For 17 years, oval track racing was the definition of the sport in Edmonton. Those who followed the drag racers to Highway 14X and the sports cars to frozen lakes were vastly outnumbered by others who made it a weekly habit to travel to Speedway Park on Wednesday evenings. No drag or sports car racers were as well known as Norm Ellefson, Ray Peets, or Eldon Rasmussen.

All this changed when Speedway Park became a modern motorsport complex. People who had never set a foot inside the grounds of the venerable oval suddenly knew who Bruce McLaren, Don Garlits, and Stirling Moss were. They spoke knowingly of e.t. and of burnouts, Christmas trees, and black flags. The opening of the new drag strip in 1967 and the first Can-Am in '68 both drew far more press coverage and people than anything that had ever happened on the oval. In those circumstances, it is possible—although rarely admitted—that the stock car veterans felt somewhat like an only child upon the arrival of the new baby.

For all these reasons, the drivers felt that the only way to be treated fairly was to develop their own facility. In 1968 a group of drivers calling themselves Edmonton Area Racing Association—to change the old name, but maintain the same initials—acquired 40 acres of land north of Highway 16 near Winterburn Road. Heavy equipment dealer Ed Miller, on security of the land, funded paving and building costs and loaned the group machinery to grade a ⅜-mile (.6-km) track. By late 1968, the new track, named Westwind Oval, was ready. What followed was a protracted, and at times ugly, battle with Speedway Park for oval racing supremacy in the city. Despite the complaints of many drivers, the Booths still had their loyalists and continued to stage their traditional Wednesday night shows. Westwind, in addition to weekend features, went right at Speedway's heart with its own Wednesday races. Each track would send spies to the other to count cars and spectators, and wildly optimistic numbers were announced by both facilities. The Edmonton *Journal* got into the fray, regularly dispatching a reporter to both tracks on head-to-head Wednesdays. On June 25, 1970, the *Journal* announced that on the previous evening, Westwind, for the first time, had pulled ahead of Speedway in both car and spectator counts. The newspaper calculated 1,650 fans and 45 cars at Westwind, with only 25 cars and 800 spectators at Speedway. With an almost 2 to 1 margin of supremacy, Westwind would eventually prevail. E.I.S. was losing money and could not afford to subsidize its oval.

Into this messy scene stepped local businessman Tom Fox.

Fox, who over a period of decades had built a successful aviation business, first caught the racing bug in the early '50s when he built a car to compete in the Al Davey–promoted midget races. When that series collapsed, he set his racing aside until son Barry became active in the sports car scene in the mid '60s. When E.I.S. opened in 1968, Tom was a shareholder and director. Shortly thereafter he reactivated his driving career with an under-2-litre sports car he named *The Geritol Special*. Now in the winter of 1971–72, Tom Fox the astute businessman realized that without a change in direction, the finest racing complex in Canada and the pride of the city when it opened only four years earlier, was doomed. If the track were to be saved, someone with money and management skills had to step up, and Tom Fox decided he was the one. Fox put together a blue-ribbon volunteer committee under the banner of Edmonton Speedway Motor Racing Association. His eldest son, Bill, was put in charge of finances; prominent lawyer Jack Agrios handled legal matters. Other committee members were Chev dealer George Stedelbauer, Police Chief Fred Sloane, racer and businessman Ray Peets, Chief Crown Prosecutor Richard Anthony, and accountant and rally veteran David Fowler.

In an interview with *Canadian Motorsport Bulletin*,[1] Fox was quoted as saying, "Don't play me up as a hero here. There are several

---

1. *Canadian Motorsport Bulletin*, official publication of Canadian Automobile Sport Clubs Inc., February 1972.

reasons why I've elected to do this. I feel auto racing is the only major international sport in Western Canada. We have world-status events. If we choose to drop these events, we will never get them back again. We have one of the most modern and complete auto racing facilities in North America and I think we are very fortunate. People don't realize how much publicity Edmonton and Alberta get from auto racing."

In simple terms, what Fox did was make a very large, continuing, donation of cash and time. If E.I.S. ran a deficit, he covered it. If it made a profit, the money was ploughed back into the track. As one of the largest shareholders, he had an interest in keeping the track alive, and certainly he would have been aware of the capital gains to be had if the value of the land increased, but he also had a long history of public service and civic contribution. Putting time and hard cash into something he believed in, and giving back to his community, were nothing new for Tom Fox.

One of the first hard decisions the new operators made was to concede victory in the war for oval track supremacy to Westwind. The quarter mile of asphalt that was Speedway Park and that had served Edmonton for almost two decades was declared dead, and its grandstands hauled over to the road course.

The next challenge was to bring the paid attendance at major races up to somewhere close to the actual attendance. Tom Fox had identified the gap between the two figures as a major factor in the losses the track was suffering. Years later his son Barry recalled his father's sense that "everybody knew somebody who knew somebody and was getting in free on their coat-tails." On the other hand, Tom Fox also realized that it could be prohibitively expensive for a family relying on a working man's wages to attend a Can-Am or a major drag race. The answer, he felt, was a two-part strategy of promotion of less-expensive amateur regional sports car racing and corporate sponsorship of events. He made these his goals. In the latter, he was successful, but the former idea never caught on with the public.

In 1974, Fox turned control over to Ron Hodgson on a lease. Hodgson was a young entrepreneur who had worked his way through business school at Northern Alberta Institute of

A pensive Tom Fox sits in the already-decaying grandstand of the five-year-old, flat-broke speedway he has just bought. *(Edmonton* Journal *photo, Alberta Provincial Archives, J-1016/1)*

Technology by running a speed shop out of the basement of his father's home. Once out of school, he had gone to work for George Stedelbauer, and a short while later entered into a partnership with his boss and with his best friend, drag racer Bob Papirnick, in the firm of Competition Specialties, another speed shop set up in a former gas station across the street from Stedelbauer's Chevrolet Oldsmobile dealership. In 1969, Hodgson left that business and reopened his own business under the name Pacemaker, and he soon had branches in Calgary and Saskatoon. Interested in drag racing as early as age 15 when he began building a 1929 Ford hot rod, Hodgson had been asked in 1972 by racer Gord Jenner if he would like to buy out Murray Dyma's share in a Top Fuel funny car. He would, and he did, and was immediately caught up in a rookie season not soon forgotten. Gordie Bonin has just been taken on as driver, and the Jenner-Hodgson car began setting times and speeds comparable with the best anywhere. On a whim, the new team decided to enter the U.S. Nationals in Indianapolis. "We weren't really prepared—I think we went there with one spare magneto and two pistons—and we finished second! It seemed so easy, but it took another seven years until we won that race."

Ron Hodgson's tenure as track manager was marked by a more aggressive marketing program than the facility had seen. A car race may or may not attract a large number of people, but a good party almost always will. Ron relishes recounting his time as a track promoter. "I picked up this idea of a 'Fox Hunt' (no pun on his landlord's name intended)—ladies in free. It was an incredible party with a lot of racing." From memory he recites his own radio ads, "Hey guys, you got a date Saturday night? Cancel it, because all the girls are going to be at Edmonton International Speedway. Watch '240 Gordie,' Don 'The Snake' Prudhomme, and Roland Leong's legendary Hawaiian funny car." The result was crowds of up to 16,000—second in Edmonton only to the Eskimos.

In Hodgson's first year at the track, he hired his old friend Gord Jenner as manager. Jenner recalls the profit-and-loss statements in one sentence: "The drags made money, and the sporty cars lost money." Jenner's statement is probably an accurate one, but also not surprising in light of the drag racing background of both the lessee and the manager.

Meanwhile Westwind Oval closed at the end of the 1977 season. Ed Miller had died, and his heirs had little interest in maintaining a relationship with the track. The void was quickly filled when promoter Rob Byrne struck a deal—separate from Hodgson's on the drag strip / road course—to take over the long-dormant Speedway Park oval and operate it as "Cobra Raceway." Beginning in 1978, he ran cards of stock cars, and a mix of sprint cars and CAMRA modifieds.

After Jenner left, Ron Hodgson carried on with the road course and drag strip until 1976, when the time pressures of running his rapidly expanding business empire necessitated hiring a new manager for E.I.S. He kept his lease, but he turned over day-to-day operations to drag racer Graham Light. Light was one of the talented crop of Edmonton-area Top Fuel drivers that emerged in the late 1960s through mid '70s, able to challenge racers from anywhere on the continent.[2]

In 1979, Ron Hodgson sold his interest in the facility to Light's former car owner, Bob Lawrence. Lawrence was a customs broker who had a long history in the sport. Not only did he field race cars, but he was also often called upon to use his professional skills getting racing cars and equipment back and forth smoothly across the Canada-U.S. border. Now he was in for a totally new racing experience.

The tenure of the Lawrence / Light team as owner-manager coincided with a surge in Edmonton's seemingly endless real-estate boom. The new Castle Downs subdivision was moving relentlessly closer to the east gates of the speedway, and noise complaints were coming in. E.I.S. and its predecessor ovals had lived in relative peace with the existing housing to the south, but residents of Castle Downs, who should have been fully aware of the presence of the race track when they bought their homes, were unaccustomed to the noise of unmuffled engines. The advent of Fox Hunts, with their parties and loud rock music, exacerbated the problem. Graham Light recalls the complaints as coming from a "small vocal minority" whose main problem was with night racing. He talked with the complainants, explaining that night events were an economic necessity for drag racing, and scheduled his events to end at 10:30 p.m. He now acknowledges that he wasn't always able to stick with that schedule, particularly if there were weather delays. Some local residents took their concerns to their alderwoman, and later mayor, Jan Reimer. A meeting was arranged with Light in Reimer's office. Light recalls going to City Hall on the understanding that there would be discussions towards a compromise, perhaps involving a curfew. "But when I got there, there was no interest in compromise. She looked me straight in the eye, and said, 'I will put you out of business.' There was no understanding of the economic impact of the track. No appreciation that when we held a race, we drew people from all over Western Canada and down into the States. That's when the harassment started."

---

2. Graham Light, who retired from driving with personal ¼-mile records of 250 miles per hour (402 kmh) and 5.82 seconds, was inducted into the Canadian Motorsport Hall of Fame in 1996.

The "harassment" began with a drug raid during a night drag race. Light estimates that 20 police cars appeared, although other racers say it was closer to 40. "They spent the whole evening there bothering people, and all they had to show for it was one liquor possession charge. We knew a lot of the cops because they all took high-speed driver training there, and they felt bad."

By this time the battle was in the media, with some journalists, notably Eddie Keen, onside with the speedway. "But it was a mistake for us to go public—I think we embarrassed her. We weren't fighting City Hall; we were fighting one individual."

The next salvo was a notice from the City demanding that overgrown noxious weeds on E.I.S. land be controlled. Light called in a mowing contractor who told him he was familiar with the form of notice, and with the City's requirements—basically the removal of weeds along the fences and in clear view of adjacent roads. The work was agreed to, at a price Light recalls as being quite nominal: "A few hundred dollars. Then one day, I come to the track, and there's all these tractors and power mowers and machinery cutting everything on every part of the property. The City had sent them, and then sent us the bill—for $21,000."

The final round of the brawl took place in 1982 when the by-then landowners, Qualico, received notice that their land zoning had been changed from agricultural to commercial. Property taxes increased ten-fold, and neither Qualico nor E.I.S. could or would pay that. The only way to restore the previous zoning was to end the commercial use of the land. Holes were drilled in the track, and much in the manner of stakes driven through the hearts of vampires, fence posts were planted, ending the life of the finest motorsport complex in Canada.

In retrospect, there seems little question that more could have been done by the management of the track to placate the neighbours. At the end, sports cars were running 94-decibel mufflers, yet they had rarely been the worst noise offenders—the big dragsters were. There are few things on earth that create as much noise as Top Fuel dragsters, but these were the machines that ran, by Graham Light's own admission, as late as midnight. Flames of burning nitro coming out the exhaust pipes of a car travelling more than 200 miles per hour in the dark are certainly spectacular to watch and undoubtedly draw spectators, but it is unrealistic to expect people whose windows are being rattled, and children wakened at late hours, to live and let live. With an ambitious, left-wing politician prepared to take up their cause, these same people were only too happy to support the elimination of the track.

Two decades later, Graham Light, now senior vice president of the National Hot Rod Association and located in Glendora, California, is philosophical about the end of Edmonton International Speedway. "What happened probably only closed it a year or so earlier than would have otherwise been the case." He points to the growth of a city that had literally surrounded the site.

Perhaps the facility was on a short, finite, lifespan when the first oval was ploughed in 1951. Certainly, many of the investors in the larger complex in the mid '60s would have known that a race track would not forever be the highest and best use of land so close to a growing city.

After the end of racing, the land remained dormant for a few years, and then began to develop. Today the land that once shook under the machines of Garlits, Rasmussen, Hulme, Stewart, Prudhomme, McLaren, Armstrong, and Villeneuve supports a typical nondescript suburban blend of strip malls, big-box retail outlets, and housing.

CHAPTER 19

ALLEN BERG

Persistence can grind an iron beam down to a needle.
—Chinese proverb

It would be easy to dismiss Allen Berg as just another well-to-do kid who, with some family money and whatever corporate backing he could find, bought a ride in Formula One, then quickly failed miserably as a race driver. It would be as wrong as it is easy, for Allen Berg is a driver who paid his dues both before and after his abbreviated tour of duty in Grand Prix racing, and in the process acquired a thorough understanding of how the business of modern motor racing works.

To be sure, his Formula One career of nine races in 1986 was, in itself, no success story. But then no one else was able to achieve anything with the badly underpowered and pathetically unreliable Osella–Alfa Romeo either. In nine races, Berg's car died on him four times. At the British Grand Prix at Brands Hatch he was caught up in the multicar crash that ended the Formula One career of Jacques Lafitte. Of the remaining four races, he had a top finish of 12th in the German Grand Prix at Hockenheim. Other Osella drivers that season, Christian Danner, Piercarlo Ghinzani, and Alex Caffi, combined for a total of 33 entries. Danner and Ghinzani didn't qualify at Monaco, and of the remaining 31 starts, the cars failed to finish an abysmal 24 times—77.4 percent, for the statistically inclined. At the end of the season, the team had collected the princely sum of one championship point, that for a sixth-place finish by Danner in Austria.

This was not a team that Allen Berg let down. As Rob Walker said in his season review in *Road & Track* magazine, Allen was "thrown in at the deep end."

Allen's first exposure to auto racing took place in 1969 when his father, Ben, took him to the second-ever Can-Am race in Edmonton. He decided then that he wanted to be a Grand Prix driver. A short while later Ben agreed to sponsor a Top Fuel dragster running under the name *The Digitizer.* Young Allen was taken to a race where someone gave him a worn-out drag slick. Allen took it home and, even though the tire stood taller than him, rolled it to school the next day where he presented it to his Grade 1 class as his "show and tell" project. The exposure to dragsters hadn't taken Allen's eye off road racing, and he began with a kart in 1977. He was working a paper route to raise money for his first kart when an appendicitis attack left him unemployed. Ben, feeling that Allen had worked hard enough to earn a ride, agreed to pay the portion of the cost his son had not already saved. Once Allen was again healthy, he began competing. He was immediately successful, winning Alberta Junior Rookie of the Year followed the next season by Alberta Junior Champion, and then in 1979, Alberta Senior Champion. He also tried Formula Ford in 1979, driving a used Lotus 69 on tracks as diverse as Edmonton International Speedway, the mountainous Westwood Circuit in Port Coquitlam, BC, and the airport at Gimli (Allen refers to it as "Grimly"), Manitoba. Still in Formula Ford, he had one race at Mosport, east of Toronto, where he qualified fifth in a rented car, but he was punted off the track on the second lap of the race.

Interestingly, Allen feels that some of the most valuable experience he gained at the amateur sports car level came in ice racing. Running with the Calgary Sports Car Club on Little Red Deer Lake, he competed in a Datsun 510 sedan. Allen's memory is vague on exactly how well he did ("I might have won a championship—I'm not sure, but I know I won something"), but he is firm in his belief that running a rear-wheel-drive car on ice is great training in car control. He likens it to a slow-motion version of driving a Formula One in the rain, and he is actively considering bringing one of his rookie Formula Atlantic drivers to Alberta in the winter just to experience ice racing.

In 1981, Allen relocated to Mosport and took employment as a racing instructor. From that base he was able to compete in the Ontario- and Quebec-based Canadian Formula Ford Championship (2nd overall), and in the North American Formula Ford Championship (5th place). In 1982, he had his first taste of Formula Atlantic competition and enjoyed the benefit of master-tuner Carroll Smith working on his car. At the end of the season he joined the jet set and took his car to Australia, where he raced in, and won, the Formula Atlantic Winter Pacific Series. This is a tour that began many years earlier as the Tasman Series, and in the 1960s it drew many internationally known drivers. The premier event in the series is the Lady Wigram Trophy Race. Allen won that race, and his name is now engraved on the trophy alongside those of Stirling Moss, Jack Brabham, Bruce McLaren, Jackie Stewart, and Jim Clark—reflective of an era when top drivers were free to race wherever and whenever they wished, as long as there was no conflict with their Formula One schedules.

From Australia Allen went to England and signed on with Eddie Jordan's Formula Three team. His first season in Formula Three was overshadowed by a year-long points battle between Ayrton Senna and Martin Brundle. Allen was arguably the best of the rest, but he was not competitive with the front two. At season's end, he was fifth in championship points, having taken one win.

Much like major junior hockey is the standard path to the National Hockey League, British Formula Three is a traditional stepping stone to Formula One for drivers from all over the world. And like its hockey equivalent, it is the first level at which the participants are effectively professionals at their sport—albeit badly paid ones. The principal difference between the two sports is in what the athletes do when they are not competing. Hockey players—and other stick and ball athletes for that matter—spend as much time as possible in training: lifting weights, skating, and taking practice. The money needed to run their teams is of little concern to them. Racers on the other hand must be constantly on the search for sponsorship.

Allen (#68) driving the wheels off a kart, 1978. *(Ben and Allen Berg collection)*

Allen (right) sharing a Formula Three podium with the late Ayrton Senna (left) and Martin Brundle, 1983. *(Ben and Allen Berg collection)*

In the Osella, 1986, leading, however briefly, Michele Alboreto's Ferrari.
(Ben and Allen Berg collection)

Good rides in good cars are out there, but they will go to the drivers
who bring with them not only a high level of skill, but also sponsorship. While at the start of his career Allen enjoyed the financial support of his family, he was largely on his own in England. He admits
to being somewhat shy in his younger years, but he forced himself
and did the requisite door-knocking in search of sponsors. With
Eddie Jordan's help he managed to get backing from Unipart, *Grand
Prix International* magazine, Quest Explorations (a Calgary-based
oil company) and Acorn Computers. "Driving is the easy part; finding the sponsorship to make that happen is the hard part. Looking
for sponsorship is a full-time job," is how Allen sums up the life of a
professional race driver.

In his personal life, Allen also felt somewhat isolated in England.
"It's a different culture; you have no family or close friends. I didn't
socialize much with other drivers. They're your competitors—they
want the same rides and sponsors you want."

Besides the cultural and personal isolation, Allen had another
challenge to deal with—one faced by all drivers at that level—that
being the higher level of driving skill needed to compete. As he
explains, "The cream rises to the top. All the guys in Formula Three

are already champions somewhere, and they all want to be Formula One world champions. At Formula Three you're near the top of the pyramid. That's where you really learn how to outbrake other people, and you also learn to carry your speed through the corners, because a Formula Three car hasn't got enough power to make speed. One little bit of oversteer you can correct, but it might cost you two-tenths of a second down the following straight."

In 1984, Brundle and Senna having moved up to Formula One, Allen returned with Eddie Jordan's F3 team. What should have been his year to shine was overshadowed by the arrival of the newest British phenom, Johnny Dumfries. The year-end standings had Dumfries first, and Berg second. Nonetheless, this was progress, as was the fact Eddie Jordan had arranged a Formula One test for Allen in a BMW-Arrows.

Allen berg in a Porsche 962, Daytona 24 hours, 1989. *(Ben and Allen Berg collection)*

At the end of the season, Allen was named Canadian Driver of the Year.

In 1985, with no Formula One offers after two years in F3, Allen made his first foray into Mexico. Journalist Gerry Donaldson called Allen to say he had heard of an opening for a good formula-car driver in Mexican "Formula K," a series for small single-seaters with Chrysler K-car engines. Allen jumped at the chance, and in his five starts, he won three times. He also spent time that year in Calgary trying to raise sponsorship money, but he was only modestly successful. "Because I had been racing in Europe for two years, I was largely unknown in Calgary."

In 1986, while effectively unemployed but still keeping in touch with his industry, Allen learned through his friend Michel Koenig of *Grand Prix International* magazine that a rallying accident had injured Arrows Team driver Marc Surer. Christian Danner of the Osella Team was being given a chance to take over Surer's seat in the faster BMW-Arrows. That would leave a ride available at Osella. Allen flew to Montreal for the Canadian Grand Prix to meet the

Allen Berg driving a Mexican Formula Three race, Vera Cruz, 2000.
(Ben and Allen Berg collection)

Osella team. A deal requiring a relatively small amount of sponsor-ship was struck, with Allen making a short-term loan. "We signed the deal on top of a fuel barrel in the garages at Montreal. It was all in Italian and I couldn't understand a word of it, but it was a Formula One contract, so I signed it."

Allen Berg drove in the United States, French, British, German, Hungarian, Austrian, Portuguese, Mexican and Australian Grand Prix races, and the results of that adventure are detailed earlier in this chapter. Certainly, being known as a Formula One driver, if only for part of a season, is a major boost to any driver's résumé, but equally important is the continuation of the learning curve that the young driver experiences. "At that level, you just have to understand the engineering of the car," he says.

"In F1, (race engineer) Steve Nichols was known as 'Ayrton Senna's secretary' because Senna had such an innate and profound knowledge of the car that he was able to tell Nichols exactly what had to be done to set it up properly," recalls Allen. "The days of a driver coming into the pits and just saying 'it's oversteering,' and expecting someone to fix it for him are gone. The driver has to be able to communicate with the engineer, on the engineer's terms."

There was a chance of a Formula One ride in 1987, with backing from Labatt, but a legal brawl between that company and arch-rival Molson resulted not only in Allen being left on the sidelines, but also the cancellation of the Canadian GP that season. Allen came back to Calgary and drove for part of the season in the Player's / GM Challenge for Firebirds and Camaros.

Allen accepts that his Formula One career was short, but strong-ly feels that as a driver, without the commercial and political com-plications of racing at that level, he could have competed. "We had 900 horsepower compared to 1150 for the top teams, so we couldn't hope to stay with them, but I was competitive with my teammates and probably faster in the rain. It's that ice-race training."

Allen Berg, who describes himself as "spiritual" rather than "reli-gious," remains philosophical: "I had my shot. I'm really grateful for the opportunity God gave me to do what I've done with my racing career."

In his early 40s, Allen Berg still fits the modern image of a Grand Prix driver: an athletic body on a short frame, moving quickly with a controlled energy. He speaks in crisp, articulate sentences, reflective of a man in the habit of giving interviews and making sales pitches. In the years following his Formula One experience, he had innumerable opportunities to practice those two skills, particularly the latter.

The next five years of Allen Berg's life were spent in continuous search of racing employment. In 1987 he had brief stints with the Kremer Porsche and TWR Jaguar sports car teams. 1988 found him back in North America running in the Trans Am series for sedans. He spent the major part of 1989 and 1990 in Porsche 962s, earning a 10th-place finish in the 24 Hours of LeMans with fellow ex–Formula One drivers John Watson and Bruno Giacomelli. In 1991 he drove a privately entered BMW in the German Touring Car Championship.

In 1992, Allen's persistence finally paid off when he received a call from the Marlboro cigarette company asking if he would be interested in driving full time for them in the Mexican Formula Two series. He was indeed interested, and he spent the next three seasons with Marlboro, in this unique Mexican class, driving cars he describes as mechanically similar to Formula Atlantic, but with some extra bodywork designed to make them look more like their Formula One cousins. He adapted quickly, finishing third in the series in 1992, then winning the championship in 1993. In 1994 he finished second.

While F2 was the focus of his energies, Allen still found time to compete in the Mexican Prototype (sports car) series, partnering with various Mexican drivers, normally ending up at or near the front of the pack.

For the next six years, Allen was a full-time competitor in another Mexican series, that for Formula Three cars. After finishing 3rd and 4th respectively in 1995 and 1996, he won the championship in 1997 and 1998. He finished third in the same series in 1999. The following season he only competed in a few F3 races, moving over to the more powerful cars of the Indy Lights Panamericana (I.L.P.) series.

In 2001 Allen was a full-time driver on the I.L.P. circuit and, for the first time in his career, a team owner. In both roles he dominated the series. Going into the eighth and penultimate race of the season, he already had three wins as a driver. A win there would clinch the drivers' championship, but he qualified a disappointing fifth. Within two laps of the start—including a restart—the four cars in front of him had all taken themselves out with accidents or spins, and he cruised to an easy win, his fourth of the nine-race season. His teammate, Waldemar Coronas of Argentina, finished second. "All these guys took themselves out and let me easily win the championship. At that point in time I was thinking that was a lucky win—everybody but me had contact. That was God saying to me, 'Here's your damn championship—retire already.' I retired right there—didn't even compete in the last race of the season. Waldemar drove, and just dominated the race."

For 2002, Allen moved to San Diego, California, with his Mexican-born wife, Erika, and established his own Formula Toyota Atlantic team, Scuadra Fortia. His drivers for the 2003 season are Waldemar Coronas and Mexican Eduardo Figueroa. "You know, after 25 years, I don't even miss driving a bit. I'm completely consumed by running my racing team. There's so much to do and so much to learn."

CHAPTER 20

TIM GEE

"Chasing a ruined mile-track groove from top to bottom lane and back again...picking out cornering patterns that straddle trenches...putting arms and souls into keeping control and bouncing and roughhousing from rut to rut, making crash landings without crashing—mile track racing is an art."
—From *The American Dirt Track Racer,* by Joe Scalzo.
Used with permission of MBI Publishing,
www.motorbooks.com

Dirt-track sprint car racing is one of the lesser-known variations of the sport. One problem it has, as the name implies, is dirt. We live in a society that truly does rate cleanliness next to godliness. We have automatic laundry machines, car washes, daily showers, and an apparently endless variety of cleaning products designed to keep our bodies, hair, houses, clothes, dishes, and machinery spotless. To abandon this sanitized world, if only for a few hours, and inhale the dust and eat the mud of cars racing on packed dirt is a challenge for many people.

Commercial support is also a difficult reach on dirt. Far better for a sponsor to be sure his message on the side of either the car or the track will remain visible for the duration of the event, and not be covered in gumbo by lap three. And think of the poor vice president of marketing who has to walk across the muddy track in his expensive shoes to present the company trophy to the dirt-splattered winner—the promo picture just doesn't look as good as it would if it were in front of a shining Indy car or a dragster.

Nevertheless, some people apparently like playing in the mud because, in spite of the obstacles, dirt-track sprint car racing has its devotees, and those people are rewarded with some of the most intense racing found on our planet. Cars with a power-to-weight ratio not significantly inferior to that of Indianapolis cars, running on half-mile tracks of bumpy dirt, can and do provide a thrilling spectacle. It is here that Tim Gee of Edmonton made his mark.

Tim does not look like a successful open-wheel racer. Surpassing both 6 feet and 200 pounds, he could more easily pass for a retired football player. Lightweight race cars are generally driven by lightweight men.

Born in Estevan, Saskatchewan, Tim spent his early childhood in Edmonton. He recalls his father, Gordie, taking him, at perhaps age four, to watch racing at Speedway Park. At the time Tim found the cars less interesting than climbing to the top of the grandstand and marvelling at how high he was. The family moved from Edmonton to Whitehorse, Yukon, where Gordie owned and operated Yukon Freight Lines. Through YFL, Gordie was persuaded to sponsor a local stock car. When the track held its annual Sponsors' Race, Gordie tasted the sweet thrill of motor racing for the first time. So taken was he by the sport that he offered to work on the car so he could qualify for the upcoming Mechanics' Race. Soon after, Gordie bought the car outright and began racing regularly, with nine-year-old Tim as his biggest fan. By 12, Tim was working in the pits.

When Tim was 14 and, by his own admission, "getting into a lot of trouble with another kid; just being shitheads," he acquired, by default, his first race car. Looking for a way to keep the two boys busy, their fathers bought an old stock car for them. The youngsters worked on the car and then took turns "hot lapping" it in the four-acre Yukon Freight Lines yards. As soon as he was old enough, Tim began racing the stocker.

In 1973, no longer satisfied with racing just stock cars, Gordie, with help from brother Allan, Tim, and friend John Robertson, built his first modified. The team set a 1930 Ford Model A body on a 1958 Ford truck frame and installed a Chev 307 V-8. Gordie and Tim shared the driving. Over the next four years, father and son won more than their share of races, and that only whetted Tim's appetite for more and faster racing.

In the fall of 1977 Tim moved to Edmonton, intending to work at YFL's Edmonton terminal and compete on the asphalt at Westwinds Speedway. Unfortunately his timing was wrong and he arrived just in time to watch the last-ever race on the track. Not knowing what to do with his racing plans now, he called Central Tire, the sponsor of the Larry Fleming sprint car that had caught his attention. He was put in touch with Fleming, who not only welcomed Tim to his shop, but also let him know that the old Speedway Park was being resurrected for the 1978 season by promoter Rob Byrne; it would be renamed Cobra Raceway. The fastest class was to be sprint car, and that was what Tim wanted to race. With advice from Fleming, he bought a turnkey used car from a Wyoming racer and ran it through the 1978 and 1979 seasons. He principally raced on pavement in Edmonton and Calgary, and dirt in Wetaskiwin, but did make it as far south as Great Falls, Montana, in 1978 for that track's major race with over 40 cars entered. In 1979 he travelled to Skagit, Washington, for his first World of Outlaws (W.o.O.) race.

A note here about the World of Outlaws. In spite of (or perhaps because of?) the bizarre name, W.o.O. has since 1978 become the premier sanctioning body for sprint cars. Born of competitors' frustration with the restrictive United States Auto Club, W.o.O. has popularized the ferocious beast that is the winged sprint car. Incredibly, in an age when Formula One runs only 16 races a year, and NASCAR Winston Cup competitors complain about a 37-race season, the rough-and-tumble W.o.O. drivers race between 100 and 120 times each year.

Tim recalls the W.o.O. race at Skagit being "a real eye-opener. The Skagit guys were fast, but the Outlaws' cars were light years ahead of them—at least at that time." Tim explains that the Outlaws were among the first to run sprint cars with wings, and then aluminum cylinder heads. In fairness, he is quick to credit the drivers as much as their cars and engines, noting that people who race over 100 times a season tend to develop a high skill level.

An early win for Tim Gee: mid 1970s, Whitehorse. *(Gee family collection)*

Tim Gee at Cobra Raceway (nee Speedway Park), Edmonton, 1978. This was an era in which genuine sprint cars began to run with the established CAMRA super-modifieds. *(Gee family collection)*

World of Outlaws, Knoxville, Iowa Nationals, 1982. Tim was out of the car before this photo was taken. Amazingly, both car and driver were back racing two nights later. *(Gee family collection)*

The happy road warriors: Tim, Ruth, and Gordie Gee at Devil's Bowl, Texas, 1982. *(Gee family collection)*

In early 1980, Gordie Gee sold his trucking company and was free to spend more time on his son's racing. They ordered a new chassis from renowned builder Jerry Barnett in Phoenix, Arizona. When they drove south to pick up the car, they found it "still on the tubing rack." They stayed for a month and helped with the final assembly. When they unloaded their "killer" cast-iron 350 Chev motor to install in the new chassis, Jerry Barnett opined that it might not be quite enough to keep up with the California Racing Association cars they planned to race with. Nevertheless, the family team—Mom, Dad, Tim, and wife Ruth—spent the spring and early summer in their motor home commuting weekly between the Manzanita track outside Phoenix and the historic Ascot track near Los Angeles—an 800 (1,300-km) round trip each week. In July they went back to Skagit for a big race, still running the iron 350, and were pleasantly surprised to qualify for the A Main, a first for Tim at that track. They continued north, racing at Cobra Raceway in Edmonton and then at Fort McMurray, where the old engine finally blew up.

They had already ordered a state-of-the-art motor from Ron Shaver in Los Angeles, so it was now time to head back south and take delivery. They arrived at night, found their way to Shaver's by-then closed shop. Satisfied that they had their bearings in the huge city, they took a room in a nearby motel. They were up before dawn and into a car wash to scrub the race car prior to its transplant. As they made the short drive from the car wash to the shop, they began to notice that they were in a rough-looking neighbourhood. They arrived at Shaver's shop, and in the daylight saw that all its doors and windows were barred and wired. Once inside, the first thing they saw was a shotgun. Loaded. Then they met Ron Shaver. Tim recalls Shaver's reaction to hearing of the Canadians' late-night reconnaissance of the neighbourhood. "You guys came down here at night? You crazy? This is Watts. Nobody comes down here at night."

"I'll tell you," says Tim, "it was real culture shock for a boy from Whitehorse."

Once the Gee team had the new engine in the race car, their first race was at Chula Vista, near San Diego. Tim qualified well, ran in the top four in his heat race, and found himself on the pole for the feature. The flagman, nervous about the pack being led to the start by an unknown kid, spoke to Tim and reminded him that the driver on the outside pole was one of California's most accomplished sprinters, Bubby Jones. "You just kinda take 'er easy, and do what Bub does," advised the starter.

Tim didn't reply. "I'm thinking I'd been down here racing for a couple of months now and I hadn't won a race yet, so to hell with Bub, I'm going to try to win this thing. I sailed 'er into the first corner on the first lap and spun it out in front of the entire pack. They all missed me though."

From California the family team travelled to Dallas, Texas, where they hooked up with the World of Outlaws and joined their tour. The Gees were one of the few teams without sponsorship, but they found they could actually support themselves on prize money. "In California we'd been wiring back home for money every few weeks, but with the Outlaws racing three times a week, we could make it work."

The W.o.O. Tour took Tim and his family to Tennessee, Missouri, and then back west to Northern California. In autumn when they told W.o.O. President Ted Johnson they were heading back home for the year, he invited them to join his tour full time for the next season. "I told him, yeah, that's what we want to do."

They had decided that before they could join the tour full time, they needed a better hauling package. Their old motor home's automatic transmission had a propensity to overheat on long hills, and steering was difficult in crosswinds. The trailer would need upgrading too. While few sprint cars travelled in enclosed trailers at that time, Tim felt their team needed one to haul and shelter all the tools, parts and luggage needed to stay on the road for ten straight months.

Long-distance travel was by now second nature. They bought their new motor home in Red Deer, drove to Sacramento, California to hook up the trailer, then east to Dallas to load the new race car they had ordered, found it wasn't finished yet, headed to Florida with their old car for the first W.o.O. race of the 1981 season, and then right back to Dallas again to get the new car.

The year 1981 brought a steep learning curve. "Our crash-and-learn season," recalls Ruth Gee. No wins, but enough progress to want to stay on tour, and enough money to do it. This was also the year Tim and Ruth bought a house in Jamestown, Indiana, to be closer to the centre of their wandering world.

1982 saw Tim move closer to the top ranks of W.o.O. drivers, and he ended the season 10th in overall point standings. The following year was the breakthrough year, as Tim won his first Outlaws feature at Martin, Michigan, and moved up to 9th in points. He was 10th in 1984, 11th in 1985, and reached his peak in 1986 with a 7th-place finish, ahead of such notables as Doug Wolfgang, Brad Doty, Dave Blaney, and Sammy Swindell. Interestingly, that was also the season that the incomparable Steve Kinser set a record of 46 feature-race wins.

When Gordie Gee sold Yukon Freight Lines to Kingsway Transport in 1980, Kingsway signed on for two years as Tim's sponsor at $30,000 per season. The cost of racing for the first full Outlaws season was $35,000, so the family was able to live comfortably on the prize money. By the time the sponsorship ended, costs were beginning to rise far quicker than prize money, and over the next five

Tim Gee today, thrilling race fans with rides in his two-seat sprinter. The happy passenger in this photo is Japanese Rotary exchange student Ami Watanabe. *(Photo by the author)*

years, Tim's finances became progressively tighter. The 1986 season cost $210,000, and even with his improving performance, he didn't earn that much in prizes.

1987 began, literally, with a bang. As he had done in previous years, Tim opened his season by travelling to Florida, but that year the race there was not sanctioned by W.o.O. In one memorable week he not only crashed the race car, but also blew the motor in the motorhome. The result was that he missed the first week's W.o.O. racing in California. World of Outlaws paid travel and hotel-room subsidies to the top ten drivers in points. Starting late, Tim was no longer in that group. He struggled for a few months, but by June recognized that there was no way he could afford to stay on the tour. He drove back to Jamestown and for the next three years contented himself with local races, and W.o.O. events whenever they were in the Indianapolis area.

In 1990, Tim's old friend from Edmonton, Terry Gray, called to tell him about the development of the new Capital Raceway, planned to include a clay oval, a drag strip and a road course. There might be some opportunities on the business side of racing, as well as a place to compete on a weekly basis. Perhaps it was time to come home?

After some thought and discussion, Tim and Ruth decided to make the move. Since then, along with Gordie, they have operated Gee and Gee Racing, just across Highway 2 from Capital Raceway in Leduc. Their shop sells new and used race cars and parts and does fabricating and repair work for the local racing community. As an adjunct, Tim rents sportsman-class sprint cars to drivers in the lower classes, and he sells rides in a purpose-built two-seat sprinter to fans.

CHAPTER 21

DOCKTOR PRESCRIBES A RACE TRACK

The starting field came out of turn 4, headed for the green flag,
rumbling and roaring...it sent goose bumps up my spine,
and I turned to my wife, and she had tears in her eyes.
— Track owner Ben Docktor at the official
opening of Race City Speedway, 1986

There wasn't much for racing facilities in Calgary when Ben Docktor arrived from the United States in the mid 1970s. The ¼-mile Circle 8 Speedway paved oval on the city's north outskirts adequately served its market, but it had only a few years to live. Calgary International Raceway—formerly Shephard Raceway—a proper ¼-mile drag strip and 2.0-mile road course, was about to be reduced because of the loss of land for construction of Deerfoot Trail, to just a shortened strip that Ben dismissed as "an eighth-mile with a press box over a toilet."

Ten years later, in 1987, Docktor had created the most comprehensive motor racing complex in Canada. Calgary, the city that had watched with envy in the 1960s and '70s as Edmonton hosted the superstars of the sport at Edmonton International Speedway, was now taking the lead role. While E.I.S. was being transformed into houses and strip malls, Calgary suddenly had a new, and arguably better, facility.

Ben Docktor grew up in North Dakota as a drag racing fan. While still a teenager, he joined the United States Army and was quickly posted to the Deep South. When he got there, he found there to be little interest in straight-line racing; stock cars were the only game in town, and a very big game they were. In short order, he became hooked on ovals too. He didn't compete in those days, but describes himself as a huge fan.

After leaving the army, he tried his hand at a variety of businesses, including running a nightclub in Wyoming, but eventually settled on the oil industry. Calgary's vibrant oil patch attracted the young entrepreneur and he chose that city in which to set up his companies, dealing in many aspects of the industry. Once his business became established, he tried racing on the dirt Stampede City Speedway oval with some success. More importantly, though, he discovered that one of his employees, Harold Browne, was already an accomplished racer. Browne wanted to progress in the sport, and Ben's businesses, the Platinum Group and Cape Oil Ltd., were doing well enough to help out.

A NASCAR North-West Tour car was ordered, and then a Kenworth tractor-trailer rig with which to haul it. On some weekends, the pressure of work made it difficult to get owner, driver, and families to the various tracks—so they flew in.

Before long, their race weekends were costing five to ten thousand dollars each. "I soon figured out for that much money we could build our own track," recalls Ben.

By late 1984 the basic plan of a new race facility had quietly been struck. The track would be located in the far southeast corner of Calgary, well beyond any foreseeable housing encroachment. The site was 160 acres of City-owned land on which a 25-year lease was signed, with an adjacent 90 acres available, should it be needed.

As commonly happens when a race track is proposed, there was local opposition. Neighbouring landowners, fervently believing that they could protect the value of their holdings by telling the world how a nearby racing facility would terribly undermine that same value, packed public meetings. "We had to go to their homes, sit at their kitchen tables and hold their hands." And when Ben sat at their

Harold Browne (facing camera), Ben Docktor, and their wives, and Mayor Ralph Klein (glasses), at the official sod-turning for Race City Speedway, June 19, 1985. *(Ben Docktor collection)*

Asphalt-laying on the Race City oval. *(Ben Docktor collection)*

Concrete launch ramp under construction at the Race City drag strip. *(Ben Docktor collection)*

American Speed Association racing action, 1989: Spinning guest star Geoff Bodine brings out the yellow flag. *(Photo by the author)*

tables, the story he told them was of a first-class racing facility, unlike anything Calgary had ever seen. A facility with good pavement, painted buildings, and a security staff to make sure families felt safe bringing their children. Ben had seen many small-to-medium sized race facilities in the United States run as "Mom and Pop" operations. They were clean, attractive, safe, and successful, and it was those tracks that he planned to model Race City after. Ben Docktor wanted the "nicest facility in Canada." From the beginning, Ben had Mayor Ralph Klein onside, but he was largely on his own when it came to dealing with the neighbours. Gradually, however, his kitchen-table meetings began to pay off, and the building permit was issued in mid-1985. Ben, Harold, and their wives were on hand June 19, 1985, to witness Mayor Klein turn the ceremonial first sod. By the time construction was complete, over six million dollars had been invested: some Ben's, some from his companies, some the banks' and some from sponsors. And that figure doesn't include the value of the land or the discounts and work-for-advertising deals made with some contractors. "We had a ten-million-dollar race facility," says Ben proudly.

When word of the development first hit the newspapers in March 1985, Ben's projected timeline called for the oval to be complete for the May long weekend, and the drag strip and road course ready July 1. It didn't work out that way. The oil industry was experiencing difficulties, slowing down all Ben's activities. The oval was finally ready to go September 29, 1985, when it hosted the Hard Hat Invitational. Seventy-five stock cars and 3,500 spectators showed up to launch the track. The feature race was won by Calgarian Bob Lowe.

The drag strip opened June 1986, almost a year later than originally projected, and there was no sign of the road course. When asked, track General Manager Murray Munsie said, "We have no projection at this time as to when the road course will be done. We'll just take it one step at a time."

Calgary Sports Car Club president Barry Sansom was quoted in the Calgary *Herald* as saying, "We're not impressed at the moment. Our people have been building road-racing cars since last August and they feel they should be able to go racing this summer. Obviously they feel a little left out." Ben pointed out that drag and stock car racing normally draw bigger crowds, and these money-makers would be needed to make a road course viable.

From the beginning, Ben understood that the quality of facility he envisioned could not be built and maintained without substantial sponsorship. The traditional corporate backers of race tracks in Calgary were small, automotive-based companies: gas stations, car dealerships, tire shops, and the like. These enterprises simply did not have the wherewithal to support Race City Speedway, so it was the large corporations who were approached. By 1986, Player's Tobacco, Molson Breweries, and General Motors had signed on. A year later, Shell Oil chipped in for the road course.

With the advice and help of NASCAR North-West's chief steward, Ken Clapp, the oval had been designed to replicate exactly the track in Bakersfield, California. It measures one-half mile along the outside wall, and .42 mile on the racing line. It is big enough to allow for side-by-side racing by full-sized stock cars, but not so big that it can't be driven by novice racers.

In the summer of 1986, Race City Speedway staged its first three major races. The Jet Car Nationals on the drag strip on June 15 drew 7,300 spectators and resulted in a line-up to the gate over a kilometre long.

The Coca-Cola 100 stock car race on July 12 was a NASCAR-sanctioned race. It drew 5,700 fans to watch Ron Eaton top a field of 26 cars. This was effectively the track's grand opening, and Ben was determined to make a lasting, positive impression on Calgary. There was a band, there were balloons, and formal opening ceremonies. Then there was a race. Ben recalls watching the starting field come out of turn 4, headed for the green flag, "rumbling and roaring, and it sent goose bumps up your spine, and I turned to my wife, and she had tears in her eyes."

Did Ben?

There is a pause as this tough-talking oilman collects his thoughts.

"Yeah, I know I did."

On August 3, a second NASCAR race took place, this one the Player's 500 for a purse of over $110,000, the highest on the North-West Tour. The green flag was waved by guest starter Cale Yarborough, and 6,500 people watched Bill Schmitt of Redding, California, take the win ahead of Winston Cup star-to-be Chad Little, and Bill Hitchcox of Victoria.

The NASCAR events had been a success, but the relationship with the North-West Tour, now called NASCAR Winston West, was to be short-lived. Ben received a phone call from Ken Clapp. "Ben, we have a problem."

The Winston cigarette company was aware of the Player's sponsorship of the 500 and was becoming uneasy with the high-profile presence of another tobacco company. If Winston West were to continue to come to Calgary, Player's would have to go. Ben had a hard decision to make: give up his NASCAR date, or turn his back on Player's, which had supported him from the day he opened and was soon to bring him the biggest road-racing series in the country: the Player's Challenge Series for showroom-stock Camaros and Firebirds. After a lot of thought, he took the decision that there was more future with the company that sold its products in his marketplace than with the American company.

A second question was whether the track could take another 500-lap feature. The 1986 Player's race had damaged the track surface. Repairs had been made, and the surface resealed, but should the race be shortened to protect the track? Ben decided to chance staying with the 500-lap format.

The Player's 500 it was to be, but who was coming to race? The 1987 Player's 500 ended up as an invitational race between a mixture of NASCAR, American Speed Association (A.S.A.), and various freelance entries, with American Rich Bickle, Jr taking the win. *Circle Track* magazine covered the race and praised Race City as "easily the best short-track racing facility in Canada, and possibly the best new track anywhere."

For 1988, Ben invited the American Speed Association, centred in the American Great Lakes states, to stage the race. The closest this group had ever come to Calgary was Cayuga, Ontario. The head of

A.S.A., Rex Robbins, was open to the idea of travelling to Calgary, but it would be costly. Ben asked Player's if they would help out with the costs. The answer was yes, and the Player's 500 was reborn.

Ben Docktor and his staff recognized that they had to take advantage of the excitement surrounding the event if it were to continue to thrive. To bring the racing closer to the people, they arranged with City Hall to have a block in the downtown core closed off for a pit-stop competition the Friday afternoon before the race. Hundreds of office workers, some of whom had probably never seen a race car in the flesh, watched in amazement as an athletic crew changed two tires and added ten gallons (40 litres) of fuel in 15 seconds. Calgary, the city of the Stampede, the Stampeders, and the Flames, was beginning to take to racing.

The Player's 500 continued under A.S.A. sanction until 1993, when the Ontario-based Canadian Association for Stock Car Racing (CASCAR) took over the major race. CASCAR had begun racing in Calgary in 1992, and within a year it had developed a local Alberta cadre of skilled drivers including Harold Browne, Kevin Dowler, Paul Gilgan, Gary Grote, Wade Lee, and Don Mossman. With the body (CASCAR) that sanctioned the local stock car races now also running the major race of the year, local flavour was brought to the event. Like I.M.C.A. of seven or eight decades earlier, A.S.A. had been strictly a travelling show—the few locals that participated were there simply to fill out the field. With CASCAR in place, the situation more closely resembled CAMRA of the '60s and '70s. The local drivers were a legitimate, competitive part of the big race.

The year 1987 marked the completion of the Race City facility with the opening of the two-mile Shell Oil–backed road course. While virtually flat, the track's 12 turns, with asphalt width varying from 30 to 60 feet (9 to 18 metres), promised a challenge for both cars and drivers. The opening of the road course was timely in that it enabled the Player's Challenge (later to become known as the Player's Ltd. / GM Motorsport Series), a series for showroom-stock Chevrolet Camaros and Pontiac Firebirds, to expand westward from the Ontario and Quebec base it had established for itself in 1986. The Player's GM series would be followed by the similar Honda /

Michelin series for Honda Civics, and by the Canon / Yokohama series for Formula 1600 (nee Formula Ford).

The Race City oval, with its wide surface, banked turns, and paved pit lane was without doubt the finest facility of its kind in Western Canada. It drew all manner of race cars, not only those commonly found on ovals. The Player's / GM, Canon / Yokohama, and Honda / Michelin cars ventured over from the road course occasionally. The Toyota Formula Atlantic series paid a visit and set a lap record. Big-Rig racing, for large trucks weighing a minimum of 12,000 pounds (3,400 kg.), and modified for speed and safety just as are stock cars, was added to the program. Some of these vehicles develop over 1,000 foot-pounds of torque and can be surprisingly fast. Unfortunately for the track owner, when the trucks hit a wall, they often demolish it. They draw good crowds, but the front four rows of grandstand seats must be closed off for safety.

In 1995, Ben Docktor sold Race City to Art MacKenzie. As this is being written, almost two decades after the sod was first turned, Race City continues to operate under McKenzie's leadership. The fact that it is surrounded by heavy industry including a railway line, a sewage lagoon, a landfill site, and other deterrents to residential development, makes its future seem secure.

CHAPTER 22

"240 GORDIE"

In this day and age of social security, retirement plans,
life insurance, the "safe" job, annuities, three dental visits
a year, calm pills, happy pills, and 25-year-old executives with
rimless glasses, we had Eddie Sachs…and we needed him.
— Warren Weith, in an obituary for oval track racer
Eddie Sachs in *Car and Driver* magazine, September 1964

Interviewing Gordie Bonin can best be likened to guessing which
way spit on a griddle is going to move. Or perhaps trying to catch
a snowflake in a windstorm. Only the most delusional interview-
er would believe that he is in control of a discussion with this near-
manic energy source seated across the table.

Idle conversation about living in Washington State suddenly
leads to an outrageous story heard from Gordie's Loon Lake,
Washington, barber about a dead black astronaut.

A pause before a photo in Gordie's scrapbook of a beautiful,
bikini-clad model standing by his Top Fuel dragster and he com-
ments that the lady is really car owner Ron Hodgson's secretary.

"You're kidding."

"You don't think Ron hires secretaries like that?"

The banter carries on, and minutes later it still isn't clear who the
model is.

What does he do when he's not racing?

"I think I'm a sales rep for Prolong Lubricants."

"Do you have a business card?"

"On me? Should I? "

"Do you save all your trophies?"

"No, I gave them all to (Ron) Hodgson. He still owes me the freight."

After a while, it becomes difficult to reconcile the man behind the constant barrage of witticisms with the one who has made his living in the upper echelons of professional drag racing for thirty years. This is a driver whom wealthy men pay to guide their ridiculously expensive, 6,000-horsepower cars from standstill to almost 300 miles per hour (486 kmh) in five seconds. This is a racer whose accomplishments warrant his inclusion in any history of the sport in Canada. Writing his story might well be easy. Finding it is another matter.

So who is the real Gordie Bonin?

Gordie Bonin was born in Prince Albert, Saskatchewan, in 1948. While he was still quite young, his family moved to Red Deer. The racing bug bit early, and by his mid teens he and his friends were chasing one another on the streets with their 50-cc Hondas. Drag racing began in 1966 with a 1956 Chev. In 1967 he moved to a '62 Pontiac and began to find some success. "We got lots of practice, racing at night on the Highway 2 bypass. Sometimes Pine Lake Highway."

A year later, Gordie's friend Ted Sinclair acquired a 1955 Chev show car. Gordie persuaded him to take it racing, which Ted did, but with little success. "Couldn't drive worth a shit," recalls Gordie. "So he put me in and we started winning. Trouble is, we kept tearing up transmissions. We'd take them into Red Deer Motors, and for a while they'd fix them on warranty, but then they cut us off. They knew what we were doing."

In 1969, Gordie "followed a girl to Saskatoon," where he was able to get some support for a Rambler "Scrambler" drag car. Gerry Ackerman of Rambler Saskatoon Ltd. got Gordie into the car, and the factory provided performance parts. The season went well, as he regularly beat Ford and GM muscle cars. But by 1970 he was back in Red Deer—having married Ingrid (the first of his two marriages), and adopted her son, Scott—selling Chevs for Red Deer Motors. That same year, Ted Sinclair bought a purpose-built race car, a Junior Fuel dragster. Again Ted tried driving, and again Gordie ended up behind the wheel.

Despite the innocuous-sounding name, a Junior Fuel dragster was a very fast, serious, race car. With 700–800 horsepower propelling a car weighing perhaps 1,500 pounds (680 kg), it had performance far removed from the stock-based "door-slammers" Gordie had driven to that point in his career. What did he think of it?

"At first it was, 'Oh shit, this is wild!' But then it's, 'OK, what's the next step?' Since I was like three years old, I wanted to be a racer. When I was a kid, I dreamt of living with palm trees and flying to my next drag race. This car was one step towards that."

The Sinclair and Bonin car was successful, racing everywhere from Winnipeg to Seattle and winning a Western Canadian championship. But perhaps more importantly, this car was moving Gordie's skill level to where it would have to be to handle the extraordinary speeds he would soon be seeing.

Late one night in 1971, returning to Red Deer from Sylvan Lake, Ted and Gordie decided to follow some emergency vehicles they spotted. They were led to a serious accident just off a Highway 2 exit. A badly damaged station wagon was in the ditch, the flat-bed trailer behind it was empty, and a Top Fuel dragster was sitting precariously atop the wagon. Tools, parts, and tires were scattered along the road and the ditch. The driver, Gordon Jenner of Edmonton, was being loaded into an ambulance. Ted and Gordie offered to pick up the pieces and take them to Ted's home for safekeeping. Jenner, seriously injured (he spent a month in hospital), agreed.

Gordon Jenner was, by the time of his chance meeting with Gordie Bonin, one of the most successful drag racers in Western Canada. His succession of cars bearing the name *Royal Canadian* had achieved almost legendary status. Partnering first with Nick Kozak, and later with Ron Hodgson, Murray Dyma, and Don Kohut, Jenner's Royal Canadians were serious threats any time they raced. Among notable *Royal Canadian* victories was the inaugural race at Edmonton International Speedway in 1967.

A year after the highway mishap, while Gordie was working for Beneficial Finance in Red Deer, he received a call from Jenner in California. Would Gordie be interested in trying out as driver for a Top Fuel funny car?

Amateur racers rarely get phone calls like that. Gordie Bonin admits to being thrilled by the invitation to drive the *Royal Canadian.* "I didn't sleep much that night, and I was down there in two days."

Murray Dyma had just sold his 50-percent share of the car to Ron Hodgson, while Jenner owned the remaining half. Dyma was also stepping aside as driver, and the three men had agreed on a short list of possible replacements. Gordie was on the list because Jenner had watched him after their chance meeting and felt he would be able to handle a faster, more difficult car.

When Bonin arrived in California, Gordon Jenner met him at the airport ("I can't believe I wore a suit and tie") and took him directly to Lion's Drag Strip. Before he would be allowed to race the 2,500-horsepower funny car, he had to upgrade his licence by making several passes under the supervision of National Hot Rod Association officials. Thirty years later he still talks excitedly of the experience. "Those things are noisy as hell, but once I got in and they lowered the body over me, it was almost quiet. All the noise points away from the car. But open the throttle, and oh shit, you talk about a need for speed! This is what I want to do for the rest of my life! I just didn't ever want to get off the pedal. Trouble is, on the first run, I had to back off. Murray Dyma was a huge guy, and the way the shift lever was set up for him, I couldn't reach it. I couldn't get high gear, so I brought the car in and they had to heat the lever and bend it back for me. It was still too far, so they stuffed Murray's fire suit in behind my back so I could reach."

Despite the problems, by nightfall Gordie Bonin had turned in a best time of 206 miles per hour (334 kmh)—substantially faster than Dyma had ever taken the car—and had his N.H.R.A. Funny Car licence. Three days later he was racing at Seattle, where he finished the weekend runner-up to Jerry Ruth.

The team raced throughout the summer, while both Jenner and

Bonin held down regular jobs. In August they ran at Seattle, Washington, where they hit a top speed of 221 miles per hour with an elapsed time of 6.56 seconds. The records then were 222 miles per hour and 6.46 seconds, set at different times by different drivers. Jenner and Bonin now knew they were competitive with the best teams. Driving back to their jobs in Alberta—Bonin still with Beneficial and Jenner with Otis Elevator—they reflected on their near-record time and the many racers at Seattle who had urged them to go to the biggest drag race, the U.S. Nationals in Indianapolis. It simply didn't seem practical, or even possible. The time off from work, the cost, and the fact that they didn't have a hauler they could rely on for that distance were all obstacles to making the trip. When they arrived home, they had yet to decide, but Jenner was determined. "We'll figure it out," Bonin recalls him saying. The next day, Jenner's decision was made for him when fellow racer Mike Lycar arrived at his door with his larger, newer hauler, and offered to lend it for the trip. A week later, having borrowed a plane ticket, Bonin was able to join his teammate in Indianapolis.

This was the weekend that Gary Beck and Ray Peets of Edmonton shocked the drag racing world by winning Top Fuel Dragster. Every bit as big a surprise was the Bonin / Jenner / *Royal Canadian* team finishing second in Funny Car, behind Ed McCulloch.

On the basis of points gathered at Indianapolis and at the other races they competed in, the *Royal Canadian* team was invited to the "World Finals" in Amarillo, Texas. This would be the final race of the season—the top ten cars from the East vs. the top ten from the West: fastest 16 qualify. Gordie made it to the semifinals, up against Phil Castronova. At half-track, he was running away with the race, already telling himself he was in the final, only to be stopped by a blown rear end. "Servicing the car? What did we know about servicing the race car?"

He had to sit on the sidelines and watch while Castronova won the title race.

"That close! I'm thinking, 'Hell, I'm a pro now. Quit my job. Move into a little motel in California. I figure I'll do the match-

The Ackerman Rambler, Saskatoon, 1969. *(Gordie Bonin collection)*

Gordie Bonin (standing) with Ted Sinclair and the Junior Fuel dragster. *(Gordie Bonin collection)*

Murray Dyma (dark glasses), Gord Jenner (hands on hips), and a bevy of beauty queens wait patiently as Miss Deer Park and Gordie celebrate the latter's first pro win, 1972. *(Gordie Bonin collection)*

racing thing, and I got it made.' But I didn't bother to think that it was the end of the season. By about February I came back and got a job at Associates Finance."

Gordie's second stint in the finance business didn't last as long as the first one. By mid 1973 he was again touring with Gord Jenner and the *Royal Canadian* when he received a call from famed Hawaiian racer Roland Leong: "Hey, boy, you want to drive my hot rod?"

Roland Leong's "hot rod" was a new, state-of-the-art, Don Long–built car. Driver Leroy Chadderton had just quit Leong, and the seat was open if Gordie wanted it. "I talked to Gord Jenner, and he understood. So I moved."

The stay with Leong was short-lived, as by 1974 the racing interests of Jenner and Hodgson switched from a car to a race track. Hodgson had taken a lease on Edmonton International Speedway from the Tom Fox group and appointed Jenner his manager. Gordie took over the *Royal Canadian* race team himself. In 1975 Hodgson was back with Gordie, this time with a major sponsor, Bubble-Up soft drinks, and a highly respected crew chief, Jerry Verhuel from

Renton, Washington. In 1977, Gordie Bonin won his first N.H.R.A. National, at Gainesville, Florida. "When I went down there in '72 and got second at the Nationals, I was thinking, 'How tough can it be to win one of those?' Well, there you go, it took five years."

Gordie took a second National in 1977, winning the World Finals in Ontario, California. He also passed the 240-mile-per-hour (389 kmh) barrier for the first time, then showed a remarkable knack for doing it consistently. That earned him the nickname "240 Gordie," a title he still proudly bears, even in an age when "320" would be more a term of distinction. He won in Gainesville again in 1979 to kick off his most successful year, and he followed up with wins at Indianapolis and the World Finals. In 1981 he won for a third time in Gainesville.

Gordie the working racer assembling a Bubble-Up funny car engine, c. 1975. *(Alberta Provincial Archives, J1275/6)*

Gordie taking off in the Bubble-Up funny car, 1975. *(Gordie Bonin collection)*

Gordie in the Hodgson / Tetz Top Fuel car, 1989. Notice the rear-end lift resulting from the chute-aided deceleration at the end of the run. *(www.LesWelch.com photo)*

Shortly after that, Ron Hodgson sold the racing team and redirected his resources towards the purchase of a brewery in Prince George, BC. Without a race car under him, Gordie signed on with the brewery as a salesman, racing only part time. "I enjoyed the selling, but if you weren't with one of the big three breweries (Molson, Labatt, and Carling O'Keefe) they made it tough for you."

This probably had something to do with why Gordie called the N.H.R.A. office in 1983 suggesting they needed help—his—with their marketing program. He was hired and spent six years promoting the sport he loved. But the need for speed was still there. In 1989 Ron Hodgson and partner Dwayne Tetz of Stettler bought a new Top Fuel dragster and put it in the hands of the reunited team of Gordie Bonin and Gord Jenner. It had been seven years since Gordie had driven a fuel drag-racing car, and his N.H.R.A. licence had long since lapsed, but a series of 250–260-mile-per-hour (405–420 kmh) passes at Calgary's Race City Speedway quickly convinced officials he was ready to come back.

The team only lasted a year, and 1990 found Gordie Bonin working as sales manager for Competition Specialties of Seattle. 1989–90 was really a precursor of the decade that was to follow—race a little, sell a little. By 1993 he was back in a Roland Leong car, winning another N.H.R.A. National title, this time at Columbus. In 1994 he landed a ride with the Smokin' Joe's team, owned by Paul Candies and Leonard Hughes. In this car, he won at Columbus again and then Memphis, his last two Nationals—so far.

In 1996 Gordie was back into sales, this time as marketing rep for Las Vegas Motor Speedway. By the late 1990s he was in Europe with backing from Prolong Lubricants, and he was crowned 1999 European Champion at an elaborate Monaco awards ceremony for all branches of motorsport. "I was up there with (Formula One World Champion) Mika Hakkinen, and the world rally champ. You know Bernie Ecclestone (referring to the notoriously egomaniacal Formula One boss) gets himself put up there, ahead of Prince Rainier?"

As this is being written, Gordie Bonin is 56 years old, but he doesn't want to hear or talk about retirement. There are records he still holds, and feels he can better. He has a career-high top speed of 297.6 miles per hour (in the Smokin' Joe's funny car), and a Top Fuel car sitting in Seattle that he's sure is good for over 300 mph. Between sales calls for Prolong, he spends his time looking for times and places to drive it.

How long does he plan on racing?

"As long as I can. Still got the need for speed."

CHAPTER 23

PRO SPORTS CARS

*I may be prejudiced, but I think race drivers are the
heroes of the 1970s. The superheroes of today—movie
stars and astronauts—need heroes of their own,
and they find much to admire in race drivers.*
—David Lockton, president of
Ontario Motor Speedway, 1970

There was a time, not long before the story you are about to read
took place, when the title of this chapter would have been an
oxymoron.

Sports car racing, as it developed in North America in the late
1940s, the 1950s, and early 1960s, was anything but professional. It
was a recreation for amateur sportsmen. Commercialization, of the
kind seen in oval track racing, was not only frowned upon, but also
simply banned. For instance, in 1959 when Edmonton racer Gene
McMahon first put his home-made racer "The Beast" on the track,
he wanted to use it to advertise his used-car lot by painting the name
"Empire Motors" on the sides. This was prohibited under Canadian
Automobile Sport Clubs (C.A.S.C.) regulations, so instead,
McMahon wrote on the car "Team Empire." This was allowed.
Teams were OK; companies were not.

In 1961 with the opening of the Mosport race circuit near
Toronto, C.A.S.C. softened its stand. Grand Prix superstar Stirling
Moss, LeMans winner Olivier Gendebien, and top Swedish driver Jo

Bonnier were invited for the Player's 200; and they weren't coming simply to share the joy of amateur competition—there was money on the line. C.A.S.C. dropped its Olympian amateur fantasy, the three Europeans came and were paid, and the rest of the race field filled out with Canadians. South of the border, progress was somewhat slower, and many American drivers, who would have loved the chance to come to Mosport and test themselves against the big names, were barred from doing so by the Sports Car Club of America (S.C.C.A.), under pain of losing their competition licences. American amateurs could not be permitted to besmirch themselves and their sport by swimming in water tainted by filthy lucre.

If the S.C.C.A. could afford to ignore a race in Canada, it could not do the same with the mighty United States Automobile Club (USAC) in its own country. USAC was an oval-track sanctioning body that had among its calendar of races the Indianapolis 500. It had become the major racing organization in the United States in the late 1950s when the American Automobile Association (AAA) had, in the wake of far too many tragedies, closed its racing division. USAC ran championship (Indy car), sprint, midget, and stock car divisions, and it was now expressing interest in sports car racing. USAC sports car races, beginning with an event at Riverside, California in 1958, unabashedly offered prize money. S.C.C.A. essentially turned a blind eye and let the local California club run its own show. The resultant annual "Fall Series" of races on the U.S. west coast quickly grew into a major event involving American sports car drivers, European professionals, and some of the better oval track drivers, including A. J. Foyt and Parnelli Jones. Knowing that many of these top drivers would be in North America in autumn, the British Empire Motor Club scheduled the first Canadian Grand Prix for sports cars for the weekend of September 23–24. By then—only three months after the Player's 200—the pressure on S.C.C.A. had become too much and they lifted their ban on pros, and a number of Americans showed up to compete at Mosport.

While these major changes in the conduct of the sport were happening, equally significant shifts were taking place on the shop floors where the cars were built. When the tiny Cooper factory of

England won its first World Formula One Championship in 1959 with a mid-engined car, all race car manufacturers were forced to reconsider the design of their products. What they discovered was that not only did the engine-behind-the-driver layout provide intrinsically better handling, it also offered better aerodynamics (the driver wasn't stuck up in the airflow, sitting above the drive shaft; nor did he have to see over the engine), better accelerative traction, and lower overall weight. The advantages were so great that mid-engined Cooper Monacos and Lotus 19s with 2.5-litre-displacement motors had no trouble staying ahead of front-engine Jaguars and Ferraris with engines 50-percent larger, let alone the numerous specials with four- and five-litre V-8s. "Just think what we could do with bigger motors in the rear," became the thought process of many builders, and by 1961, Bill Sadler of St. Catherines, Ontario, had put a Chevrolet V-8 in the rear of his Sadler Mk 5. While the car was not a great success, it ran well enough to confirm that such a pattern was practical, and it became the precursor of sports-racing car design for much of the ensuing decade.

Professional sports car racing grew immensely in popularity throughout North America in the early to mid 1960s. People enjoyed watching the fast two-seaters with the noise and power of stock cars and the braking and cornering pace of Formula cars. It was a spectacle. In 1964, some 52,000 fans showed up at Mosport for the Player's 200—a record attendance for a Canadian sports event at that time—and even larger crowds appeared at the Los Angeles Times Grand Prix at Riverside. Nevertheless, these races remained much like exhibition games in team sports in that they were simply stand-alone events. There was no Grey Cup or Stanley Cup or World Championship at the end of it all, and no organization to provide contiguous support and governance. The big-name drivers were paid appearance money by the promoters on a race-by-race basis. Lacking was the driver commitment to a series such as was found in Formula One, or the USAC National Championship. But with the success of the races, it became inevitable that a series would be built around these cars, and the formal announcement of the Canadian American (Can-Am) Challenge Cup came in February 1966.

The original plan was to hold races at St. Jovite, Quebec; Mosport, Ontario; Laguna Seca and Riverside, California; Kent, Washington; and Las Vegas, Nevada. In addition to the tourist crowds of Las Vegas, the schedule effectively captured the population centres ("big market" in today's sports parlance) of Toronto, Montreal, Los Angeles, San Francisco, and Seattle. By the time the rubber hit the track, Kent had dropped out, and that track's date was taken over by Bridgehampton, New York. To avoid any scheduling conflicts, the races would take place in September, October, and November, after the Formula One season had ended in Europe.

Beginning with St. Jovite on September 11, 1966, the series was an immediate success, bringing such world-renowned drivers as Bruce McLaren, John Surtees, Dennis Hulme, Dan Gurney, and Chris Amon to the doorsteps of North American fans. The big sports cars were far more powerful than their Formula One cousins, and in practice for their first race they had two of their number do backflips after becoming airborne on the Quebec track—fortunately without serious injury to either driver. This had never happened to a Formula One car, and it put drivers, builders, fans, and the media on notice that the new series was taking racing to unknown, and frightening, levels of performance.

The 1966 and 1967 Mosport Can-Ams were organized, as were many major races at that track, by a Toronto sports car club, the Canadian Race Drivers Association (C.R.D.A.). In 1967 the operators of the Mosport facility, bypassing their traditional partner C.R.D.A., went out on their own and brought in two USAC races: one for champ cars and one for stockers. C.R.D.A., sensing that Mosport's next move might be to try to gain control of the Canadian Grand Prix and the Can-Am, moved to protect its interests. It began looking at alternatives to Mosport. But where? Westwood outside Vancouver was too small, and St. Jovite already had a Can-Am date for 1968 (or at least it thought it did). But Edmonton was just building a new track, long enough to stage a race and spacious enough to accommodate the tens of thousands of people these races were drawing.

Contact was made and arrangements quickly put in place to have the 1968 Can-Am at Edmonton. The race, named the Klondike 200

1968 Edmonton Can-Am: Bruce McLaren warms the engine of his car before qualifying. *(Photo by the author)*

Stirling Moss, with Bob Stokowski as passenger / spotter, leads the 1968 Edmonton Can-Am field on its pace lap. *(Pete Lyons photo www.petelyons.com)*

1969 Edmonton Can-Am: Starter Don Sharp flags home the crippled car of Toronto's George Eaton to a third-place finish. Car #55 in background is the damaged McLaren of Roger McCaig. *(Pete Lyons photo www.petelyons.com)*

1970 Edmonton Can-Am: *Spirit of Edmonton* driver Graeme Lawrence and mechanic, their faces reflecting the season they were enduring. *(Mike Dean photo)*

after the city's annual fair, Klondike Days, would be run by C.R.D.A., but there would be an Edmonton committee responsible for the plethora of local details that could not be efficiently handled from Toronto. The local committee consisted of Don Arason, Ian Natrass, Willie Bass, Hal Pawson, Frank Hutton, Bob Russell, John McNeill, Dave Fowler, Ed Bryant, Fred Sturm, John DeLooper, Don Clarke, Nancy Magnee, Winifred McIntryre, Ernie Smalian, Dave Williams, Don Sharp (race starter), Gordon Lloyd, Paul Fee, Bryson Stone, Ron Clarke, Lloyd Martin, Norm Dick, Dick Porteous, and Dick Anthony.

The official announcement of the race was made on Victoria Day Monday, 1968, with simultaneous press conferences in Edmonton and New York, connected by telephone. The press conference, coming at the end of that particular long weekend, was a landmark proclamation of the state of auto racing in Edmonton in the late 1960s. The announcement, taken by itself, was enough to mark the beginning of a new sports era in the city, but immediately prior were three events that solidified Edmonton's growing reputation as a racing town. On Friday and Saturday, the Regals Car Club held their annual car show at the Sportex Building, attracting 12,000 people. On Sunday, the first drag race of the year drew over 16,000 fans, who watched not only some excellent racing, but were also witness to one of the early signs that Edmonton racers would be able to compete with anyone, as local boy Geoff Goodwin set a new national record in the Competition Eliminator class. On Holiday Monday, 3,700 people filed into the Speedway Park oval to see a weak race card offering only a demolition derby and the slowest of the track's three standard racing classes, Early-Late stock cars. In one weekend, 31,700 people had paid money in Edmonton to see fast cars in some form or another.

If one were to take a map of North America and mark on it the locations of Elkhart Lake, Wisconsin; Bridgehampton, New York; Edmonton, Alberta; Laguna Seca, California; Riverside, California; and Las Vegas, Nevada, Edmonton would immediately stand out, not only as being the only Canadian location of the lot, but also for being so remote from the others. In hard numbers, Edmonton is 4,118 kilometres from Bridgehampton and 2,558 from Laguna Seca, and those were the sites of the Can-Am races immediately before and after Edmonton. Luckily for everyone concerned, the authors of the season schedule had left a two-week gap on either side of the Edmonton date of September 29, because not only was there a lot of highway to be covered, but the teams were also not as well equipped to do the job as they would be now. In the 1960s, race teams—even top professional ones—typically hauled their cars, tools and spare parts on open trailers towed behind half-ton pick-up trucks powered by passenger-car V-8s. In this instance, these lightweight rigs were at the limit of their capabilities hauling that much weight, that far, that fast. Before they reached Edmonton, the Chaparral, McLaren, and Caldwell teams had all had highway breakdowns. Fortunately, with the extra time available to make the trip, everyone arrived safely and on time.

The crews that arrived early must have wondered why they were coming to this sub-arctic outpost. A heavy blizzard had shut down much of the province's highways the weekend prior to the race. The weather then took its sweet time recovering from the pre-winter storm, and most of the following week was cool, cloudy, and wet; but by Saturday the 28th, clear skies, bright sunshine, and relatively warm temperatures prevailed, much to the relief of the organizers, who must have known from Day 1 that they were flirting with disaster in staging a race this far north so late in the year.

Looking back from 35 years later—an era when Western Canadian cities have difficulty supporting major-league professional hockey teams let alone auto racing—it all seems so improbable. But on Saturday, September 28, for the price of a pit pass, one could literally rub shoulders with the greats of the sport. They were all there: World Champions Denny Hulme of New Zealand and John Surtees of England; Formula One winners Bruce McLaren from New Zealand, Jo Bonnier from Sweden, and Dan Gurney and Peter Revson from the United States—along with future Indianapolis 500 winner Mark Donohue. Not to forget Grand Prix legend Stirling Moss, who arrived from London, England to drive the pace car—sports car racing having recently abandoned the accident-prone standing start in favour of a rolling one.

Opinions of the track expressed by the professional drivers were mixed. Stirling Moss, touring it in a street car, found it to be a "difficult, demanding circuit." American Sam Posey called it "challenging." Bruce McLaren and Jim Hall criticized the track for "too many slow corners," while Jo Bonnier declared it to be "not terrifically interesting." John Surtees said the track's layout was "OK," but like several others, was concerned that the lack of any sort of curbing or other barrier to define the edge of the track surface was encouraging drivers to cut corners, thus throwing dirt onto the asphalt. The race organizers were listening, and by race day the insides of the corners had been guarded by a series of half-buried old tires.

Saturday qualifying went much as expected, with the McLarens of Hulme and McLaren taking the front row with identical 1-minute, 26-second laps. In the second row, within half a second of the two Kiwis, were Jim Hall in his Chaparral and Mark Donohue in a McLaren. In all, an impressive 25 cars made the grid. With the official business of qualifying out of the way for the day, Bruce McLaren took Olympic gold-medal skier Nancy Greene for some quick laps in the tiny second seat of his racer. With his passenger, McLaren was unofficially timed at 1:29.1, a time that would have put him 9th on the starting grid, ahead of 16 other cars. Miss Greene wore a huge smile when she got out of the car.

The gates were opened at midnight for an estimated 1,500 people wanting to camp overnight in the huge parking lot to the south of the track. Sunday dawned another clear, sunny day, but with track founder Reg Booth realizing that the campers had been let through the gates without buying tickets. At 7:30 a.m. he took a car onto the front straight and began revving the motor and squealing the tires. Track promotions manager Donald McKay recalls Booth saying, "I wanted to wake them up to make sure they bought tickets."

By early morning, a group of Edmonton Telephone and Calgary Power employees was busy building their own private grandstand atop a telephone pole. Other enterprising fans built grandstands out of oil drums and wood planks. Some brought stepladders to gain a better view.

There was really no scale to aid the organizers in predicting how many fans would pay to see the city's first big sports car race. There had never been a major sports car race in Edmonton, and the closest Calgary had ever come to watching this style and quality of racing was the Player's Prairie in Calgary the year before when the McLaren of Ross de St. Croix had decimated the field. Reg and Percy Booth were hoping for 18,000 paid admissions, which would have been enough to cover their $100,000 investment on the weekend. C.R.D.A. optimistically predicted 30,000. By 10:00 a.m. Sunday, both predictions had been passed. Incredibly, in a city where the football park barely seated 20,000 and the hockey arena less than half that, 41,200 people, the second-largest crowd to ever witness a sporting event in Canada at that time, paid to get in the gate for Edmonton's first taste of big-time sports car racing.

Preliminary races for amateurs filled the morning, although for some reason, Can-Am driver Brett Lunger took a Formula A car out with the locals in the open-wheel race and allowed the Formula Ford Merlin of Edmontonian Mike Atkin to close within ¹⁄₁₀ second at the finish. The sedan race was won by the Mini-Cooper S of Neil McGill, while the Lotus of Carl MacKenzie took the Sports and Sports Racing heat.

The feature race was preceded by a parachuting demonstration and a parade of drivers. For the preliminary races, the pace car had been driven by veteran Edmonton driver Bob Stokowski, while the Can-Am was to be led by Moss, with Stokowski riding as spotter. When Moss was signalled by the starter to move out, Stokowski was watching the starting grid, and seeing it still crowded with pit crew and photographers, told Moss to wait. The great English driver just shook his head and floored the Camaro. "They'll catch up." At the second corner, Stokowski looked over his shoulder and was shocked to find that the entire pack had done just that. "With Moss driving, I thought we were just flying, and there's all those guys right on our bumper. That's the first time I realized how really fast those Can-Am cars were."

In the race, Hulme and McLaren jumped into an immediate lead, but Hall soon made his way into second on lap four and successfully

1971 Can-Am: Fans show how to enjoy racing in Edmonton in late September. *(Mike Dean photo)*

1971 Edmonton Can-Am: Peter Revson, in toque, watches as his crew frantically works to remove the foreign bolt stuck in his intake manifold. The author, upper left of photo, stands ready to offer his unsolicited, yet remarkably inexpensive, advice. *(Mike Dean photo)*

1972 Edmonton Can-Am: Winner Mark Donohue shares a victory drink (Molson's, apparently) with the race queen. *(Mike Dean photo)*

A mid 1970s Formula Atlantic race. Despite great drivers racing in well-matched cars, crowds for road racing have dwindled badly since the late 1960s. *(Edmonton* Journal *photo from Provincial Archives of Alberta, J2151/1)*

held off McLaren until a rear brake-caliper failure put him in the pits for 15 laps. In the latter half of the race, Hall put on a driving show, setting fastest lap of the day, and repeatedly unlapping himself, moving from dead last to 11th by the finish. At the end, Hulme prevailed, taking home first-place money of $8,000, followed by McLaren ($5,000), with Donohue, who had to make a pit stop to have leaves cleared from his radiator, third ($4,000). The rest of the pack was at least four laps in arrears.

The success of the inaugural event meant that even with Mosport back on the schedule the following year, Edmonton would keep its race, and on a much better date. July 29 promised far less risk for the organizers than late autumn had the first year. The growing importance of the Can-Am series in international racing meant that drivers and, in the case of McLaren and Ferrari, entire teams, would work around overlapping Formula One and Can-Am schedules, enabling the big sports cars to run all over North America without having to worry about being snowed out.

As well as a better date, the 1969 race also offered more variety with the 6.2-litre V-12 Ferrari of New Zealander Chris Amon joining the show for the second time in the season, and Jim Hall with his new driver John Surtees debuting the radical 2H Chaparral. Completely different than the previous year's model, the new Chaparral featured an almost-coupe body with only a small opening for the top of the driver's helmet. An additional novelty was a clear-plastic door panel enabling spectators to watch the driver at work. The Ferrari worked quite well, qualifying third, but the Chaparral showed itself to be in need of a lot of development work, with Surtees qualifying fifth in the obviously ill-handling car, more than five seconds behind the pole. For the second year, McLaren and Hulme sat on the front row with identical times, this year almost five miles per hour faster than last. More powerful engines, massive high-mounted wings, and a philosophy of development by evolution rather than revolution appeared to be working well for them. In the race, however, Amon's Ferrari proved a handful for the McLarens, and by the end of the first lap the big red car was ahead of Hulme, its driver obviously looking for a way past McLaren. On the second lap he found it and held the lead for two laps. The pattern continued and in the first 40 laps of the race, the lead changed hands among the three New Zealanders 14 times—almost unheard of in Can-Am competition. On lap 36, McLaren dropped out with a broken piston, and Hulme, apparently realizing he would have to carry the team himself, got in front of Amon one final time and stayed there for the final 42 laps, winning by 5 seconds.

Again, the race was organized by Toronto's Canadian Race Drivers Association, but significantly, with the exception of chief starter Don Sharp who was an Edmontonian, each C.R.D.A. official had an N.A.S.C.C. member listed on the program as assistant. The locals were learning how to do the job, and in 1970, N.A.S.C.C. would be the organizing body.

The year 1970 saw the Can-Am joined by the Continental Formula A Championship as a professional race at E.I.S. Formula A—or Formula 5000 as the class was known in Europe—called for single-seat, open-wheel cars powered by stock-block American V-8s of no more than 5000-cc (305-cubic-inch) capacity. The rules provided for a 3-litre (186-cubic-inch) pure racing engine as an option, but that was rarely used. Less costly and less powerful than their Can-Am cousins, the Formula A cars were nevertheless formidable racing machines, and when they arrived in Edmonton on May 24, their qualifying times were only three seconds or so slower than the big sports cars. Some of that speed differential—perhaps most of it—was attributable to the drivers rather than the cars. Whereas the front rows of a Can-Am starting grid were filled by drivers of international repute, with journeymen and wealthy sportsmen rounding out the field, this latter group of drivers was the entire field in Formula A. Ron Grable, an American who had won some S.C.C.A. class championships in production cars, dominated the Formula A weekend with his Lola-Chev, setting fastest qualifying time, fastest race lap, and overall win in a field of 27 cars. Second was Torontonian Eppie Wietzes.

When the Can-Am cars paid their annual visit in late July, it was without Bruce McLaren, who had been killed in a testing crash at Goodwood, England the previous month. To his enduring credit, the team that McLaren had founded and staffed with top engineers, managers, and mechanics was now strong enough to survive on its own. His seat was taken by European Formula 5000 star Peter Gethin, and in what was becoming habitual fashion, the orange McLarens qualified for the two front starting positions. Denny Hulme had burned his hands in a practice crash at Indianapolis and was driving in pain, but he managed pole position. In the race itself, Hulme, Gethin, and Lothar Motschenbacher ran in close company for a short time, but the inevitable gaps opened up, and by the end, Hulme had won his third straight Klondike 200 by over half a minute from his teammate, with Motschenbacher a lap and a half down. The locally sponsored *Spirit of Edmonton,* with Graeme Lawrence driving, failed to finish, as did the much-touted BRM of George Eaton.

The year 1970 was also the first time the glow that had surrounded the Can-Am began to fade. In 1968, it was undeniably the sporting event in Edmonton. Pages of newspaper coverage were devoted to it, companies ran ads based on their support for, or attendance at, the race, and tens of thousands of people who had never been to an auto race before were there. But the repeated McLaren triumphs, the wide performance gap between the top cars and drivers and the rest of the field, and the long, flat nature of the track were all mitigating against the spectacle many had expected. Newspaper coverage shrank to the level one might expect for a good football game. With no tension left in the 1970 race after the three leaders began to pull apart, Terry Jones of the Edmonton *Journal* described it as "the most boring race since the days of Barney Oldfield"—this in spite of his employer donating the eponymous first-place trophy. Why Jones picked Barney Oldfield as a comparison to the Can-Am is also a bit curious, as Oldfield always had close finishes in races he promoted. This year, the crowd was announced as 45,000, but many weren't buying it. There were many empty reserved seats in the grandstands, and Reg Booth's explanation that many of those people were walking to the corners to watch the racing simply wasn't credible.

A new pro series came to town in 1971 with the arrival of the Trans-Am race for sedans. Unfortunately this series, which had been running since the mid '60s, had lost most of its factory teams at the end of the '70 season. Chevrolet and Chrysler were out, leaving only American Motors backing the Roger Penske / Mark Donohue Javelin, and Ford sponsoring the two-car Bud Moore team of George Follmer and Peter Gregg. A 23-car field was announced, but when the green flag dropped, only 14 answered the call. For a while, the three factory-backed cars engaged in a thrilling race, but gradually Donohue pulled ahead, and Gregg dropped out. Donohue and Follmer finished six laps ahead of the third-place car. There was a separate race for under-2-litre cars, and that was a walk-away for the factory-backed, superbly prepared Datsun 510 of John Morton. The field was so thin for that one that organizers invited a number of locals to join the pack. Mike Atkin, Jamie Browne, Bob Hawkins, and Ray McGowan, all competent amateur race drivers in decent cars, were added, bringing the total car count to just 11.

This was the only year the Trans-Am would appear in Edmonton.

The real entertainment that day—unless you count the pit fire at the Ford Mustang of Vancouver's John Hall as entertainment—was the Formula B race, which counted towards the Canadian Championship. Without question the best race to take place on the 2.5-mile track to that time, it featured no less than 23 lead changes over 40 laps. At the end, Jacques Couture of Quebec led David McConnell across the finish line by half a second, and Craig Hill by another $\frac{3}{10}$ second. This race marked the change in the format of the Canadian Championship from one of Formula A and Formula B running for two separate awards, to only Formula B with a single championship.

The Continental Formula A series visited again in August, and Englishman David Hobbs took the win from the previous year's winner, Ron Grable.

The Can-Am returned to its high-risk, late-September date in 1971. McLaren was again back with two cars, this time Peter Revson backing up Denny Hulme. Competition came from the Jo Siffert Porsche 917, Jackie Oliver in the new Shadow, and World Formula One champion Jackie Stewart in a Lola. Nevertheless, the McLarens arrived in Edmonton holding the top two positions on the Can-Am points list. A sign of the declining popularity of the race was the fact that race sponsor Molson had to take out a paid advertising feature in the Edmonton *Journal* to get back to the amount of ink that had been used on the event in the late '60s.

On race day, the Northern Alberta weather did its worst, bringing rain and a cold wind. Revson was 11 laps late to start because a bolt—not one that would fit a McLaren car—was found in the intake manifold of his engine. Someone, apparently intent on sabotage, had been allowed too close to the car. With Hulme on his own, he trailed both Stewart and Oliver. Stewart very uncharacteristically spun out twice, and Revson, once on the track, did a fine job of delaying Oliver. Siffert, who might have been expected to be part of such an entertaining scrap, seemed to fight his ill-handling Porsche all afternoon. In the end, only 15,000 people watched the best Can-Am race yet, as Hulme took his fourth-straight Edmonton win.

The Formula B national championship was back in 1972, this time with some local participation. Ric Forest was an Edmonton driver who had done well in regional races in Formula Ford, but now had a brand new March Formula B. Edmonton would be his first race in the series. When qualifying began, it was raining, and Forest had no wet-weather tires. He soon bought a set and installed them on his only set of wheels, in place of his slicks. They worked well, and in qualifying, he earned pole position. Race day dawned cold and dry, but Forest, still owning only one set of wheels, was stuck with the wets. Just before the race, the rain came, helping him and his wet tires to a lead of over 40 seconds. With 15 laps to go, the rain stopped, and as the track dried, the pack began to close in on him. In the end, he held on, despite gearbox problems, for a nine-second victory. In his first-ever Formula B race, the local boy had conquered a field of over 20 drivers, most with far more experience than he. After enduring various mechanical problems, fellow Edmontonian Barry Fox was classified 20th. Regrettably, the weather, and the lack of the big names that Edmonton race fans had come to accept as normal, meant only 2,000 people witnessed the event. Ric Forest would not win again that year, but he would accumulate enough second-

and third-place finishes to end the season in third place overall in the Canadian championship.

Also in 1972, Continental Formula A paid what would be its final visit to E.I.S. The race was won again by David Hobbs. Ron Grable's record of good fortune on the track ended when he slid straight into the earth bank on the outside of the bridge turn.

Still tempting fate, the Can-Am organizers scheduled the 1972 Edmonton race for October 1. Since the last Edmonton race, the Roger Penske team had signed an agreement to field a team for the Porsche factory. As in previous races, the front row of the grid was composed of two cars of the same make; but this time, they were turbocharged Porsche 917/10s, not McLarens. Porsche drivers Mark Donohue and George Follmer qualified a full second ahead of the McLarens of Hulme and Revson. In the race, Hulme and Revson bulled their way into an early lead, but pit stops by Revson and Follmer left it a two-car race between Hulme and Donohue. After 30 laps, Donohue, with apparent ease, passed the McLaren and went on to a comfortable win, ending Denny Hulme's four-year hold on the race. The crowd was announced as 30,000 fans.

1973's Can-Am confirmed what many had sensed was happening the year before: the McLarens had been caught and defeated. But that only meant that another team had taken the dominant role in the series. The Porsches, with their rumoured 1,000 or 1,200 horse-power, left the rest of the field as little more than also-rans. Same show, different star.

To add interest to the Can Am races, the organizers split their races into two heats. In Edmonton, this meant 30 laps on Saturday, and 50 on Sunday. At the end, it made no difference, as in the final Donohue lapped everyone but second-place man George Follmer. The stated Sunday crowd was 22,000, or roughly half of that seen in the late 1960s races.

There was no Edmonton Can-Am in 1974. The series struggled through that season, its last, with only half the calendar of four years earlier. Audiences throughout North America joined Edmontonians in voting with their feet and staying away from races that seemed unable to break the pattern of single-marque domination set first by

McLaren, then Porsche. The unlimited engines that had created so much speed and excitement in the series' early years were ultimately its downfall. McLaren was able to get from General Motors 500-cubic-inch engines before anyone else, then Porsche built their five-litre, double-turbocharged motors with over 1,000 horsepower. At one point, Porsche built and tested a 16-cylinder monster, but never used it in competition. No other team could match the horsepower available to these two teams, so there was never a level playing field.

As the major road races came and went, the one professional constant throughout the years was the Player's Canadian Championship. From 1969 through 1978, first the Formula A, then the B, and finally the Atlantic cars showed up, generally staging a good, competitive race. Spectator counts were low, but for those who took the trouble to attend, there was the opportunity to watch some of the future superstars of the sport, including 1986 Indianapolis winner Bobby Rahal and the spectacular Gilles Villeneuve, who would later go on to be the first Canadian to win a World Championship Formula One race. Villeneuve, arguably the fastest (recognizing how subjective that word can be) driver of all time,[1] raced in Edmonton 1974 through 1977, winning the latter two years.

By 1981, the Can-Am series had been resurrected, but as a cost-controlled program. In place of the unlimited sports-racing cars were Formula 5000 single-seaters, with fenders added. New, too, were the drivers. Donohue, McLaren, Revson, and Siffert were dead. Amon, Eaton, Hall, Hulme, and Motschenbacher had retired. In their place came a cast of journeyman competitors, with a few up-and-coming stars such as Al Unser, Jr. Edmonton Oilers hockey team owner Peter Pocklington used his abundant promotional skills to attract Lethbridge Brewery as title sponsor for a renewal of the Edmonton Can-Am on August 16, 1981. The winner was Australian sports car driver Geoff Brabham.

The 1981 Can-Am was to be the final major road race at Edmonton International Speedway. As is detailed elsewhere in this

---

1. Villeneuve, who was killed in a practice crash in 1982, so dominated Formula One during his brief career there, that at the United States Grand Prix in 1979, he qualified an incredible 11 seconds ahead of his nearest rival on the 5.5-kilometre circuit—in pouring rain.

book, economics and politics would put an end to the great racing facility. The changing nature of the sport, with Formula One drivers contractually prohibited from taking part in different racing series, meant Alberta would never again see world champions on its soil.

Until it was gone, we didn't know how lucky we had been.

CHAPTER 24

CAPP AND FEDDERLY

Persistence of vision
— Peter Egan, *Road & Track* magazine

While Edmontonians Bernie Fedderly and Terry Capp have spent the past two decades of their drag racing careers on separate paths, they were admitted together to the Canadian Motorsport Hall of Fame, and that is entirely appropriate because it was as a young partnership that they achieved their earliest successes and came to the notice of the drag racing industry.

The two met in the early 1960s while attending St. Joseph's High School and quickly found common interest. Bernie was enrolled in the automotive program, and Terry was a guy who just wanted to drive fast. Terry's driving career goes back to the age of 11 when living in Highvale, near Lake Wabamun. He was enrolled in weekly boxing lessons in Stoney Plain, and he needed a ride. A neighbour had agricultural association meetings to attend the same evenings in the town, and offered to drive Terry. The only complicating matter was the neighbour's habit of stopping at the nearest beer parlour after his meeting and prior to picking up Terry at the gym. One night, realizing he was in no condition to drive, he handed the keys to Terry and told the youngster to drive them home, an order that was promptly obeyed, and repeated almost every week for a year. The trip was over 30 miles, and it gave Terry practice that he would put to good use in later years.

Of the thousands of partnerships that formed in the early years of drag racing, most failed, mainly because they lacked a clear and defined division of responsibilities. As Bernie recalls, "There were too many drivers, but never enough mechanics." If everyone wanted to drive the car, who was going to build it? The strength of the Capp-Fedderly partnership lay in the fact that the talents of the two men complemented, rather than matched, each other. Terry wanted to drive race cars and was quickly developing skills in that direction, whereas Bernie's passion was for the designing, building, modifying, and maintaining of cars. When the two met, Bernie was building a 1936 Ford coach, and Terry had just acquired a 1932 Ford pick-up that he was planning to turn into "the ultimate street machine." Bernie pitched in on Terry's project, but the '32 never made it as far as the street.

At about the time in 1960 when the "deuce" had been fitted with a small-block Chev V-8, a drag race was scheduled at the Royal Canadian Air Force base at Namao, just north of Edmonton. It only made sense to see how the car would perform, so its builders towed it to the meet, where it turned in a respectable, if not winning, time of 15.42 seconds at 86 miles per hour (137 kmh). That naturally led to questions about what could be done to make it go even faster. Improvements were made, and in the end, the car that was to be the "ultimate street machine" was never licensed for the street, but enjoyed an honourable career as a racer. The old Ford was sold in the mid 1960s, but in 2002 Terry was able to track it down and buy it back.

Building race cars does not always go according to schedule, and one weekend Terry and Bernie found themselves without an operable car on the eve of one of the early Highway 14X races. Terry's sister Frances, who at age 19 was already employed as a schoolteacher,[1] owned a Jaguar XK-E, a 1948 Ford, and an Austin-Healey 3000. On this particular weekend, she was planning to take her XK-E to Fort MacLeod for a sports car race. Terry asked if he could borrow the

---

1. Frances Capp graduated from high school at age 16, and by 19 had achieved her university degree, honours with distinction. Tragically she died at the age of 26.

Healey while she was gone, and Frances agreed, not enquiring as to where he planned to drive it. Terry and Bernie hopped in and quickly entered it in the drag meet. English sports cars were never intended to be drag race cars, and this one was no exception—by midafternoon the transmission was in pieces. "Bernie had never worked on English stuff before," recalls Terry, "but he managed to figure it out and got it back on the road for her."

In 1967 the two racers, while on a weekend hunting trip, found a 1951 English Ford Anglia in the proverbial farmer's field. It wasn't in running condition, but the body was sound. They bought it from the farmer for $50, then they immediately stripped off the running gear and sold it, recovering all but $10 of their original investment. Within a year, the little car, with help from Richard Chevalier of Pioneer Automotive among others, had become the 327 Chev-powered Capp-Fedderly *Pioneer Anglia.* A true hot rod, the Anglia used parts from Corvette, Chevrolet, Willys, Ford Econoline, and Triumph TR-2 donor cars, as well as home-built traction bars, front axles, and roll cage.

Just as the car was being completed, the organizers of the inaugural Can-Am race for sports cars in Edmonton invited them to give a demonstration run prior to the start of the sports car feature. The partners had to scramble to get the car ready in time, and when they arrived at the track, they hadn't driven a single practice run. Not knowing what to expect, Terry wound the engine up and dropped the clutch. "Right now I'm doing this massive wheel-stand. The front end came up about four feet. I knew I couldn't just back off, because if I dropped the front end back down real fast, the suspension would break. So I kept my foot down. I couldn't see ahead because the nose was so high, so I watched out the side window to see if I was getting closer or further away from the guardrail. You know, that car was so stable, it didn't even try to go sideways on me. I shifted to second fast enough to keep from dropping the front, and then in third it started to come down gently. I think the sports car crowd liked it."

The Anglia was a success, but the two racers were continually moving up to higher classes. Their motor came out of the Anglia and into a C-class dragster which they ran for two years. This was followed in 1970 by a Dickson-chassis top Fuel Dragster with a 392-cubic-inch Chrysler hemi. The new car was a consistent performer in the mid-six-second range, at one time holding the Canadian top speed record of 225 miles per hour (364 kmh). At sea level in Seattle, they were able to reach a very impressive 236 miles per hour (382 kmh), but by that time the technology of drag racing was moving the engine from the front to the rear, rendering their car obsolete. The remaining front-engined Top Fuel cars were looking for places and points, not wins. For a while, they held the record as the fastest front-engined dragster in the world, but Terry and Bernie wanted more than a consolation prize. In 1972, they joined with a third partner, Wes VanDusen, in the ownership of a new rear-engined chassis with one of the second-generation Chrysler hemis, a 426. The car ran as *Wheeler Dealer,* the name of the speed-equipment company Terry owned.

The early 1970s were great years for drag racers in Edmonton. They had a world-class facility on their doorstep, and a perfectly serviceable strip three hours down the road in Calgary. At one time Edmonton was home to six Top Fuel dragsters, the greatest concentration outside of Southern California, and arguably the highest number per capita anywhere. Of the drivers, at least four—Gary Beck, Terry Capp, Gary Egbert, and Graham Light—were capable of running with the best in the business. Sponsorships, never really easy to come by, were now at least possible. Pacemaker, Bubble-Up, Export A, and Reliable Engine were all major backers of Edmonton dragsters. An example of the openness of the Edmonton business community to racers was Ken Haywood of Kentwood Ford, who offered Terry and Bernie a truck, "take your pick," to haul their car. The two racers nervously checked out the huge inventory of pick-ups and chose a very plain half-ton. When they showed their selection to Ken, he shook his head. "That won't do the job." He took them back onto the lot and pulled out a fully optioned three-quarter-ton with a super-cab and a big-block V-8. "This should work for you. I know you boys will take good care of it. Bring it back at the end of your season."

1968: The Capp-Fedderly Anglia does one of its famous wheelstands.
(*Terry and Rachelle Capp collection*)

The eyes of a
champion: Terry in
an early funny car.
(*Terry and Rachelle
Capp collection*)

Indianapolis, September 1980: Crewman Al Mah waves the flag in victory circle. L to R: Mah, N.H.R.A. Founder-President Wally Parks, Miss Winston, Terry Capp, Bernie Fedderley. *(Terry and Rachelle Capp collection)*

1988: Rebirth of a career: Terry in the *Royal Canadian*.
(Terry and Rachelle Capp collection)

In 1973 the team had its first success, winning the American Hot Rod Association's version of the world championship in Tulsa, Oklahoma. The following year they moved up to the sport's major league, the National Hot Rod Association, and finished ranked 7th. Two years later they were 5th, and by 1979, 3rd. During this time, Terry had also gained his Top Funny Car licence and was competing in both classes—often on the same weekend.

In 1980, the team achieved its greatest success, winning the N.H.R.A. U.S. Nationals at Indianapolis—the second Edmonton-based team to accomplish the feat, after the Beck-Peets wins of 1972–73.

By 1982, the individual talents of Terry Capp and Bernie Fedderly were so highly regarded in the sport that each was receiving invitations to join other teams. Edmonton was certainly a hub of professional drag racing activity, but it wasn't the centre of this sport's universe—that was still Southern California. Bernie decided to move there to further what was by now his career. Terry was negotiating with the giant Miller brewing company on a sponsorship deal, and had reached a tentative agreement that would have required him to move south too, but instead decided to end his career. The idea of packing up his wife, Rachelle, and their children Jaret, who was ten, and Terra-Lynn, just one, and moving thousands of miles to a different country was not attractive. "I was a Canadian and proud of it." A further irritant was the amount of time racers spend away from home. "I left home one spring when my son was in the cradle, and by the time I came back, he was walking."

For six years, Terry kept his back turned to his sport, not even following it in the media. He went into the car business and concentrated on career and family, but racing, like any addiction, never entirely left him.

Meanwhile, Bernie Fedderly, having moved to California, worked for a number of teams, ultimately joining the John Force Top Funny Car team in 1992. Depending on one's point of view, 1992 was either the worst or the best year to join the Force-Castrol team; it was the first season in three that Force had not been crowned N.H.R.A. Funny Car Champion. That would soon turn around as the team, with Bernie working alongside crew chief Austin Coil, would become the highest-profile, most successful team in the sport. It would claim the next nine consecutive titles, a record unmatched in the major leagues of any sport.[2]

Back in Alberta, Terry Capp's retirement ended in 1988 when Edmonton car dealer and long-time race supporter Ron Hodgson called one winter day to invite Terry and Jaret to travel with Ron and his son Jeff to the Winternationals N.H.R.A. race at Pomona, California. Terry, still in denial, refused the offer. A short while later, Ron appeared on Terry's doorstep, holding the paid-for Winternational tickets. "It was pretty hard to say no at that point," recalls Terry.

Once at the big race, Terry quickly re-established his old contacts. Bernie Fedderly was working for Larry Minor's team, which had a chassis for sale. Ron bought it. Terry and Ron began comparing notes on what parts each owned, and they soon realized they had a race car between them. Dale Adams and Gord Jenner were brought into the nascent team, and then a second car was acquired in partnership with Dwayne Tetz of Stettler. A two-car team needs a second driver, and Gordie Bonin, who, like Terry, had been out of the driver's seat for a while, was picked. Terry's car would carry the by-now legendary Alberta drag-racing name, *Royal Canadian*. The team, labelled the "Over the Hill Gang" by Edmonton *Sun* sports writer Terry Jones, then renamed the "Over the Belt Gang" by Capp, soon proved it was more than just a nostalgia trip for a bunch of has-beens. Terry, still wearing the trimmed beard that had been his trademark in the 1970s, took the *Royal Canadian* to Race City in Calgary and promptly broke the track record by 25 miles per hour (40 kmh). In August, in only his third race, he erased the old track record, held by Don Garlits, with a pass of 5.39 seconds at 271 miles per hour (439 kmh), to win the American Hot Rod Association World Finals. A month later he was up to 280 mph (453 kmh) at the

2. The second-best record for consecutive championships is eight, held by the Boston Celtics of the National Basketball Association. Next are Formula One driver Michael Schumacher with six, and the Montreal Canadiens of the National Hockey League and the New York Yankees of the American Baseball League with five each.

N.H.R.A. U.S. Nationals in Indianapolis, qualifying ninth. The following year he was also driving Dave Korzan's Top Fuel funny car. For a decade, the once-retired racer ran in events all over North America, keeping both his Top Fuel and Funny Car licences current. In 2000, at the age of 56, Terry went back to the A.H.R.A. World Finals in Spokane and took that title for a third time.

As this is being written in 2003, Bernie Fedderley and Terry Capp are still involved in the sport they love. Their admission to the Hall of Fame in 2002 didn't mark the end of their active careers. Bernie is now co-crew chief of the John Force team, sharing responsibilities with Austin Coil, supervising the work of 40 employees. Terry works full-time in the insolvency department of Price Waterhouse and races every chance he gets. With career-best figures of 299 miles per hour (484 kmh) and 5.02 seconds, he wants to clear 300 mph and get under five seconds before he retires—again.[3]

---

3. On July 4, 2004 Terry Capp, at age 59, achieved his goal. Driving a new Capp-Hodgson car, again bearing the *Royal Canadian* name, he completed a run of 4.75 seconds / 317 miles per hour (514 kmh) at the Rocky Mountain Nationals at Edmonton's Budweiser Park.

CHAPTER 25

VINTAGE ON THE PRAIRIE: THE SPORTS CARS MATURE

The cost? He shrugs: "Whatever...You only live once."
—Ken Staples, Alberta racer for 38 straight seasons

The opening of Edmonton International Speedway in 1968 took place at a time when racing in general, and road racing in particular, were passing through a period of profound change.

Safety, which had been of marginal concern for the first decade of the sport in Alberta, became a major issue in the mid 1960s. Roll bars, seat belts, shoulder harnesses, driving suits, fuel tanks, helmets, and oil catch cans were all either required for the first time, or subject to greater scrutiny. Rules permitting or mandating the removal of non-essential material in street-based cars made it far less practical than before to use a racing car for day-to-day transportation.

Canada Class disappeared as Formula Vee, for cars based on stock Volkswagen components, and Formula Ford, for more sophisticated racing chassis powered by English Ford engines, took over the low-cost end of the single-seat market. These were joined by the engine-displacement-based formulae: A, B, and C. The sedans, which for years had raced as the poor cousins of sports car fields, now came into their own, encouraged by the immense popularity of the Mini-series cars from Britain, and the powerful sports sedans of the American manufacturers. By 1969 there was a separate championship for four classes of sedans, the Sedan Challenge Cup.

While the multiplicity of classes ensured there was a class just right for every taste, it also badly watered down the competition in an already-fractured sport. In 1969 C.A.S.C. listed 21 separate racing classes. Normal entry lists had no more than 60 cars, so there were often only one or two cars in each of several classes. With trophies or dash plaques awarded to the winners of each class, meaningful car-to-car racing was not common. After the initial glow of enthusiasm created by the early Can-Ams, crowds at regional-level races shrunk to all-but invisible levels. As Gavin Breckenridge had discovered so many years earlier, fans like lots of action, and small fields of sports cars strung out over a long race track don't provide much of that. A driver may know that he is travelling over 200 kmh, and feel the pull of the wind on his helmet, but seen from a distance, he provides little more excitement for a spectator than does a truck passing by on a highway.

Nevertheless, fuelled by growing numbers of drivers, sports car racing continued, much in the manner of other amateur sports, with the participants prepared to pay for the sheer joy of competition and the exhilaration of speed—crowd count be damned.

The sprawling, thinly-populated nature of Canada makes genuine national sporting championships difficult to organize and expensive to contest, but C.A.S.C. tried. Beginning in 1962, it ran a National Racing Championship for sports cars, but found there were few cars in the country capable of keeping up to the handful of truly world-class racing machines with a chance at the title. In most seasons, not more than two or three teams travelled the breadth of the country seeking the championship. A typical national championship starting grid would have a front row of Lotuses, Coopers, and RS Porsches, and a field filled out with the mainly production-based cars found at any regional race. Only rarely, as in the case of the memorable wheel-to-wheel, wire-to-wire Phil Smyth / Lotus 23–Ludwig Heimrath / Cooper Cobra battle at Davidson in 1964, was there much of a race for the overall win in a national event. In any case, the national championship had nothing to do with 95 percent of amateur racers.

In 1972, C.A.S.C., with sponsorship from the Player's cigarette company, began the "Player's Race of Champions" for the sedan and production sports car classes, and formulas Ford and Vee. The concept, which was pioneered successfully by S.C.C.A. as the "Run-Offs," was to bring the best regional competitors together from across the country for a weekend of races for each individual class. The top ten racers from each formula in each region, together with the top five in each production and sedan class, would be invited. A modest travel allowance (tow money) would be provided, varying with distance travelled.

In the 23 years the Player's event was run, it only appeared once at Edmonton, that in 1973. The majority of the races were set at Le Circuit–Mont Tremblant, Quebec, and Mosport, Ontario. Given their large numbers and their familiarity with the tracks, it is not surprising that Ontario and Quebec drivers were the most consistent winners. Alberta drivers, though, remained competitive, and did take some titles:

David Morris, Formula Ford, 1973
Cappy Thomson, Formula Vee, 1973
Harald Hubka, Formula Vee, 1974
Ric Forest, B Sedan, 1973
Fred Del Piro, GT-3, 1982, 1983, 1984
Don Rushton, B Sports Racing, 1974
Don Robertson, Formula Vee, 1988

In 1978, C.A.S.C. finally came to grips with the problem of the plethora of classes within the sport. The eight production sports car and four sedan classes were dissolved and replaced by performance-based classes GT-1, GT-2, GT-3, and GT-4.

In 1982, Edmonton International Speedway closed, leaving the province without a road course. Sports car racing was either on ice, primarily with N.A.S.C.C.'s ambitious program, or it involved travel. The venerable Westwood Circuit near Vancouver was still operating, as was the Gimli, Manitoba airport track, attracting those Alberta racers with the motivation and resources to make the long treks.

Alberta remained without a road-racing facility from 1982 to 1987, when the Shell road course opened at Race City Speedway in Calgary. At two miles, it was slightly shorter than the long track at E.I.S., and was similarly flat. It lacked the pit garages and paved paddock of the Edmonton track, but after four years of having to travel to an even shorter track at Westwood, or to an old airport on the shores of Lake Winnipeg, no Alberta racers were complaining.

The opening of the Calgary road course was timely in that it enabled the Player's Challenge (later to become known as the Player's Ltd. / GM Motorsport Series), a series for showroom-stock Chevrolet Camaros and Pontiac Firebirds, to expand westward from the Ontario and Quebec base it had established in 1986. For 1987 there would now be separate Eastern and Western series, the latter involving three races each for Race City and Westwood. The first Calgary race, held July 12, 1987, was won by local boy Paul Gilgan.

Drawn by the fixed price of the cars and good prize money, drivers from a variety of racing backgrounds appeared. Formula One driver Allen Berg returned from Europe; sprint car star Gary Miller tried road course racing. Older drivers like Calgary veteran Norbert Glimpel came out of retirement. Suddenly, the thin, widely disparate fields typical of a normal amateur sports-car weekend were replaced with huge swarms of virtually-identical cars crowding, bumping, and scratching for every advantage.

The Player's / GM rules required the competitors to buy special-order cars. The cars were reasonably priced at around $18,000, and purchasers had to place a bond of $5,000, forfeited if they failed to participate in the series. The cars were completely street-legal, and in fact Player's and General Motors encouraged competitors to use them for day-to-day transport—but no speeding! All cars were checked on a dynamometer to ensure a minimal horsepower variance, and their main engine, ignition, and fuel-delivery components were sealed against tampering. Nevertheless, there were always rumours that so-and-so had found a way to cheat. "We went around the slowest turn nose-to-tail, and then he pulls out four car lengths on me down the next straight! Legal? I don't think so!" Policing became a major challenge for the organizers, particularly in the area of electronic engine-management systems. Post-race inspections included searching winning cars for switches that could be activated by the driver to alter anything from fuel injection to ignition advance.

To be sure, there was some cheating, but probably not as much as some drivers would have us believe. The most blatant example came in the Calgary race in the final season when the two leading cars, both of the same team, suddenly caught fire. The initial explanation by the team was "brake fluid leak." GM impounded the cars and rumours—credible ones—came out to the effect that inspectors had found fuel-return lines that had been crimped, thereby increasing fuel-injector pressure. The crimping left the steel lines dangerously thin and vulnerable to leaks, thereby causing the fires.

In 1988, the Player's / GM series was joined by a similar event for Honda Civics, the Honda / Michelin Challenge. Like the Player's / GM cars, the Hondas raced at both Calgary and Westwood, with the season champion being decided on the basis of combined results. Both series offered good prize money and close, wheel-to-wheel competition—rarities in amateur road racing.

Qualifying times in both series were, of necessity, measured to the 1/1000 second, and racers' imaginations were stretched trying to find any advantage. A popular technique in the Honda series was "bump drafting." This involved two cars working together in qualifying sessions. The following car would attempt to run into the rear of the leading car, particularly on corner exits, in effect giving it a push down the next straight. Later, by agreement, the two would reverse positions and do it all over again.

A year after that, a third semi-pro series joined the mix. Canon and Yokohama combined to back a Western series for Formula 1600 (nee Formula Ford) single-seat racers. Like the two sedan series, these cars had already run a season in Ontario and Quebec, and in the West would run at both Race City and Westwood. Perhaps because of the higher cost of a good car—new ones were selling for $30–35,000 at the time—the series never attracted near the car count of the two sedan series.

Unfortunately for the racers, each of these series was, at its core, an advertising program for the sponsors, and like any advertising program, each had a finite lifespan. In the early '90s, all three disappeared within a short time. The end of the Player's / GM series came at a time when GM was struggling financially, and the market for the V-8 sports sedans that had grown almost exponentially in the '60s ands '70s with the rise of the baby boomers, suddenly shrank as that

Changes over the years in what is considered a "production car" are illustrated in these two photos. The first is of Bob Stokowski in his MG in 1962. There is a single roll bar, the bumpers have been removed, and the windshield is cut down. That's it. *(Bob Stokowski collection)*

The second photo is of Ken Staples some 30 years later. The Volkswagen is completely stripped, with a roll cage effectively acting as a supplementary frame. The stock body is augmented with various plastic pieces designed to improve aerodynamic performance, and to cover the wide tires and wheels. The lights are fake, and the car cannot be legally driven on the street. Sedans are now in the majority. *(Gerry Frechette photo)*

By the mid 1970s, the gentlemen racers of two decades earlier had been replaced by more aggressive drivers not afraid to "trade paint," as witness this 1976 ice-racing scene near Edmonton. *(Alberta Provincial Archives photo, J-3000, courtesy Edmonton* Journal*)*

Typical of the two late '80s / early '90s single-marque sedan series is this Honda / Michelin race scene from Calgary's Race City Speedway. *(Gerry Frechette photo)*

same demographic found their needs better satisfied with sedans and mini-vans. Honda / Michelin came to an end when the principal backer of the series within Honda left the company. The Canon / Yokohama series really died from a lack of participation.

Some drivers left the sport; many carried on in sports car racing, their talents now honed by the intense competition of one-make racing, and a few, particularly from Player's / GM, went oval track racing with the new CASCAR stock car series.

In recent years, vintage car racing has been a growing part of the sport. Vintage car racing began many years earlier in England, with people restoring cars such as Lagondas, Bentleys, Bugattis, and Alfa Romeos from the 1920s and '30s. In Canada, the history doesn't go that deep, but it doesn't need to. Auto racing is based on technology, and technology is always moving. By the late 1980s, the cars that first attracted many people to the sport—the sleek little sports cars of the 1950s and '60s, the "pony cars" of a decade later, and even the early Formula Vees and Fords—were no longer competitive in open racing. They may be fun to drive, but the level of fun diminishes quickly if entire races are spent simply trying to stay out of everyone else's way. By 1993, there were enough people enthused about the idea of racing older cars that the Calgary Vintage Racing Club was formed. Since then the club has held races in conjunction with regular sports car cards at Race City Speedway, and it also runs its own annual race meet, Vintage on the Prairie. Competing vehicles range from aging sedans to Ford GT-40s and McLarens. It costs money to enter, and once in, there is no prize money. The amateur sportsmen who began it all in 1953 would be pleased.

*   *   *

Auto racing can consume unlimited amounts of time and money. Racing is a world where the life of tires is measured in minutes—hours if you're lucky; where four miles to the gallon (58 litres per 100 km) is considered reasonable fuel consumption; where cars crash and engines explode. In racing, "all-nighter" refers not to a party or hitting the books, but to a dusk-to-dawn scramble to repair a damaged car so it can race the next day. "It's midnight. Can we send someone out to the chicken place to get supper?" There is also the chance, albeit slight these days, that someone might get killed. Not surprisingly, racing is a world that puts huge strains on family budgets and social lives. Many an eager new racer in May has decided by September that his first season will also be his last.

If a year of racing is that much effort, imagine the determination and love of the sport required to carry on for four or more decades. Here are three drivers who have done just that.

Ken Staples began his career in 1966 in an MGA, and has not missed a season of racing since. The MG was replaced by a Sunbeam Tiger, then a Corvette. Over the next 17 years, he won seven C.A.S.C. Prairie Region class championships, set two class lap records at Edmonton International Speedway, one at the Knox Mountain Hill Climb at Kelowna, BC, and lost count of his ice-race wins. Beginning in 1988, he concentrated on the two hyper-competitive showroom-stock classes: Honda / Michelin, and Player's / GM. Over the next three years, he took three outright wins and a lap record (Westwood, BC) in his Honda, and was a consistently high finisher in the Camaro. Many times, he drove both cars in lengthy races on the same day, having to adjust his driving style in minutes from a low-powered, short-wheelbase, front-wheel-drive, understeering Honda, to a very powerful, rear-wheel-drive Camaro. When Alberta was without a race track in the mid '80s, he travelled as far as Montreal to race.

When Ken Staples thumbs through the pile of booklets that are his racing logbooks, and looks at the hundreds of races he has competed in, he wonders aloud how much money it has all cost, then shrugs, "Whatever. You only live once…"

Bob Stokowski is 68 years old, and, as he was at 28, is still a very difficult man to beat on any ice-race course. In the 1960s, he would take his MGA out against Porsches and Citroens—cars with their engines above the drive wheels and theoretically far better suited to icy roads—and regularly beat them. With a little parts help from the car's maker, British Motor Corporation, and often with only his wife Bev as pit crew, he was just as tough on asphalt. From the MG he moved to a Porsche, and then to a Formula Vee, enjoying success in both. Bob quit asphalt racing in the 1970s, then served as chief steward for the Honda / Michelin series. He still competes on ice in his Datsun 240Z, and often wins, adding to his collection of 65 trophies, and an almost equal number of dash plaques. Retirement from racing is planned for age 70, but Bob becomes less sure about that when reminded that actor and amateur racer Paul Newman is still competing at 79…

Like Stokowski, Jack Ondrack began his career in the late 1950s. His first car was a T-series MG, bought from an Edmonton used car dealer with a colourful reputation. Within days, it was obvious the car was in need of a lot of work—engine, steering, and transmission to start with. Jack took it to Bill Chevalier at Pioneer Automotive, who told Jack the car wasn't safe to drive. Jack couldn't afford to have everything that was wrong with the car fixed, and so prepared to leave. Chevalier called him back. "I told you it's not safe to drive, now leave it here." Some weeks later, Chevalier handed back the now completely overhauled MG to young Jack, along with his bill for $175, a fraction of what the work was worth. "Bill helped out a lot of young guys that way. Kids got their start in racing because of him."

In the intervening four and a half decades, Jack has raced often, in a variety of cars, including a Buick he had to ask the N.A.S.C.C. board of directors for permission to run with sports cars on ice in 1962. There have been gaps in his racing career as he concentrated on other interests. He has had a variety of businesses, and in the 1980s took time to write a book on big-game hunting in Alberta. Now approaching 70, Jack still competes in a variety of cars. Success in his career enables him to travel not only to races in the Western provinces, but also to compete in such places as California and New Zealand. In 2002, he took a turbocharged Porsche 911-6 to an overall win ahead of more than 60 entrants in the Open Track Challenge, a series of seven races on seven tracks in the southwestern United States spread over just seven days. Not bad for a guy receiving pension cheques.

CHAPTER 26

CAPITAL CITY RACEWAY

If there is one thing auto racers and land developers share, it is optimism.
—The author

"If you want to know anything about how that place got going, you have to talk to Liz Oglu. She's the one that made it happen."

That is Geoff Goodwin's answer to a request for information about the founding of Edmonton's Capital City Raceway, later Labatt Raceway, later Budweiser Park. Goodwin has at times been a shareholder, a director, and general manager of the facility, but he takes no credit for the years of effort it took to move it from a wish to reality.

Liz Oglu's enthusiasm for the sport goes back to the mid 1950s, when she attended stock car races at Speedway Park. Later when she married Wally Oglu, she became actively involved with his Super Gas drag car, and deeply enough committed to the sport that she became the first female president of Capital City Hot Rod Association.

After the final drag race at Edmonton International Speedway in 1982, Northern Alberta racers had no track of their own, and Calgary had only a ⅛-mile strip. The sport that had flourished beyond all reasonable expectations throughout the 1960s and 1970s found itself in worse shape than it had been since 1954. There was no place to race, and this time there was no Gordon E. Taylor to come to the rescue. If the drag racers wanted a place to ply their sport, they would have to find it themselves. Liz remembers the winter of 1982–83 as a time spent "listening to everyone bellyaching and moaning 'woe is me.' People had lots of ideas about getting Edmonton International started again, but Graham Light told them it just won't work. The track was dead, but a lot of people didn't want to believe it."

From the time E.I.S. closed, Liz realized a new facility would have to be built, but the cost of land and improvements would be enormous. As long as Edmonton-area racers harboured any fantasies that E.I.S. could be resurrected, raising serious money for new construction would be even more difficult than usual in such ventures. However, by late 1983 the racing community, seeing fence posts planted in the now-crumbling asphalt of E.I.S., had largely turned around and faced the reality that a new plant was needed. Beginning with C.C.H.R.A., Liz canvassed the car clubs and racing associations of the greater Edmonton area, and with 12 on board, formed Alberta United Racers Association (AURA). Each club chipped in $100 seed money, and then the real business of fund-raising, under Liz's leadership as project coordinator, began. By the following year when C.C.H.R.A. held its 25th-anniversary banquet, enthusiasm for the project was growing. Volunteers were signing on to work at bingos, car raffles, swap meets, and car shows, and by 1990, a half million dollars had been raised. Not enough to build a proper multi-use racing facility, but enough to get one started.

Hand in hand with the fund-raising was the search for a location. If raising money to build a race track is tough, finding a piece of land to sit it on is far more so. Most urban areas are now surrounded by acreages owned and occupied by people who either guard the reality or harbour the fantasy of quiet, peaceful, country living. The very mention of any sort of commercial development in their neighbourhood, let alone an auto race track, is enough to send earnest citizens bustling from door to door with petitions demanding that such an outrage be immediately stopped. Liz knew, particularly after witnessing the acrimonious end to E.I.S., that she would face opposition no matter where she found land, but she started looking. The first likely piece of property was an industrial site east of Highway 2, south of Edmonton. Local opposition killed that one. Further from the critical population base of Edmonton was a site at Wetaskiwin. This was more promising than the first candidate in that Wetaskiwin Mayor Frank Dyck and most of his city council were supportive. Nevertheless, after an extensive campaign, a municipal plebiscite was held and the proposal defeated by 11 votes.

The next site was near Morinville to the north. While further removed from residential development than the first two properties, this proposal too died, this time at the hands of planners, responding to a small, but vocal, opposition.

Finally, in 1986, a friend who knew of Liz's search called to say that Transport Canada would soon be offering for lease the lands adjacent to Edmonton International Airport. Because the land was so close to the airport, it was exempt from any local noise bylaws. When the land was formally put on the market, AURA contacted Transport Canada, and was told that a lease was available at $2,000,000 per year. That figure was obviously unrealistic and far more than any race track could afford, and so the serious bargaining began. In the end the parties settled on a 20-year lease with a 10-year renewal option, at $60,000 per year, with a $60,000 security deposit up front. A reasonable rent, but the security deposit cut a large piece from AURA's bank account.

AURA now had land, but much more cash would be needed. Liz Oglu, armed with an independent feasibility study prepared by a branch of the engineering firm Stanley & Associates, went looking for investors to buy share units of $50,000 each. The first unit of $50,000 went to a group of 22 individuals calling themselves Racers Investment Group. At that rate, it would have taken a long time to get the funding needed, but Liz's next sale was the real groundbreaker as Robert Dunn, publisher of the *Auto Trader* papers, agreed to take three units and find investors for another three. Next up was Red Deer racer and hotelier Geoff Goodwin for two units, Edmonton businessman Gil Cook for two, and Jim Bell of JB's Automotive for one. Jack Hampton, one of the racing Hampton brothers of Youngstown, agreed to do the construction and roadbuilding in exchange for share units.

June 13, 1990: Sod-turning ceremony. L to R: Gil Cook, Robert Dunn, Geoff Goodwin, Terry Gray, Liz Oglu. *(Liz Oglu collection)*

Capital City Raceway, summer 1990: Grading fresh clay onto the oval. *(Liz Oglu collection)*

January 1991: Richard Chevalier introduces guest speaker John Force.
(Liz Oglu collection)

July 1991: AURA volunteers dismantle 1,800 grandstand seats at Kinsmen Field
House. *(Liz Oglu collection)*

The project had begun as a volunteer effort, and now even with $50,000 share units being taken up, there was still room for unpaid work. Liz heard that the operators of the Kinsmen Field House were planning on replacing the bleachers in their facility. She struck a deal to buy the old ones for $300 on condition that she would dismantle and remove them. The AURA volunteer network showed up in force, complete with a flatbed semi-trailer, and got the job done on a weekend.

With a reasonable amount of capital in place, Liz Oglu as project coordinator was joined by Geoff Goodwin as general manager, and long-time oval racer Terry Gray as operations manager.

AURA's original plan called for a paved oval, drag strip and road course, but Terry Gray pointed out that a small dirt track was operating successfully at nearby Calmar, with a consistently good field of cars, including crowd-pleasing sprinters. The lease on the Calmar land was soon ending, so why not save the cost of paving and build a clay oval? If tiny Calmar had been able to support a track, certainly a new location closer to Edmonton would be a success. The initial cost-saving would be substantial,[1] and dirt was agreed to. This would be important once construction began, as costs quickly began coming in over budget, and in some cases unbudgeted. Engineering and development studies had been allowed for, but additional drainage costs and $100,000 for a left-turn lane off the adjacent highway were not things that had been considered. Nevertheless, if there is one thing auto racers and land developers share, it is optimism, and the official sod-turning ceremony took place on June 13, 1990.

After the sod-turning, progress was slower than hoped for, although cash continued to flow out. Liz organized a fund raiser in January of 1991 with soon-to-be-superstar drag racer John Force as guest speaker. The dinner sold out, with 380 in attendance. Work was able to continue through the spring of 1991, and finally on May 11 the gates were opened to the first race on the new ⅜-mile (.6-km) oval. First-year champions were Sean Moran in Sprint Car, Levis Dumont in Late Model Stock, Tim Erlam in Stock, and Stan Fearon in Mini-Stock.

---

1. In the end, the saving was less than first thought, the existing dirt being found unsuitable for racing.

The plan had been to run the oval track events in 1991 to provide some needed capital for the construction of the drag strip. The races were run, but they were not in themselves profitable enough to finish the job. A cash call went out to the investors, and Robert Dunn, who had just sold his *Auto Trader* business, came up with the shortfall in exchange for control of the project.

Concurrent with the construction of the drag strip, the road bed was laid for a road course, but as this is written more than a decade later, it remains unpaved. The demise of the Player's / GM and Honda / Michelin racing series in the early 1990s seemed to kill any enthusiasm for investment in new road-racing tracks. Terry Gray recounts how one car manufacturer offered just $5,000 towards completion of the track. "How much asphalt are you going to lay for $5,000?" he asks rhetorically.

Since completion of the facility, ownership and management have changed several times. It has gone from being called Capital Raceway to Labatt Raceway, to Budweiser Motorsport Park. The drag strip offers a steady program of bracket racing, with a few major shows added each season. The oval, supported by a hardcore fan base, has over the years run various classes of stock cars, modifieds, and sprint cars, with the spectacular 360 sprints being the prime draw. The track is nowhere close to being the facility Edmonton International Speedway was in the 1960s and 1970s, but it continues to provide a much-needed venue in a city that went without one for almost a decade.

Since 1992, Liz Oglu has not been involved with the track except as a casual spectator. As others invested large amounts of cash, there was progressively less room for volunteer initiative. In the fall of 1992, the drag strip was completed and a formal grand opening ceremony held. Liz was not invited. Perhaps if the road course is ever completed, someone will recall the gracious gesture of the Booth brothers in 1968, and name various parts of the track for people who contributed to the sport over many years. "Liz Oglu Straight" doesn't exactly roll off the tongue, but it would somehow seem appropriate.

E P I L O G U E

The game is bigger now, but it will
never be bigger than a small boy's dreams.
—Bobby Hull

O ver a span of almost 100 years, automobiles and automobile racing have progressed far beyond anything the adventurous celebrants of 1906 could have imagined. Three hundred miles an hour? Cornering or accelerating so fast that the driver weighs more laterally than vertically? Racing week after week, year after year, with little risk of injury? Tires as wide as a man's arm is long? One engine creating as much power as 6,000 horses? Parts made of aluminum, titanium, carbon fibre, and magnesium? And why aren't passengers allowed? To hear of these things would baffle, excite, and perhaps frighten those pioneers.

While regular, home-grown racing has not been continuously active in Alberta for that long—only a little over 60 years—the progress in that relatively short time has been immense. But as with any great movement, not all change has been progress. In six decades, the cars we race have become much faster and yet safer, and the tracks much more suited to the job than were the soft-earth fairgrounds tracks. But we have also had our losses. The great CAMRA and Can-Am circuits are no more. The magnificent Edmonton International Speedway has come and gone. Today, in an age when professional athletes work under personal services contracts, obligating them to one team or a small number of sponsors, the greatest drag and road race drivers in the world are not likely to compete in our "small market" cities. The National Hot Rod Association no longer sanctions our drag strips.

The zenith of Alberta racing took place from the mid 1960s through the mid 1980s. CAMRA brought us great oval racing. A remarkable corps of talented drag racers was just learning its craft. A world championship rally came here. Established Formula One and N.H.R.A. drivers paid regular visits. Formula One and Indy-car stars of the future raced wheel-to-wheel in their Formula Atlantic cars, just north of 137 Avenue. We had Albertans in the major leagues of NASCAR, Indy car, N.H.R.A., and Formula One. We were over our heads. Large population centres across North America lusted for what we had.

Then, just as quickly, it was gone.

By 1982, aside from small ovals, we had nowhere to race. Like deposed dictators or the paper millionaires of 1929, we went from all to nothing. But nothing lasts only as long as it is allowed to last, and with the persistence and vision of a few determined people, small tracks and strips survived and kept the sport alive. When new facilities opened in Calgary, and then Edmonton, we had the cars and drivers to put them to quick use. Today, hundreds of drivers compete every weekend from mid-May to late September. Alberta doesn't garner the international media coverage it once did, but with tracks across the province, the sport is strong. From that strength will come talent, and we will again contribute skilled racers to the major leagues of the sport, just as we have in the past. . . .

Go to your nearest race track, and take a child with you, for as Bobby Hull once said about hockey, "The game is bigger now, but it will never be bigger than a small boy's dreams." And together watch carefully. You and your young friend may well be seeing the next Gordie Bonin, Trevor Boys, Terry Capp, Tim Gee, Eldon Rasmussen, or Frank Weiss behind the wheel; or Dale Armstrong, Bernie Fedderly, or Rob Flynn doing their magic in the engine bay.

Enjoy.

GLOSSARY OF RACING TERMS

Anti-roll bar — A bar of spring steel, connected to both the left and right suspension arms at either end of the car, pivoting on the frame of the car, thus enabling the vertical movement of one side to act as a spring on the other. Not to be confused with **Roll bar.**

Blow, or blew
(past tense) — *(v.)* Suffer a major mechanical failure.

Blower — See **Supercharger.**

Blown — a.) *(adj.)* Supercharged.
b.) *(adj.)* Mechanical part that has been destroyed.

Bracket racing — A form of handicapped drag racing in which each competitor states, or "dials-in", the fastest time he feels his car is capable of achieving in a race. The start of the race is staggered, representing the difference in the stated "dial-in" times of the cars. This allows cars, no matter how slow, to be competitive. If a competitor finishes the race in less time than his dial-in time, he is said to "break out" and is disqualified. Probably the only type of racing—human, animal, or vehicular—wherein one can be disqualified simply for being too fast.

Burnout — *(n.)* A drag racing practice whereby prior to the start of the race, the rear wheels are spun on an area of pavement that has been watered. The resultant friction heats up the tire surfaces, thereby providing more traction when the race begins.

Christmas tree — The arrangement of coloured lights facing the competitors at the start line of a drag race. The lights signal the drivers when to start, and also indicate if a driver has started too early ("jumped the start" or "**Red-lighted**"), thereby being disqualified.

DNF	Did not finish.
DNS	Did not start.
Dice	(*n.*) Road racing term used to describe a close race between two or more drivers. Also (*v.*) to participate in such a close race.
Draft	To follow another car so closely as to use that car as a wind-break. The lead car absorbs the wind resistance, while the following car rides in a virtual vacuum. This technique can be used to save fuel, or to gain sufficient momentum as to accelerate or "slingshot" past the leading car.
Drag race	A car race in which two competitors accelerate in a straight line to the end of a ¼-mile track, or "strip." In rare cases, the race covers only ⅛ mile. The term "drag" is believed to be derived from the expression "main drag," meaning the major automobile thoroughfare through a town or city—a place often used for racing in the early days of hot-rodding. The term may also have originated with the term "dragging the gears," which meant holding the car in a lower gear longer than normal while accelerating.
Drag chute	A parachute attached to the rear of a drag racing car. It is activated by the driver at the end of the race to assist in bringing the car to a stop. Chutes are mandatory in most drag racing jurisdictions on any car capable of over 140 miles per hour (226 kmh).
Dragster	a.) Any car competing in a drag race, or b.) More correctly, a single-seat, open-cockpit, open-wheel, long-wheelbase, purpose-built drag racing car, and normally (since the 1970s) one with the engine in the rear.
Elapsed time (e.t.)	The time a drag racing car takes to accelerate from stand-still to the end of the strip.
Formula (car)	A set of rules standardizing the specifications for a class of race car, particularly single-seat, open-wheel, road racing cars.

Fuel	a.) The flammable liquid, usually gasoline, diesel oil, or methanol, which when combined with air is used to power internal-combustion engines. b.) In drag racing, a mixture of methanol (alcohol) and nitrous oxide, or nitro-methane. Allows for the creation of vast amounts of horsepower, but severely limits the life-span of the engine. c.)*(adj.)* A drag racing car competing in a class permitting the use of "fuel" (see b.) above), e.g. "fuel funny car."
Funny car	A front-engined drag racing car in which the driver and the drive train are enclosed together under a lightweight removable body that bears some distant visual resemblance to a production or street car. The class is limited to a wheel-base of 125 inches (318 cm), which can cause handling problems, or "funny" steering, thereby the origin of the name.
Grand Prix	French; literally "big prize." Some people believe the term should only be applied to races counting towards the Formula One World Championship, but many promoters and sanctioning bodies use it in the title of any races important to them.
Hemi	An engine having combustion chambers of roughly hemi-spherical shape. Such a shape will normally provide room for more and / or larger valves. Specifically, the term "hemi" is often used to describe Chrysler's 392-cubic-inch engine of the 1950s and their 426-cubic-inch engine of the 1960s and '70s.
Hot lap	In oval track racing, this term refers to practice laps.
Hot rod	A stock passenger car, modified for improved performance and / or radical appearance. In recent years, the name has come to encompass purpose-built cars with new bodies designed to resemble early models, such as 1932 Fords.
Ice dice	See **Ice race,** also **Dice.**
Ice race	A race on the frozen surface of a lake. Usually laid out as a road course, although in the mid 1950s, there were ice drag races.

Kart	A miniature, open-wheel racing vehicle with no suspension or body, and in most classes, no transmission. Karts are normally powered by a small air-cooled engine. Karts are raced by children as young as 5 years, and have for many years been the earliest racing experience for many of the world's top drivers. Previously called go-karts.
Lap	*(n.)* One trip around a road course or an oval. *(v.)* To pass a competitor who is already behind, thus putting him one or more full lap(s) in arrears.
LeMans start	In sports car racing, a start that involves parking the cars diagonally on one side of the track, with the drivers standing opposite. At the green flag, the drivers run across the track to their respective cars, jump in, start the engines, and begin racing. In response to outrageous rumours that some drivers were starting without first being properly buckled-up, LeMans starts were discontinued shortly after seat belts and shoulder harnesses became mandatory.
Loose	See **Oversteer.**
Modified	a.) *(adj.)* Any car-particularly a passenger car-or part that has been altered to improve its performance, e.g. "modified sports car." b.) *(n.)* An oval-track racing car, based on stock components, but reconstructed to improve performance. These cars are normally single-seat, open-wheel cars.
Monocoque	Race car (and airplane) construction in which the body and frame are one. The strength and curvature of the body panels, rather than conventional framework, provides the structural rigidity.
Oversteer	A handling condition in a car whereby when cornering the rear tires tend to develop a greater **Slip angle** and lose lateral traction prior to the front. Also referred to as **Loose.**
Paddock	Areas near a race track where cars are kept prior to racing, where haulers are parked, and where major repairs are carried out.

Parc fermé	In rallying, a secure area, commonly a fenced compound or a parking garage, in which competing cars are held during rest periods. The parc fermé not only protects the cars from vandalism, it also prevents unauthorized repairs or modifications by the teams.
Pari-mutuel	A system of betting on races in which the winners share in the total stakes, minus an administration fee. Can be very profitable for the proprietor, or "house." Most commonly found at horse races.
Pit	(*n.*) Area adjacent to the race track where cars are serviced during the race. (*v.*) To stop a race car at its assigned pit.
Pony car	An American sport sedan, generally with two front bucket seats and minimal, child-size seating behind. The term "pony car" derives from the name of the first model of this genre, the Ford Mustang. Most pony cars have powerful engines.
Push	See **Understeer.**
Rally	A form of motorsport in which cars carrying both a driver and a navigator follow a prescribed route, normally on public roads. In a Time-Speed-Distance (TSD) rally, competitors must travel at precise average speeds, penalty points being given for going off route or completing the route too fast or too slow. Prior to the early 1970s, TSD rallies were the norm throughout North America. Modern rallies typically include "special stages" on closed-off roads where the object is to cover the route as fast as possible, with penalty points given for being slower than either a predetermined target time or the fastest car.
Red-lighted	(or "red lit") In drag racing, a car red-lights when it leaves the start line prior to the green light on the **Christmas tree** coming on.
Restrictor plate	A metal plate attached to the top of the intake manifold and beneath the carburetor, usually on a stock car. The plate has holes of a regulated diameter so as to restrict the amount of fuel passing into the manifold and the engine. Restrictor plates are mandatory in some racing jurisdictions, particularly on larger and faster tracks, as a means of controlling horsepower and speed.

Ride	*(n.)* Employment driving someone else's race car.
Road race	A race taking place either on public roads temporarily closed to accommodate the event or, more commonly, on a closed race track featuring turns of both left and right and usually varying in elevation.
Road course	A road race track.
Roll bar	A protective hoop, usually of steel tube, attached to the race car's chassis and rising above the driver's head. Not to be confused with **Anti-roll bar.**
Roll cage	A system of multiple roll bars and braces, both behind and in front of the driver, typically connected to key points on the frame to stiffen the chassis.
Skid	Condition wherein a tire's limits of adhesion have been exceeded, and the tire slides on the road surface, with no control of direction.
Slick	An asphalt-track race car tire with no tread grooves, lugs, or void.
Slip angle	The variance, measured in degrees, between the direction of the wheel, and that of the tire tread while under cornering forces. Slip angle is not the same as skid. A passenger car travelling through a corner at normal speed develops a slip angle, albeit much less than a race car at competitive speed. See also **Oversteer** and **Understeer.**
Slipstream	See **Draft.**
Special	*(n.)* A one-of-a-kind race car, often home-built. The term special is also commonly used to identify a car with its sponsor, e.g. "The Rotgut Whiskey Special."
Special stage	A section of a **Rally** run on a closed-off road, the object being for competitors to cover the route as fast as possible.

Sports car	a.) A two-seat passenger car offering exceptional performance, but at the expense of minimal passenger accommodation, harsh ride, and often noise. b.) A race car used on road courses, based either on a particular road-going sports car or on a generic description of a sports car detailed in the rules. Such rules typically require fenders and sufficient cockpit space to accommodate two people.
Sprint car	A front-engined, single-seat, open-wheeled race car, often with a large wing on top, used in oval racing, primarily on dirt-surfaced tracks.
Stagger	Difference in circumference between the left and right tires on one axle (either front or rear) of an oval track car. Stagger has a substantial bearing on how the race car will handle; e.g. more stagger at the rear (greater difference in circumference, with the right being larger than the left) leads to **Loose** handling.
Stock car	Originally an American production passenger car, altered only enough to make it safe for racing (passenger seats removed, doors fastened shut). Over years, except in the lower amateur classes, the stock car has evolved to become a specialized racing machine with only the engine block, and in some cases the rear axle housing, coming from its namesake passenger car. Stock cars have bodies that bear some resemblance to their road-going counterparts.
Supercharger	A device to force air into an engine's induction system at greater than atmospheric pressure, thereby increasing the amount of fuel than can be used and resulting in greater horsepower. True superchargers are mechanically driven. When driven by the force of exhaust gases on a turbine, they are properly referred to as **Turbochargers.**
Super-modified	An oval-track race car using an engine based on a production American V-8, but otherwise being a purpose-built race car, normally single-seat and open-wheeled (see **Modified**).
Strip	Drag strip. Straight paved race track, normally ¼ mile long, but occasionally as short as ⅛ mile.

Sway bar	See **Anti-roll bar.**
Turbocharger	A device to force air into an engine's induction system at higher than atmospheric pressure, thereby increasing the amount of fuel than can be used, and resulting in greater horsepower. Turbochargers are driven by a turbine propelled by the force of the car's exhaust gases. See also **Supercharger.**
Top Fuel	The fastest classes of drag racing cars. Can be either a **Dragster** or a **Funny Car.** They are powered by massive, supercharged V-8 engines burning **Fuel** and often creating 6,000 horsepower or more.
Understeer	A handling condition whereby, when cornering, the car's front wheels tend to develop a greater **Slip angle,** and ultimately lose lateral traction prior to the rear. Also known as **Push.**
Wedge	Chassis height variance between left and right sides of an oval-track race car, determined by spring rate, spring height, and adjustments to the spring tension or "preload." Wedge is a major factor in setting the handling of the car for **Loose** or **Push.**

BIBLIOGRAPHY

Brockington, Robert J. *Mosport International Raceway: Four Decades of Racing.* Bowmanville, Ontario: Mosport International Raceway, 2001.

Buziak, Kelly. *Roaring Lizzies: Model T Ford Racing in Alberta, 1941 to 1951.* Wetaskiwin, Alberta: Friends of Reynolds–Alberta Museum Society, 1992.

Colombo, John Robert. *Famous Lasting Words: Great Canadian Quotations.* Vancouver: Douglas & McIntyre, 2000.

Friedman, Dave. *Trans-Am: The Pony Car Wars 1966–1972.* Osceolla, Wisconsin: MBI Publishing, 2001.

Gray, James H. *A Brand of Its Own: The 100 Year History of the Calgary Exhibition and Stampede.* Saskatoon, Saskatchewan: Western Producer Prairie Books, 1985.

Holmgren, Eric J. & Holmgren, Patricia M. *Over 2000 Place Names of Alberta, Third Edition.* Saskatoon, Saskatchewan: Western Producer Prairie Books, 1976.

Klopfer, Wolfgang. *Formula A and Formula 5000 in America.* Norderstedt, Germany: Wolfgang Klopfer Books on Demand GmbH, 2003.

Lyons, Pete. *Can-Am.* Osceolla, Wisconsin: Motorbooks International, 1995.

McArthur, Dr. Ian. *The Early Years of the Rocky Mountain Rally.* Unpublished.

McLennan, William N. *Sport in Early Calgary.* Calgary: Fort Brisebois Publishing, 1972.

Nolan, William F. *Barney Oldfield: The Life and Times of America's Legendary Speed King.* Carpinteria, California: Brown Fox Books, 2002.

Purdy, Ken W. *The Kings of the Road.* New York: Little, Brown & Company, 1952.

Rendall, Ivan. *The Checkered Flag: 100 Years of Motor Racing.* Secaucus, New Jersey: Chartwell Books Inc. / A Division of Book Sales Inc., 1993.

Scalzo, Joe. *The American Dirt Track Racer.* St. Paul, Minnesota: MBI Publishing, 2001.

Taylor, Rich. *Indy: Seventy-Five Years of Racing's Greatest Spectacle.* New York: St. Martin's Press, 1991.

Williams, James N. *The Plan.* Stittsville, Ontario: Canada's Wings Inc., 1984.

INDEX

A

Ackerman, Gerry, 231
Acteson, Henry, 141, 153, 154
Adams, Dale, 268
Advocate, 21, 44
Airdrie airport, 29, 57, 72, 77, 135–37, 147
Alberta Auto Racing Association
  (A.A.R.A.), 36–38, 44, 63, 94, 166
Alberta Beach, 81
Alberta Cup, 107
Alberta Modified Racing Association
  (AMRA) Championship, 171
Allan, Peter, 156
Allen and Sharpe (rally team), 156
Allison, Tony, 60
Amarillo, Texas, 234
Amato, Joe, 189
American Automobile Association (AAA),
  6, 7, 8, 242
American Hot Rod Association
  (A.H.R.A.), 267, 268
American Speed Association (A.S.A.),
  224, 227–28
Amon, Chris, 244, 253–54, 259
Amusements Act, 30
Andretti, Mario, 93, 175
Anthony, Richard "Dick," 195, 247
Arason, Don, 247
Armbruster, Rolf, 78
Armstrong, Dale
  builder / craftsman, 181–82, 186, **187,**
    188–90, 192
  crew chief, 181, 188–91
  Hall of Fame, vi, 191
  Lifetime Achievement Award, 192
  N.H.R.A. Nationals / World
    Championship, 186
  racing career, 64–65, 131, 181–82,
    183–84, 185–86, 188–92,
Armstrong, Grant, 114
Ascot, California, 217
Ashley, Sid, 96
Atkin, Mike, **101,** 107, 250, 256

B

Badger, Terry, 57–58
Baker, Harry, 156
Bakersfield, California, 226
Ball, Tony, 72
Bambush, Orv, 57, **61**
Barnaschone, John, 79, 100, **101–2,** 103,
  106, 110, **112**
Barnett, Jerry, 217
Bartels, Dick, 156
Bass, Willie, 247
Beast, The, 78, 79, 241
Beck, Gary
  Hall of Fame, 109
  top drag racer, 64–65, 93, **115,** 145,
    191, 264
  Top Fuel Dragster, 234
  U.S. Nationals, 116–17, 267
  with Ray Peets, 114–17
Becker, George, 103
Beckman, Ralph, 156
Bennett, Darrell, 103
Bennett, Lillian, 11
Bennett, Vic, 32, 39
Benz, Karl, 1–2
Berg, Allen
  Driver of the Year, 208
  early career, 203–4
  Formula One, 202–3, 207, 208–9, 273
  I.L.P. championship, 210–11
  Lady Wigram Trophy, 204
  Mexican championships, **208,** 210
Berg, Ben, 203
Bernstein, Kenny, **184,** 188–91
Bickle, Rich Jr., 227
Bighorn Rally, 159
Bird, John, **151,** 153, 154
Bland, Eric, 72
Blaney, Dave, 219
Blumenschein, George, 142
Bobek, Vaclav, 150–53
Bon Accord, Alberta, 81, 99
Bone, Peter, 150

Bonin, Gordie
  European Champion, 239
  Hall of Fame, vi
  Interviewing, 230-31
  top drag racer, 64–65, 145, 231–34, **235,**
    238, 239, 268
  U.S. Nationals, 237, 239
  with Gordon Jenner / Ron Hodgson,
    197–98, 232–34, 236–37, **236, 237**
  with Roland Leong, 237
Bonnier, Jo, 241–42, 248
Booth brothers, Percy, Reg, and Russell
  and stock car drivers, 96, 98, 193–94
  businessmen, 138, 140, 114, 249–50
  and E.I.S., **101,** 102–4
  founding CAMRA, 161–62, **163**
  track building, 95–96, **97–98,** 99-100,
    134–35, 137, 138, 140, 193–94
Bordeaux, E., 74
Bower, Mr., 136–37
Bowett, Reg, 142
Boyce, Walter, 158
Boys, Buddie, 51–52, 118–19, 126, 178
Boys, Trevor
  and Wheeler, 124,126
  Cale's engine, 123–24
  racing career, 52, 119–20, **121–22,** 123,
    126, 131–32
  with Buck Heberling, 131–32
Boys, Wheeler, 119, **122,** 124, **125,** 126
Brabham, Geoff, 259
Brabham, Jack, 204
Brands Hatch, England, 202
Breckenridge, Gavin, 37, 39, 94–95,
  106, 271
Brennan, Pat, **69,** 72
Brickman Hill, 6
Bridgehampton, New York, 244, 247–48
British Columbia International Trade Fair
  (B.C.I.T.F.), 149
British Commonwealth Air Training Plan
  (B.C.A.T.P.), 29, **31,** 57
British Empire Motor Club, 242
Brown, Harold, 63
Browne, Harold, 142, 222, **223,** 228
Browne, Harry, 170
Browne, Jamie, 256
Brundle, Martin, 204, **205,** 207
Bryant, Ed, 247

Budweiser (racing team), 188, 189, 191
Budweiser Motorsport Park, 280, 286
Byrne, Rob, 198, 214

C

C.A.S.C. Prairie Region Championship,
  119, 141, 278
Caffi, Alex, 202
Caldwell Team, 248
Calgary Drag Race Council, 63, 136–37,
  142
Calgary Exhibition (and Stampede), 12,
  14, 24
Calgary Eye Opener, 1, 2
Calgary International Raceway, 146, 221
Calgary Regional Planning Commission,
  142
Calgary Sports Car Club (C.S.C.C.)
  Alberta's first, 72–73, 74
  elitism, 71–72
  Gendebien visits, 79
  Happy Valley hill climb, 141–42
  ice racing, **69**
  rallying, 76–77, 157–59
  wrath of, 82
Can-Am (Canadian American
  Challenge Cup)
  announcement / opening, 243–44
  at E.I.S., 107, 194, 244, 247–50, 253–55,
    256–60
  cost of, 196
  popularity, 30, 114, 194, 250, **251,**
    255, 258
  resurrection, 259–60
Canada Track and Traffic, 150
Canadian American Modified Racing
  Association (CAMRA)
  car safety, 166
  Championship, 89, 165
  formation, 50, 88, 113, 161–62, **163**
  popularity, 88, 138, 140–41,
    166–67, 171
  promoting, 50–51
Canadian Association for Stock Car
  Racing (CASCAR), 168, 228
Canadian Automobile Sport Clubs
  (C.A.S.C.), 74, 241
Canadian Motorsport Hall of Fame
  (CMHF)

Alberta drag racers in, 54
Bernie Fedderly, vii, 261, 269
Dale Armstrong, vi, 191–92
Elson Rasmussen, viii, 53, 93
Gary Beck, 109, 117
Gord Jenner, vii
Gordie Bonin, vi
Graham Light, vii, 199
Maurice "Mo" Carter, 153
Ray Peets, vii, 109, 117
Ron Hodgson, vii
Terry Capp, vii, 261, 269
Tom Johnston, vii
Canadian Race Drivers Association
   (C.R.D.A.), 244, 254
Candies, Paul, 239
Cantin, Art, 40
Cape Oil Ltd., 222
Capital City Hot Rod Association
   (C.C.H.R.A.), 60, 104, 280
Capital City Raceway. *See* Oglu, Liz /
   Captial City Raceway
Capp, Frances, 262–63, 264
Capp, Terry
   family and business, 267
   Hall of Fame, vi, 261, 269
   top drag racer, 64–65, 145, 264, 267
   U.S. Nationals, 267, 268–69
   with Bernie Fedderly, 261–64, **265–66**
Car and Driver, 230
Car Craft, 192
Cardston, Alberta, 170–71
Carl Nickle Trophy, 48
Carr, Group Captain, 59
Carroll, Ed, 57–58, 204
Carter, Maurice "Mo," 113, 153
Castronova, Phil, 234
Championship Auto Racing Team
   (CART), 93, 179–80
Chaparral, 248, 249, 253
Chevalier, Jules G. "Bill," 106, 279
Chevalier, Richard, 55, 59–60, 65, 73, **101,**
   136, 263, **284**
Chevalier, Ross, 106
Chevrolet, Arthur, 22
Chicago *Press,* 9
Chinetti, Luigi, 153, 154
Chinook Raceway, 134–35
chuckwagon races, 128

Circle 8 Speedway. *See under*
   McMahon, Gene
Circle Track, 227
Clapp, Ken, 226, 227
Claresholm, Alberta, 29, 57, 77, 106, 135
Clark, George, 14, **16,** 21
Clark, Jim, 204
Clarke Stadium, 39
Clarke, Don, 247
Clarke, Roger, 154–56
Clarke, Ron, 247
Cline, Bob, 14, 22
Coad, Dennis, 136
Cobra Raceway, 198, 214, **215**
Cochrane, Billy, 2
Coil, Austin, 267–68, 269
Collins, Emory "Spunk," 24, 35–36
Connelly, Bill, 37
Coombe, Ann, 156
Cooper, Boots, 60, 62
Copp, Bob, 81
Coronas, Waldemar, 211
Costello, Mayor M. C., 17–18
Couture, Jacques, 256
Crane, Gary, 186

D
Daily Herald, 9, 50, 54
Daimler, Gottlieb, 1–2
Danner, Christian, 202, 208
Davey, Al, 36, 39–40, 195
Davidson, Saskatchewan, 73, **76,** 107, 271
Day, Mike, 79
de St. Croix, Ross, 250
Dean, Mike, 157
Deane, Dr. Gordon, **76,** 78
Deane, Superintendent, 6, 10
Deer Park, Washington, 58, 76
Delmar, Art, 57
DeLooper, John, 247
Dent, Jim, 39–40
DePalma, Johnny, 24
DePalma, Ralph, 24
Derval, Bob, 96
Desebrais, Wayne, 142
DeWinton, Alberta, 57, 61, 77, 81, 135
Dick, Norm, 247
Didsbury, Alberta, 131, 135
dirt cars. *See* sprint cars

dirt tracks, 14, 35–36, 74, 94–95, 145–46, 212–13, 285
Disbrow, Louis, 8
Dixon's Mule Derby, 14
Docktor, Ben / Race City Speedway
  careers, 222
  finest facility, 134, 221, 229
  NASCAR / Player's / CASCAR, 226–28, 229
  opening, 225–26, 272
  plans / construction, 146, 222, **223–24,** 225
  downtown racing, 228
  sprint cars, 52–53
  See also Race City Speedway championships
Doherty, Ron, 127, 167
Donaldson, Gerry, 208
Donohue, Mark, 248–49, **252,** 253, 256, 258, 259
Doty, Brad, 219
Dowler, Eric, **164**
Dowler, Kevin, 168, 228
Doyen and Gibbs (rally team), 150
Doyle, Larry, 22
Draper, Mrs. Richard, 80
Duimel and Jackman (rally team), 156
Dumfries, Johnny, 207
Duray, Leon, 22–23
Durward, Geo. Huff, 13
Dyer and Jackman (rally team), 156
Dyma, Murray, 197–98, 232–33, 234, **236**
Dyson, Paul, 141

E
East African Safari Rally, 150
Eaton, George, **246,** 255
Eaton, Ron, 226
Eby, Lloyd, 131, 142
Ecclestone, Bernie, 239
Edmonton International Speedway (E.I.S.)
  Can-Am races, 243–44, 247–50, 253–58
  closing, 221, 272, 280–81, 287
  first / final race, 107, 259–60
  going public, 103–4
  history, 99–100, 103–4, 106–7
  model / plans, 100, **101–2**
  opening, 64–65, 82, 104, **105,** 106, 270
  troubles, 193–94, 198, 199–20

Edmonton Journal, 5, 7–8, 21, 110, 195, 257
Edmonton Light Car Club (E.L.C.C.), 73, 157–58
Edmonton Sports Car Club (E.S.C.C.), 73
Edmonton Timing Association, 60
Edwardes, Robin, 150, 153, 154
Egan, Peter, 261
Egbert, Gary, 145, 264
Eken, Lutz, 156
Elizabeth II, Queen, 57
Elks Lodge, 5
Ellefson, Norm, 96, 162, **163,** 165, 194
Ellingboe, Jules, 14, 22
Endicott, Bill, 22, 23
Erlam, Len, **27,** 36
Erlam, Tim, 285
European Drag Race Champion, 239
Ex-American Day, 2

F
Fairs, Geoff, 142
Fedderly, Bernie
  builder / craftsman, 261, 262–63
  top crew chief, 64–65, 261, 269
  Hall of Fame, vii, 261, 269
  U.S. Nationals, 267
  with John Force, 267–69
  with Terry Capp, 261–64, **265–66**
Fee, Paul, 247
Ferworn, Ron, 137–38, 171
Festor, Eric, 72
Figueroa, Eduardo, 211
Finnigan, Ken, 73–74, 78
Firecracker 400, 120
Fisher, Craig, 153
Fleming, Larry, 214
Flood, Curt, 191
Floyd, Hunter, 156
Flynn, Rob, 65
Follmer, George, 256, 258
Force, John, 64, 192, 267, 269, **284,** 286
Ford, Henry, 32
Forest, Ric, 257–58, 272
Formula Atlantic, 204, 211, 229, **252**
Formula One
  car safety, 79–80
  drivers, 202, 206–7, 243, 260, 287–88
  stepping stones to, 204, 206
  winners, 54, 248–49

Formula One World Championship, 239, 243, 248, 256, 259

Fort MacLeod, Alberta, 29, 77, 81, 107

Foster, Billy, 88, 89, 113, 162, 165

Foust, Jim, **183,** 186

Fowler, David, 153, 154, 195, 247

Fox, Barry, 107, 153, 154, 257

Fox, Thomas "Tom," 39, 103, 195–**97,** 236

Foyt, A. J., 52, 242

Fraser, Simon, 148

Fraser, Tom, **28,** 32, 34

Frère, Paul, **70,** 79

G

Gainesville, Florida, 237

Garlits, Don "Big Daddy," 65, 117, 144–45, 194, 201, 268

Gaunt, Rod, 72

Gee, Gordie, 213–14, 217–20

Gee, Ruth, 217–20

Gee, Tim
  family team, 213–14, **216,** 217–20
  sponsorship, 219–20
  top sprint car racer, **139,** 213–14, **215**
  World of Outlaws tours, 139, 213–14, **216,** 217–20, **219**

Gendebien, Olivier, **75,** 79, 150, 153, 241

Gethin, Peter, 255

Ghinzani, Piercarlo, 202, 203

Giacomelli, Bruno, 210

Gilgan, Paul, 168, 228, 273

Gimli, Manitoba, 203, 272

Giroux, Ben, 14, 18

Gold Cup, 95, 96, 99, 109, 165

Goodhall, Phil, 78

Goodwin, Geoff
  and Liz Oglu, 280, 282, **283,** 285
  national record, 247
  racing career, **55,** 57, 60, 62, 65
  with Ray Peets, 110, **112,** 113

Gotoff, Ben, 22, 24

Goyman, Terry, 145–46

Grable, Ron, 254, 256, 258

Graham, Ewen, 153, 154

Graham, Terry, 138, 171

Grand Prix. See Formula One

Grand Prix International, 207, 208

Grasswick, Carl and Mrs., 6, 10, 11

Gray, Terry, 168, 220, **284,** 285, 287

Green, Oscar, 37–39, 94–95, 106

Green, Randy, 142

Greene, Nancy, 249

Greenley, Charley, 134–35, 137

Gregg, Peter, 256

Gregory, Mel, 81

Gridiron Speedway, 7–10

Grobe, Arthur, 136

Grote, Gary, 228

Gunn, Jim, 150

Gurney, Dan, 244, 248

Gwynn, Darrell, 188

H

Hakkinen, Mika, 239

Hall of Fame inductees. *See* Canadian Motorsport Hall of Fame; Sprint Car Hall of Fame

Hall, Jim, 249, 253

Hall, John, 256, 259

Hamilton, Davey, 162

Hampton brothers, 131, 282

Hampton, Bruce and May Anne, 167–68

Harkey, Bob, 51

Harris, Ron, 42, 96, 135

Hartley, Harry, 153, 156

Harvest Night Rally, **152**

Harvey, Scott, 156

Haugdahl, Sig, 22, 23, 24

Hawkins, Bob, 256

Haywood, Ken, 264

Healey, Walt, 40

Heberling, Duane S. "Buck," 127, 128, 131–32, 182

Heighington, Con, 32

Heimrath, Ludwig, 136, 271

Higgs, Pat, 39

Hill, Craig, 256

Hillary, Reg, 149

hill climbs, 74, 82, 141–42, 149, 153, 278

Hillier, W., 2

Hillin, Bobby Jr., 120, **121**

Hinton, Alberta, 87

Hitchcox, Bill, 227

Hobbs, David, 256, 258

Hodgson, Ron, vii, 197–98, 230–31, 232–34, 236, 239, 268

Hodson, J. H., 12

Hogben, Mike, 156

Honda / Michelin Series, 228–29, 274, **276,** 277, 278–79, 286
Hoover, Wendell, 79
Hopkins, Ronnie Jr., 120, **121**
Hopkirk, Paddy, **152,** 156–57
H'Orey, Fred. *See* Horey, Fred
Horey, Fred, 14, **15,** 17, 21
Howard, Allan, 81
Howe, Geoff, 156
Hucul, Cliff, 162
Hudson's Bay Company, 30
Hughes, Leonard, 239
Hughes, Ron, 153
Hull, Bobby, 287
Hulme, Denny, 201, 244, 248–50, 253–57, 258, 259
Hutton, Frank, 247
Hylton, James, 52, 132

I

ice racing, **69,** 81, **86,** 203–4, 209, 278
Indianapolis 500, 23, 24, 51, 100, 140, 175–76, 248
Indianapolis Motor Speedway, 6, 36, 37, 170
Indy Lights Panamericana (I.L.P.) series, 210–11
Indy Racing League (I.R.L.), 179
International Hot Rod Association (I.H.R.A.), 66, 189
International Motor Contest Association (I.M.C.A.), **15,** 35–37, 44, 167–68, 228
See also Sloan, J. Alex
Ivo, Tommy, 191–92

J

Jack Carter Chev Olds, 171
Jack, Peter, 167, 174
Jackson, J., 5–6
Janett, Bertha "Bea," 47
Janett, Frank
bicycle racing, 42–43
family, 47, 53
Model Ts, 26, 33, 42, 43–44, **45**
sprint cars / modifieds, 33, 36, **38,** 42, 43–44, **45,** 47–49, **51,** 52, 135
stories about, 48–50
with The Boys, 51–52, 119–20
Jeffrey, Maj. J. B., 9

Jenner, Gordon "Gord"
at E.I.S., 104, 106, 232
Hall of Fame, vii
top drag racer, 64–65
with Gordie Bonin / Ron Hodgson, 197–98, 232–34, 236, 239, 268
Jewett, Chad, 14
Johncock, Gordon, 176
Johnson, Ivan, **76**
Johnson, Kneal, 156
Johnson, Les, 72
Johnson, Stan, 81
Johnson, Ted, 218
Johnston, Tom, vii, **76,** 79
Jones, Bubby, 218
Jones, Parnelli, 242
Jones, Terry, 255, 268
Jones, Tom, **86,** 92
Jordan, Eddie, 204, 206, 207

K

Karkar, Jon, 136
Kase, Mike, 188
Katke, Bob, 174
Kent, Washington, 244
Kerry, Mike, 150, **152,** 153, 156
Kidco Construction, 145
King, Bobby, 124
Kingsway Transport, 219
Kinsella, W. P., 94
Kinser, Steve, 219
Klein, Ralph, 182–83, **223,** 225
Kline, Bob. See Cline, Bob
Klondike 200, 244–45, 247, 255
Koenig, Michel, 208
Koetzla, Dave, 14, **15,** 18
Kohut, Don, 145, 232
Kornelson, Del, 142
Korzan, Dave, 269
Kozak, Nick, 104, 232

L

Labatt Breweries, 209, 239, 280, 286
Labatt Raceway, 280
Lady Wigram Trophy Race, 204
Lafitte, Jacques, 202
Laguna Seca, California, 244, 247–48
Lalonde and Jones (rally team), 150
Land, Jim, 79

Landage, Jack, 36
Langton, John, 181
Las Vegas, Nevada, 244, 247
Lawrence, Bob, 199
Lawrence, Graeme, 114, **246,** 255
Leacock, Dr. Rosamond, 17
Leatham, Bill, 154
Lee brothers, 65
Lee, Wade, 168, 228
Lemay, George, 33, 36–37, **38,** 43–44, **46,**
   96, 135
Leong, Roland, 145, 198, 236, 239
Lethbridge Brewery, 259
Lethbridge Sports Car Club, 81
Lethbridge, Alberta, 1, 6–7, 10, 36, 40–41,
   135, 137–38
Light, Graham, vii, 198, 199, 200–201,
   264, 267, 281
Lincoln Park, 57, 73
Linderman, Paul, 137
Lions Club, 26, 30, 131
Little, Chad, 227
Ljungfeldt, Bo, 153
Lloyd, Gordon, 247
Lockton, David, 241
Loop Rally, 73
Lord's Day Act, **56,** 62–64
Lord, Ken, 72
Lowe, Bob, 225
Lunger, Brett, 250
Lutz, Ernest, 141–42
Lycar, Mike, 234
Lynch, Bud, 29
Lynch, Ron, 156

M

Macdonald, Manitoba, 107
MacEwan, Mayor Grant, 142
MacKay, Donald "Don," 95–96, 100,
   161, **163**
MacKenzie, Art, 229
MacKenzie, Carl, 250
MacKid, Stewart, 2
Maclin Motors, 30, 32
McArthur, Ian, **155,** 158–59
McCaig, Maurice, 52, 119
McCaig, Roger, **246**
McConnell, David, 256
McCulloch, Ed, 234

McDonald, Bob, 78
McDonald, Sandy, 138
McEachran, John, 89, **97**
McEwan, Tom "Mongoose", 116, 191
McGill, Neil, 250
McGowan, Ray, 256
McIntyre, Winifred, 247
McLaren, Bruce, 194, 201, 204, 244, **245,**
   248–50, 254–59
McLaughlin-Buick, 5–6, 17
McLean, Ken, 114–15
McLennan, Paul, 154
McLeod, K. A., 5, 10
McMahon, Gene
   airport drag strips, 80–81
   The Beast, 78, 79, 241
   and Bill Powers, 142–43
   and Shirley Muldowney, 144
   Circle 8 Speedway, 138, **139,** 140,
      142, 147
   gentlemen amateur, 81–82
   on Gordon Taylor, 59
   Shephard Raceway, **56,** 63, 135–36, 141,
      145, 147
McNeill, John, 247
McPherson, F. H., 22
McQuirk and McQuirk (rally team), 151
Magnee, Nancy, 247
Mais, Elfreida. *See* Maize, Mlle.
Maize, Mlle., 16, 24, 25
Malloy, Jim, 88, 89, 113, 162
Mann, Bryce, 167
Manzanita, Arizona, 217
Marchildon and Jackman
   (rally team), 153
Marlboro, 210
Marlin, Sterling, 120, **121**
Martin, Jim, 57–59
Martin, Lloyd, 247
Martin, Marion, 24
Martin, Mark, 120
Matan, Eddie "Tiger," 99
Melchin, Howard, 103
Meldau, Emil, 106, 161, **163**
Merson and Davies (rally team), 153
Metro Ford, 171
Mexican Formula Two / Formula Three
   Championships, 210
Miller Brewing, 191, 267

Miller, Ed, 194, 198
Miller, Gary, 142, 273
Miller, Harry, 23
Milligan, Jim, 73, 77–78, 81
Milton, Tommy, 23
Minor, Larry, 191, 268
Model T Fords
  business interest, 30, 32
  early drivers, 29, 31, 32, 33–34
  novelties, 33–34
  races, 26, **27–28**, 28, 34
  rules / safety, 26, 29, 30, 33
  spectators, 28, 30, 34
Moffat, Paul, 80
Molson Breweries, 209, 239, 257
Mont Tremblant, Quebec, 272
Morgan and Hartley (rally team), 153
Morning Albertan, 14, 23
Morris, David, 272
Morris, Joseph H. "Joe" 2, 5
Morros, Steve, 138, 167–68
Morton, John, 256
Moser and Ryder (race team), 5
Mosport, Ontario, 241–44
Moss, Stirling, 194, 204, 241–42, **245,**
  248–50
Mossman, Don, 133, 228
Motschenbacher, Lothar, 255, 259
Mr. X. See Breckenridge, Gavin
Muir, Miss M., 17
Muldowney, Shirley "Cha Cha", 65, 144–45
Munsie, Murray, 225

N

N.H.R.A. U.S. Nationals, 117, 186, 188,
  237, 239, 267
See also National Hot Rod Association
Namao R.C.A.F. Base, 58, 63–64, 73,
  76–77, 89, 99
NASCAR (National Association of Stock
  Car Auto Racing)
  "a closed shop," 52
  Canada West series, 166–67
  North-West Tour, 222, 226, 227
  popularity, 165
  sanctioned races, 226–28
  winners, 54
NASCAR Winston Cup series, 54, 121,
  214, 227

National Hot Rod Association (N.H.R.A.)
  cost of season, 66
  first national races, 115–16
  greatest drag racers, 54, 191–92
  promotion, 239
  sanctioning races, 287
  Top Fuel Funny Car titles, 65
  World Championship, 117, 186, 267
  See also N.H.R.A. U.S. Nationals
Natrass, Ian, 247
Nichols, Steve, 209
Nickle, Carl, 48
Northern Alberta Drag Racing Council
  (N.A.D.R.C.), 58
Northern Alberta Sports Car Club
  (N.A.S.C.C.), 73, 74, 76–78, 81–82, 107,
  157–58
Northern Light and Sports Car Club
  (N.L.S.C.C.), 73
Nutt, Inspector, 9

O

Oglu, Liz / Capital City Raceway, 280–82,
  283–84, 285–86
Oldfield, Barney, **3–4,** 6–**10,** 71–72, 255
Oliphant, W., 5
Oliver, Jackie, 256
Olson, Carl, 117
Ondrack, Jack, 82, 279
Orchard, Jim, 36
Osella (racing team), 202, 208–9

P

Pados, Franz, **70,** 72
Papirnick, Bob, 145, 197
Parker, Wally, 106
Parks, Wally, 116, **266**
Parsons, Benny, 120
Passmore (rally team), 149
Patterson, Goldie, 36
Pawson, Hal, 247
Pearson, David, 120, 153, 154
Pease, Al, 153
Pedregon, Cruz, 65
Pedregon, Frank, 137, **139**
Peets, Ray
  family, 109–10, 117
  Gold Cup Champion 109
  Hall of Fame, vii, 109

racing career, 64–65, 109–10, **111–12,**
  113–14
Reliable Engine Services, 108–9, 113,
  117
Top Fuel Dragster, 234
U.S. Nationals, 116–17
with Gary Beck, 114–17
Penhold, Alberta, 30
Penske, Roger, 256, 258
Perry, Keith, 40
Peters, Jim, 156
Petty, Richard, 120, 124
Pilkey, Arley, 77
Pinder, Fred, 142
Pioneer Automotive, 65, 106, 263, 279
Platinum Group, 222
Player's, 141, 226, 227, 242, 243, 250, 272
Player's Ltd. / GM Motorsport Series, 168,
  209, 227–28, 273–75, 277, 278
Poage, Terrell, 104
Pocklington, Peter, 259
Pocono, Pennsylvania, 90
Pollard, Art, 113, 162, **163**
Porteous, Dick, 247
Posey, Sam, 249
Powers, Bill, 142–44, 145
Price, LAC Norman, 29
Prince, John, 2
Proctor, John, 153
Prudhomme, Don "The Snake," 65, 116,
  145, 191, 198, 201
Puller, Jim, 36

Q
Quigley, Magistrate, 63

R
Race City Speedway championships, **130,**
  132, 133
  See also Docktor, Ben / Race City
  Speedway
Radbruch, Don, 25
Rahal, Bobby, 259
Rainier, Prince, 239
rallying
  defined, 71–73
  time, speed, distance, 148–49
  Harvest Night Rally, **152**
  Rocky Mountain Rally, **155,** 157–59

Shell 4000, 149–50, **151, 152,** 153–54,
  156–57
Rasmussen, Arnold, **31,** 49, 89
Rasmussen, Bert, 153
Rasmussen, Diane, 89, 90
Rasmussen, Eldon
  Hall of Fame, viii, 53, 93
  racer / mechanic, 83–84, **85–86,** 87–89,
    90, 91, 92, 162, 165, 194
  soapbox derby special, 83
  with Dick Simon, 93
  with Frank Weiss, **91,** 174–75
Rasmussen, Gordon, **31,** 33, 83, 84
Reagan, President Ronald, 120, **121**
Rebels Car Club, 57–58
Rees, Sgt Maj. J. H., 30
Regals Car Club, 247
Revson, Peter, 248, **251,** 256–57, 258, 259
Reynolds, Stan and Ted, 32
Rideout, Jim, 77, 99
Rimbey, Alberta, 81
Riverside, California, 242, 243, 244, 247
Road & Track, 203, 261
Roadents Car Club, 57, 60
Robbins, Rex, 227–28
Robertson, Don, 29, 272
Robertson, John, 213
Rocky Mountain Rally
  See under rallying
Rodriguez, Pedro, 153–54
Rogers, Bob, 36, 44
Rookie of the Year, 120, 171, 203
Ross, Klaus, 153, 154
Royal Canadian, 106, 232–33, 234, 236,
  266, 268
rules, 26, 28, 30, 74, 88, 160–62
Rupert, Frank, 104, 106
Russell, Bob, 114, 247
Ruth, Jerry, 65, 116, 145, 233
Rutherford, Johnny, 90
Rutter, Tommy, 40
Ruttman, Troy, 36

S
Sachs, Eddie, 230
Sadler, Bill, 243
Sadler, Earl, 123–24
safety equipment, 26, 28, 79–80, 158
St. Josephs High School, 261

St. Jovite, Quebec, 244
Sanders, Colonel, 9
Sansom, Barry, 225
Save, Kelly, **46,** 135
Scalzo, Joe, 212
Schmitt, Bill, 227
Seattle, Washington, 161, 244
Segar, Corporal, 30
Seigel, Fred. *See* Siegel, Fred
Senna, Ayrton, 204, **205,** 207, 209
Sharp, Don, 96, 98, **164, 246,** 247
Sharratt, Roy, **46,** 135
Shaver, Ron, 217
Shell 4000 Rally. *See under* rallying
Shepard airport, 57, 77, 135–36
Shephard Raceway. *See under*
   McMahon, Gene
Sherman, Bill, 60
Siegel, Fred, 18–19, 21
Siffert, Jo, 256–58, 259
Sikora, Pete, 40
Simon, Dick, 93, 162
Sinclair, Ted, 231–32, **235**
Skaalrud, Brian, 142
Skagit, Washington, 214, 217
Skinner and Skinner (rally team), 156
Sloan, J. Alex, 13–19, 21–24
Slogar, Tony, 162
Smalian, Ernie, 106, 247
Smith, Al, 96
Smith, Carroll, 204
Smith, Dale, 88
Smith, Rosemary, 156
Smyth, Dr. Phil, 271
Sneva, Babe, 51, 162
Sneva, Edsel, 51
Sneva, Jan, 52
Sneva, Jerry, 51
Sneva, Tom, 51, 140, 162, 175
Soules, Vern, 22
Southern Alberta Auto Racing Association
   (SAARA), 63–64
Spaulding, Cliff, 96–97, 98
Speedway Park, 81, 95–96, 98–100, 161,
   194–95, 196, 214
   See also Cobra Raceway
Spirit of Edmonton, 114, 246, 255
Spokane Washington, 58, 161, 163
Sports Car Club of America (S.C.C.A.),
242
Springbank Speedway, 48, 135
Sprint Car Hall of Fame, 17
sprint cars, 36, **139,** 212–13, **215**
Stampede City Auto Racing Association,
   137, 145
Stampede Speedway, 137–38, 145–47
Stampede Speedway Auto Racing
   Association, 145–46
Stanford, Don, 68
Staples, Ken, 270, **275,** 278–79
Stedelbauer Chev Olds, 100, **101**
Stedelbauer, George, 103, 156, 195, 197
Stewart, George. See Duray, Leon
Stewart, Jackie, **201,** 204, 256, 257
Stibbard, Tom, 156
Stiles, Pat, 156
Stinson, Katherine, 21, 23
Stokowski, Bob, 77, 82, **245,** 250, **275,**
   278–79
Stone, Bryson, 247
Stratton and Petersen (rally team), 156
Sturm, Fred, 247
Sturm, Tom, 186
Suderman, Art, 54
Sultans Car Club, 58
Surer, Marc, 208
Surtees, John, 244, 248, 249, 253
Swindell, Sammy, 219

T

Talladega, Alabama, 123
Tasman Series, 204
Taylor, E. J., 5
Taylor, Frank "Old Dad," 36–37, 47
Taylor, Henry, 153, 154
Taylor, Henry Seth, 1
Taylor, Hon. Gordon E., **55,** 57–60, 62, 99,
   104, 106, 136, 182
Taylor, J. P., 22
Tetz, Dwayne, 239, 268
Thompson, Cappy, 78, 141, 272
Thompson, Mickey, 191
Toft, Clifford, 22
top fuel dragster, 115, 200–201, 232–33,
   234, 264
Tortorelli, Louis, 72
Toupin, Bob and Teddy, 82
Trammel, Dr. Terry, 92, 178

Trotter, Daniel Webster, 7–9
Tugwell, Iain, 158–59
Tupper, Don, 109

U
United States Auto Club (USAC), 92, 100, 214
Unser, Al Jr., 259
Unser, Al Sr., 90
USAC National Championship, 90, 243

V
VanDusen, Wes, 264
Vaselenak, Leonard, 166, 167
Veney, Ken, 186
Verhuel, Jerry, 236–37
Victoria Park oval, 7, 10, 17, 43, 44, 47
Villeneuve, Gilles, 201, 259
Villeneuve, Jacques, 118
Villetard, Bob and Tom, 32

W
Wainwright Army Camp, 153
Walker, Hal, 50
Walker, Rob, 203
Ward, Jim, 37, **38, 46,** 49–50, 135
Ward, Rodger, 100
Waterson Bros., 14
Watson, John, 210
Watt, C., 5
Weadick, Guy, 12, 24
Webber, George, 11, 17–19
Weidner, Lou, 36, 38
Weisgerber, Larry, 145–46
Weiss, Frank
    accident, 52, 176, 178–79
    AMRA Championship, 171, **177**
    top modified racer, 138, 142, 162, 170–71, **172–73, 177–78**
    family, 171, 179, 180
    Racing Components Inc., 170, 178–80
    with Eldon Rasmussen, **91,** 174–75
Weith, Warren, 230
Wenzel, Werner, 141, 153, 154
Werner, Doug, 40
West Edmonton Drifters, 58
Western Speed Association (W.S.A.), 167
Westwood Circuit, 167, 203, 272–73
Wetaskiwin, Alberta, 282

White, R., 2
Wietzes, Eppie, 153, 254
Willard, Floyd, 14, 22
Williams, Dave, 247
Wilson, John, 154
Winkley, Frank R., 40–41
Winter, Ritch, 108
Wocknitz, W. A., 29
Wolfgang, Doug, 219
Wood, Keith, 136
Woods, Doug, 158, 159
World of Outlaws (W.o.O.), 214, **216,** 218–19, 220
Worth, Ian, 153

Y
Yarborough, Cale, 120, 123–24, 227
York, L., 5
Young, J. J., 2
Young, Jack, 149
Yukon Freight Lines, 213, 219